Enhancing Classroom Dialogue Productiveness

This book demonstrates how artificial intelligence (AI) can be used to uncover the patterns of classroom dialogue and increase the productiveness of dialogue.

In this book, the author uses a range of data mining techniques to explore the productive features and sequential patterns of classroom dialogue. She analyses how the Large Language Model (LLM) as an AI technique can be adapted to enhance dialogue contributions. The book also includes valuable feedback and practical cases from teachers and their dialogue transcripts, facilitating an understanding of AI use and pedagogical development.

This book makes original contributions to the field of classroom dialogue and technology, and it will encourage scholars making similar attempts at technological infusion for pedagogical improvement.

Yu Song has attained her bachelor's degree from Peking University and accomplished MPhil and PhD studies at the University of Cambridge. She works as an associate professor in South China Normal University and a visiting scholar in Peking University. Her research interests include classroom dialogue, intelligent teaching assessment, teacher professional development, and artificial intelligence. She is well-known in the intersection between artificial intelligence and dialogic education.

Enhancing Classroom Dialogue Productiveness

Exploring the Potential of Artificial Intelligence

Yu Song

Routledge
Taylor & Francis Group
LONDON AND NEW YORK

First published 2025
by Routledge
4 Park Square, Milton Park, Abingdon, Oxon OX14 4RN

and by Routledge
605 Third Avenue, New York, NY 10158

Routledge is an imprint of the Taylor & Francis Group, an informa business

British Library Cataloguing in Publication Data
A catalogue record for this book is available from the British Library

ISBN: 978-1-032-89300-6 (hbk)
ISBN: 978-1-032-89483-6 (pbk)
ISBN: 978-1-003-54303-9 (ebk)

DOI: 10.4324/9781003543039

Typeset in Times New Roman
by Apex CoVantage, LLC

Contents

Figures

Tables

Preface

Exploring the convergence of artificial intelligence and dialogic education

The first time I heard about the term 'classroom dialogue' was during my MPhil study at the University of Cambridge. Many top experts in the Faculty of Education, Cambridge, are well-known in classroom dialogue, such as Prof. Robin Alexander, Prof. Neil Mercer, Prof. Christine Howe, Prof. Sara Hennessy, and Prof. Rupert Wegerif. I am lucky that my research is built on these prestigious works. Classroom dialogue is a commonly used method for teaching and learning worldwide, and a close study of dialogue has increasingly become an active field. Nowadays, more and more researchers and educational practitioners, even government principals, have begun to realize that classroom dialogue matters significantly to the development of our children in this new area. Dialogue pedagogy when used strategically will help with critical thinking, deep understanding, and creative ability and boost learning achievement.

As technology in education continues to evolve, artificial intelligence's potential to revolutionize research and practice of classroom dialogue becomes increasingly apparent. Ever since my PhD graduation from Cambridge, I started the journey to explore a new intersection area between classroom dialogue and artificial intelligence. I want to leverage the potential of AI techniques to enhance the productiveness of classroom dialogue. To be more specific, to bring in the new technique from the AI area to upgrade the methods used in dialogic research, to increase people's understanding of the characteristics and patterns of productive dialogue in classroom settings, and to help support teacher professional development on dialogic education so that a broader range of students could benefit from this process. Six years passed, and I now lead a team with brilliant people from multiple areas, such as education, computer science, and school practitioners. Many interesting and exciting research products keep coming out. With increasingly more attention on this interdisciplinary area, it is an excellent time to have an overview of these works and share them with you. To my knowledge, few books focus on reporting the effectiveness of using artificial intelligence techniques in classroom dialogue. This book hopes to leverage the potential of artificial intelligence techniques and explore how they could be used strategically to enhance dialogue productiveness.

This book will be demonstrated in six chapters. The first chapter is an overview of the field of classroom dialogue to understand its definition, main research approaches, theoretical basis, productive features, latest research tendencies, and potential benefits. In the second chapter, the other key term of this book, 'artificial intelligence', will be introduced, as well as its usage in the educational field. The AI technique develops fast, and many of its components and strengths need to be made familiar to educators. It is necessary to be familiar with these updated, powerful tools. Chapters 3–4 are the critical areas where AI can release its powerful abilities to facilitate classroom dialogue research. The third chapter is about an automatic assessment of classroom dialogue using a neural network technique. Systematic observation and coding are essential methods for studying classroom dialogue. It matters significantly to the assessment of pedagogical performance. The first step is establishing a coding instrument for classroom dialogue. It is the basis for effectively applying artificial intelligence technology to dialogue analysis. It is critical in transforming intellectual development goals into measurable and evaluable indicators. Deep learning and neural network techniques can automate the process and allow for prompt teaching performance assessment. This technology can quickly and accurately annotate large-scale dialogic data and refine semantic features based on the coding instrument. This will overcome the problems of slow rate, low accuracy, and high cost of manual training in manual coding. It will meet the demand of large-scale data analysis and extract the key features from dialogic transcripts. In the fourth chapter, we will explore sequential patterns of classroom dialogue using data mining techniques. The data mining technique will be introduced first. Then, sequential patterns of classroom dialogue in different subjects, diverse quality levels and different educational stages will be demonstrated. Traditional analytical methods often rely on static descriptive statistics to annotate data, describing the frequency or percentages of dialogic categories. They cannot reveal the evolution patterns between the complicated interactions between the teacher and students. To address the issue, a data mining technique is brought in to uncover classroom dialogue's productive features and sequential patterns. It is advantageous to reflect on how dialogue is built collectively and constructively. After understanding the performance of classroom dialogue, next comes its improvement. The fifth chapter recently introduces one of the most attractive AI techniques, the large language model, and how it can be adapted to polish dialogic contributions. Generate AI and large language model (LLM) will be introduced about how they function. Then, I will introduce an LLM-based teaching assistant tool developed by my team and how it can be used to refine classroom talk. Finally, I share how my team used the above techniques and research products in teacher professional development and helped with their dialogic practice. Feedback and practical cases from teachers and their dialogic transcripts will allow educators to understand AI usage better.

Integrating dialogic education and AI techniques will leverage many fascinating benefits and make a more productive form of classroom dialogue accessible to a broader range of teachers and students. Like many other new inventions, it is undoubtedly true that there are potential risks and ethical problems that come along with this progress. The critical point of this is to select AI techniques wisely, use them properly with educational scenarios, and address educational issues positively. This book makes original contributions to the field of classroom dialogue and technology. Artificial intelligence techniques have the potential to break through the limitations of traditional methods. The effective use of artificial intelligence will promote methods to foster the upgrading and set a new agenda for studying classroom dialogue. This is an emerging and promising approach, and we hope that our research will encourage more scholars to make similar helpful attempts in the technological infusion into pedagogical improvement.

Acknowledgement

I would like to thank the National Natural Science Foundation of China (project number 62377014) for granting my research. I give my gratitude to my colleagues and team members for providing good assistance and advice during the studies. These include Prof. Tianyong Hao, Prof. Jia Zhu, Dr Shu Zhang, Shunwei Lei, Baihao Ye, Jiao Zhang, and Yumei Lv. I have been fortunate to work collaboratively with Guangzhou Huaqiao Foreign Language School, its headmaster Changliang Xu, and teacher participants. Their involvements strengthen our confidence in introducing artificial intelligence techniques in facilitating dialogic productiveness.

1 Understanding classroom dialogue

An overview

Introducing classroom dialogue

Classroom dialogue is a frequently explored method for teaching and learning (Howe & Abedin, 2013), and it is viewed as a main indicator of interaction between teachers and students and between students themselves in classroom settings (English et al., 2002; Wells & Arauz, 2006). The close study of classroom dialogue has increasingly become an active field of research since the 1970s (Howe & Mercer, 2017). Interest in understanding and improving the quality of classroom dialogue is higher than ever, not only within academia but also among teachers in schools and potentially in governments (Howe, 2017; Kim & Wilkinson, 2019). Publications on this topic and its related terminologies, such as exploratory talk (Mercer et al., 2017), accountable talk (Michaels et al., 2008), and dialogically organized instruction (Juzwik et al., 2013), have proliferated in recent years (Song et al., 2019). This expansion is mainly because classroom dialogue, when used strategically, will boost teaching and learning achievement (Vrikki & Evagorou, 2023).

Scholars define classroom dialogue in diverse ways based on background theories and research objectives (Howe & Abedin, 2013). There is no clear consensus about the many definitions, and scholars have been seeking one that could incorporate typical dialogic behaviours. The term 'dialogue' is derived from classical Greek, with 'dia' indicating 'through' and 'logos' meaning 'word' (Shorter Oxford English dictionary, 2002). Other than discourse, classroom dialogue is concerned with verbal exchanges occurring in classroom settings. I use the definition proposed by Howe and Abedin (2013), namely that classroom dialogue refers to verbal communication in classroom settings where one individual addresses another individual or individuals and at least one addressed individual replies. Students addressed can reply after an interval if the class does not move on to another topic or question. This definition is clear for use when searching articles and identifying dialogic behaviours in empirical studies, which has won wide recognition (Pehmer et al., 2015). Howe and Abedin (2013) recognized that some scholars use narrower definitions but felt that a narrower definition would not adequately represent the field. Thus, the broad definition presented earlier is most appropriate for this book.

A three-step pattern, initiation-response-feedback/evaluation (IRF or IRE), is taken to be the dominant pattern within classroom dialogue (Howe & Abedin,

DOI: 10.4324/9781003543039-1

2013; O'Connor & Michaels, 2007). This pattern involves a participant, typically the teacher, launching a discussion by asking a question or bringing up a subject. Subsequent responses are typically provided by students, followed by the initiator offering feedback on those responses, which can be categorized as brief assessments ('good', 'interesting') or comprehensive evaluations (Wiebe Berry & Kim, 2008; Schwab, 2011). Another main contribution to sorting out dialogic patterns has been made by Mortimer and Scott (2003), who generated four types of communication approaches: 'authoritative interaction', 'dialogic interaction', 'authoritative non-interaction', and 'dialogic non-interaction'. As indicated by Howe and Abedin (2013), the first three approaches are consistent with the IRF pattern.

Small-group classroom dialogue and whole-class dialogue are two different approaches to facilitating interaction and learning within the classroom setting. Small-group dialogue involves dividing the class into smaller groups, typically three to five students each. This method encourages students to discuss, share ideas, ask questions, and support each other's learning. The teacher may facilitate these groups, providing guidance and support as needed. Small-group dialogue allows for more personalized attention and active participation from students, as it promotes a collaborative and interactive learning environment. It also helps students develop communication, teamwork, and critical thinking skills. However, small-group work is often found challenging to group effectively (Fung & Howe, 2014). Tracking each student's contributions in small group dialogue is also difficult. Also, talk among students when no teacher is involved is less common in classrooms and has typically not been regarded as facilitating productive exchanges of views when it does take place (e.g. Galton et al., 1999). Whole-class dialogue, or whole-class discussion or whole-class teaching, involves engaging the entire class in a collective conversation (Van den Veen & van Oers, 2017). In this approach, the teacher poses questions, presents information or initiates discussions that involve all students (Fritschner, 2000). Whole-class dialogue promotes active listening, as students hear their peers' perspectives and contribute their thoughts. It also allows for modelling language and thinking skills as students observe and learn from each other. The teacher guides the conversation, ensuring that all voices are heard and that the discussion focuses on the intended learning objectives (Molinari et al., 2013).

In an ideal state of classroom dialogue, individuals not only respond to previous inquiries or utterances but also initiate responses. Students and teachers actively comment and build on each other's ideas, and then explore knowledge co-constructively (Alexander, 2008; Mercer et al., 2010). As proposed by Alexander (2008), dialogic learning aims to achieve the following goal, namely, that students achieve common understanding through structured, cumulative questioning and discussion which guide and prompt, reduce choices, minimize risk and error, and expedite 'handover' of concepts and principles. The process of classroom dialogue should be collective, reciprocal, supportive, cumulative, and purposeful (Alexander, 2008, 2019, 2020). These principles are routinely used to assess the quality of this pedagogy. Teachers and students are expected to share and build on each other's ideas towards particular educational objectives, reach shared understandings, construct knowledge, and facilitate reasoning.

- *Collectivity: Teachers and children address learning tasks together, whether as a group or as a class.*
- *Reciprocity: Teachers and children listen to each other, share ideas, and consider alternative viewpoints.*
- *Support: Children articulate their ideas freely, without fear of embarrassment over 'wrong' answers, and they help each other to reach common understandings.*
- *Cumulation: Teachers and children build on their own and each other's ideas and chain them into coherent lines of thinking and inquiry.*
- *Purposefulness: The dialogue is planned and transacted with specific learning outcomes clearly in view.*

Theoretical framework: sociocultural perspective on educational dialogue

Since the 1980s, research into classroom dialogue has primarily focused on two distinct approaches, which Mercer (2010) categorizes as linguistic ethnography and sociocultural research. The former draws on the disciplines of social anthropology and descriptive linguistics, frequently engaging with the cultural aspects of classroom conversation. Conversely, the sociocultural perspective aligns with traditions in social and developmental psychology and pedagogical research, deeply rooted in Vygotsky's (1978) theories. Vygotsky advanced a sociocultural theory that connects thought, action, communication, and culture, suggesting that cognitive processes are embedded within cultural and historical contexts and that learning occurs as a shift from interpersonal to intrapersonal processes (Wertsch, 1993). According to Vygotsky, education and cognitive growth are cultural processes that are realized through interaction with others, with language serving as a crucial tool for thought and activity mediation.

Vygotsky's concepts have been widely adopted, tested, and expanded within classroom settings over the past three decades, leading to several significant applications that enhance their relevance to classroom dialogue. Cazden (2001) emphasizes the use of scaffolding to support students in their learning progression, highlighting the importance of teachers' skilled engagement with students in both whole-class and small-group settings. Alexander's (2001) pioneering research underscores the critical role of high-quality classroom dialogue in enhancing student learning, noting cultural differences in dialogic and other pedagogical approaches. He introduced the concept of 'dialogic teaching', illustrating productive dialogue in classrooms based on five core principles: collective, reciprocal, supportive, cumulative, and purposeful (Alexander, 2008). Mercer (2000, 2008, 2010) has underscored the significance of dialogue as a 'social mode of thinking' that enables collaborative problem-solving and shared responsibility for constructing understanding, a process known as 'inter-thinking'. His seminal work on peer interactions has focused on 'exploratory talk', which is valuable for its educational benefits. Exploratory talk involves critical yet constructive engagement with one another's thoughts, where arguments are challenged and built upon, seeking agreement to drive joint advancement. Mercer and his colleagues have facilitated the use of exploratory talk among British primary school children through their innovative programme 'Thinking Together' (Mercer & Littleton, 2007). Wegerif (2007) defines 'dialogic' as the space where multiple perspectives are held in tension within a dialogue, from which meaning emerges. Howe (2010) indicates in her works that participants in dialogic interactions construct meaning through chained sequences of utterances and chained lines of thinking and inquiry.

Nowadays, the sociocultural perspective has been applied widely in research on classroom dialogue and has become dominant (Hennessy et al., 2020). Research demonstrated in this book focuses on how classroom dialogue allows teachers and students to co-construct knowledge and meanings, and therefore, sociocultural theory serves as a prominent stand in this book.

Discussion of productive features of classroom dialogue

There are many debates on the productive features of classroom dialogue, which are characteristics that verbal interaction in classrooms should display to optimize student outcomes. It is traditionally believed that there are ways of organizing classroom talk, which, if achieved with sufficient frequency, will prove beneficial in terms of educational goals. Interactions are typically regarded as following fixed patterns, prevalent among which was the so-called I-R-E/F format (Mehan, 1979; Sinclair & Coulthard, 1975). Changes have occurred in recent years as scholars found that the number of occurrences of questioning and responses themselves was not typically seen as neutral concerning student outcomes. It is a function of dialogue rather than the format that matters to the productiveness of dialogue.

Numerous proposals have been made about the characteristics that productive talk should possess. Alexander (2008) has compiled various insights on what constitutes productive conversation in educational settings, identifying key types of student dialogue that foster learning: narrate, explain, speculate, imagine, explore, analyse, evaluate, question, justify, discuss, and argue. In a comprehensive review, Howe and colleagues (2019) identified five core dimensions of such dialogue. They highlighted the importance of open-ended questions, such as 'Why has Edinburgh emerged as a pivotal hub of culture?', which invite a range of responses. They also emphasized the need for participants to expand on their comments, building upon their own and others' insights. The third theme involves acknowledging and examining diverse viewpoints, with an emphasis on understanding the rationale behind each perspective. A fourth dimension calls for a cohesive examination of ideas, where students actively seek to connect their contributions and resolve discrepancies. Lastly, Howe et al. suggested that learners should cultivate a metacognitive awareness of the value of dialogue and reflect on how to improve their engagement. These five dimensions, according to Howe et al., are widely recognized and supported by numerous researchers. There is an emerging consensus about the forms of educational dialogue that seem to be productive for learning (Hennessy et al., 2021).

In essence, these focus on attunement to others' perspectives and continuous co-construction of knowledge through sharing, critiquing, and gradually reconciling contrasting ideas.

In this book, we recognize productive classroom dialogue should demonstrate characteristics that elaborations, explanations, and clarifications that make a concept or an idea explicit, thorough, and comprehensive; seeking coordination that pursues integrated lines of inquiry and connection between contributions; recognizing and evaluating varied viewpoints, building on and clarification of own or another's contribution; making explorations beyond what is being learnt, and links to the broader context.

Overview of the field: bibliometric analysis of two decades of research on classroom dialogue

As research into classroom dialogue widens, it is beneficial to compile an extensive review of scientific literature from around the world that pertains to this area. While there are existing reviews (e.g. Gillies, 2016; Henderson et al., 2018; Howe & Abedin, 2013), to the best of our knowledge, most of these have yet to employ quantitative methods. Bibliometric analysis – a quantitative approach used to study or quantify texts, especially within large datasets (Zupic & Čater, 2015) – is valuable for constructing literature structures, evaluating the significance of publications, and identifying trends and the evolution of research topics (Gimenez et al., 2018). Bibliometrics is helpful not only in researching past developments but also in discovering hot topics and trends within disciplines in a quantitative and objective manner. The outcomes of bibliometric analyses contribute to the progress and advancement of a specific research field in multiple ways. For instance, it allows for the assessment of progress, identifies the most reputable and widely cited scientific sources and significant contributors such as authors and institutions, establishes a foundation for evaluating new developments, spots emerging research interests, and forecasts future research achievements (Geng et al., 2017; Mazloumian, 2012). Additionally, it aids researchers in pinpointing potential topics, finding suitable institutions for collaboration, and identifying possible academic partners (Martínez et al., 2015). This section shows a bibliometric analysis of the scientific literature on classroom dialogue with the following specific aims: firstly, to determine the trends in publication and citation over time in this field; secondly, to identify the most productive journals, authors, and institutions; and thirdly, to trace the evolution of critical topics over time.

Data retrieval and methodology

In conducting data retrieval, one critical procedure or challenge was to identify search terms. As popular as classroom dialogue is, people have yet to reach a consensus over its terminology and conceptualization (Howe & Mercer, 2017). Besides 'classroom dialogue', terms such as 'accountable talk', 'exploratory talk', 'dialogic teaching', and 'classroom discourses' also appear in the literature (Hennessy et al., 2017). The choice of terminology is sometimes arbitrary, and there is a lack of distinction; different terms are used even though many of them are intended to describe similar phenomena (Howe & Mercer, 2017). One challenge was to maximize the identification of studies that addressed dialogue in class as opposed to other settings. Classes can be conducted either on campus within traditional classrooms or off-campus, such as through online classes. There are two types of dialogue: those that take place between teacher and students in whole-class settings or those that occur between students themselves in small groups. In the end, 'classroom' and its two associated terms, 'whole class' and 'small group', were taken as one set of keywords in the course of the literature search. Another challenge was to search the literature in a fashion that would maximize the identification of studies that were consistent with our definition of dialogue. Howe and Abedin (2013) used 22 associated terms (i.e. answer, argumentation, communication, conversation, dialogic, dialogue, discourse, discussion, feedback, ground rules, interaction, interactive, IRE, IRF, language, oracy, question, reciprocal, recitation, speaking and listening, talk, turn taking) to conduct the search in their review. The terms were identified by examining reference lists of items and iterating the process until no new ones emerged. We intended to use these terms in literature retrieval; nevertheless, tens of thousands of articles resulted, and many of them were not relevant to dialogue research but happened to contain one of the terms in titles or abstracts. In this case, it was decided to employ the Delphi method to cue terms associated with dialogue. Four relevant domain experts were invited to list any associated terms of which they were aware, and then they were encouraged to refine their earlier answers in light of the replies of other members. In the end, ten terms were identified as the other search keywords: dialogue, dialogic, discourse, conversation, discussion, language, interaction, talk, communication, and speaking.

Although the study of classroom dialogue started in the 1970s, it is from around the year 2000 that the field has experienced rapid growth (Howe & Abedin, 2013). Thus, it is reasonable to examine two decades of publications, namely, the years 2004 to 2023. As Web Of Science (WoS) is the essential bibliometric database (Cobo et al., 2015), raw bibliographic data concerning the area of research on the classroom dialogue were retrieved from it with the following advanced query, in which 'TS' (Topics), referring to the title, abstract or keywords of a publication, was used as a search field. The specification was for any publication with which at least one keyword from each of the two sets was associated. The retrieval was conducted on January 1, 2024.

TS=(('classroom' OR 'small-group' OR 'whole-class') AND ('dialogue' OR 'dialogic' OR 'communication' OR 'conversation' OR 'discussion' OR 'discourse' OR 'interaction' OR 'talk' OR 'speaking' OR 'language'))

Publications retrieved from the query were considered if they were: (1) articles, since research articles usually provide more original research findings and give more specific information on authors and their affiliations (Geng et al., 2017); (2) in English, but did not have to be conducted in English-speaking countries;

(3) published between 2004 to 2023; (4) in a Web of Science Category with 'education' or 'educational' in the name; and (5) indexed in Science Citation Index Expanded (SCIE) and Social Sciences Citation Index (SSCI). Based on the above restrictions, 14,174 publications with complete bibliographic information, as well as citations published between 2004 and the end of 2023, were downloaded in plain text. A Python program was used to extract critical elements, for example, title, abstract, journal, year published, and author address of each publication, from the downloaded raw data, which were entered into Excel for further processing. To guarantee the high relevance of the data to the research target, a filtering exercise was carried out by two researchers based on the criteria listed in Table 1.1. According to the criteria, 4,418 publications were selected for the analysis of the final data set.

The influence of the published works was evaluated using several bibliometric indicators. Initially, the traditional methods of counting publications and citations were employed, as they are the most prevalent bibliometric techniques (Ding et al., 2014). These methods quantify an individual's productiveness and the impact of their work, respectively (Svensson, 2010). Subsequently, the Hirsch index, also known as the H-index, was applied to gauge academic prowess based on both the quality (as indicated by citation count) and the quantity (as indicated by publication count) of an individual's output. The H-index was initially designed to assess a researcher's productiveness and the impact of their published works. It has since been expanded to evaluate the productiveness and impact of journals, countries/regions, institutions, and authors. An H-index value of 'H' signifies that an individual has at least 'H' citations per publication (Hirsch & Buela-Casal, 2014), with higher values indicating a more extraordinary scientific accomplishment. Further, three citation thresholds (300 or more, 100 or more, and 50 or more citations) were used to determine the influence of publications based on achieving specific citation counts (Merigó et al., 2015). Additionally, to measure the influence of academic institutions, the 2023 Academic Ranking of World Universities (ARWU), the QS World University Rankings 2023 (QS), and the World University Rankings

Table 1.1 The inclusion and exclusion criteria for manually verifying the retrieved publications

Inclusion criteria	**I1**	Talk
	I2	Textual verbal exchanges
	I3	Non-verbal behaviour (including paralinguistic and prosodic features) was only of interest when it supported language
	I4	Computer-mediated communication
	I5	Dialogue carried out in distance or online learning
Exclusion criteria	**E1**	Not focused on classroom dialogue or associated terms listed above
	E2	One individual's commentary on contrasting ideas
	E3	One individual's assertion of a single, received idea
	E4	One individual's speech
	E5	Dialogue happened outside class

2023 (THE) were consulted, which are among the most renowned global university ranking systems.

Geographic visualization is a collection of methods that enhance the analysis of spatial or geospatial data. By integrating technologies such as image processing and virtual reality, computers can assist in presenting information that highlights patterns more effectively. Typically, the location serves as the primary variable, with visualization tools enabling the visualization of hidden information in a visual context, which is often more informative than textual or numerical descriptions. A geographic visualization analysis was performed using GeoDa and ArcGIS to generate a global research heat map, which charted the publication counts for each country/region.

Since publication keywords usually represent the major research focus of a publication and can help to identify the research topic of the publication quickly (Zhong et al., 2016), author-defined keywords as well as ISI KeyWords Plus were used for topic analysis in this study. To ensure analysis effectiveness, keyword preprocessing was applied. First, for the 171 publications without author-defined keywords or ISI KeyWords Plus, keywords were manually supplemented according to title and abstract content. Specifically, keywords were mainly extracted from titles, as titles commonly reveal the nature of a work. For example, keywords 'problem orientation', 'small-group', 'discussion', and 'biochemistry teaching' were extracted from the title 'Problem-oriented small-group discussion in the teaching of biochemistry laboratory practical'. Keywords were then revisited by referring to abstracts. Second, a de-duplication process was applied (Cobo et al., 2015). Specifically, abbreviations were replaced by corresponding full names by reviewing the corresponding publication content; for example, L2 was replaced by '2nd language', L1 was replaced by 'first language', FL was replaced by 'foreign language', and SLA was replaced by 'Second Language Acquisition'. Third, all the keywords were converted to lowercase. Furthermore, keywords representing the same concepts were grouped, for example, 'color' and 'colour', 'behaviour', and 'behavior'.

Trends in publications and citations

Statistical computing was applied to the retrieved publications, and the distributions of total publications and citations by year are presented in Figure 1.1. We conducted polynomial regression analysis with year as the independent variable x to fit the trends of total publication and citation counts. In the regression modelling, the period 2004–2023 was used for regression fitting. Two polynomial regression curves with the R^2 were integrated in the figure. From the results, there is a trend towards an increase in the quantity of publications, reflecting a growing enthusiasm for research in the field. With the regression model, the predictive value for future years can be estimated. The citation counts were also recorded and analysed. There has been a dramatic increase in the number of citations, particularly from 2006. Similarly, we also employed a regression model to predict the trend relating to citation change. The publications and citations in relation to classroom dialogue

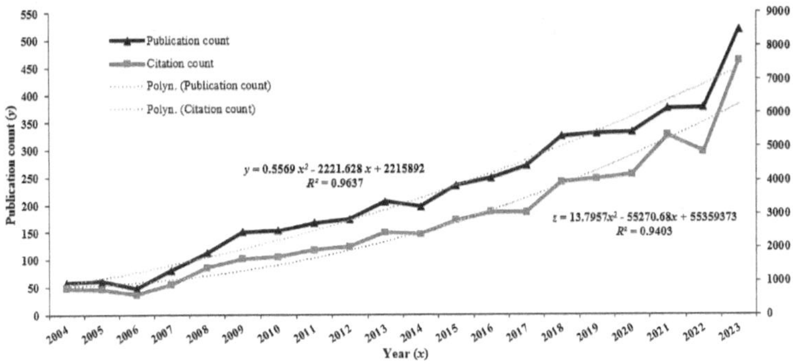

Figure 1.1 The trend analysis of publication and citation counts

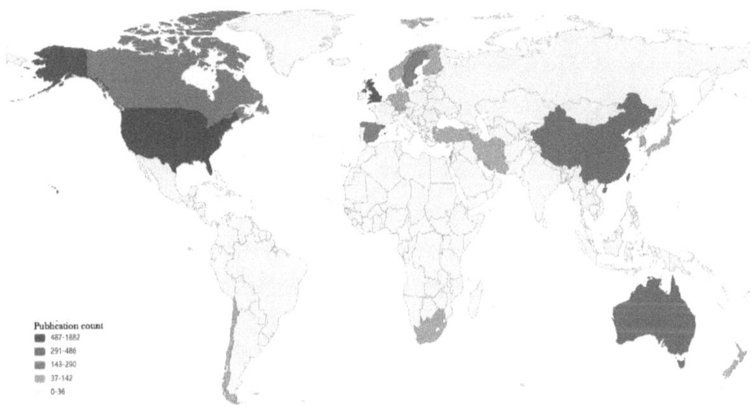

Figure 1.2 Geographical distribution of publication counts

have grown consistently across the 20 years, which can be further divided into a steady development between 2004 and 2016 and a flourishing in the periods 2016–2018 and 2022–2023.

Prolific countries/regions, institutions, and authors

The analysis focused on institutions and countries/regions involved in each published work to identify the most prevalent participants. Research articles stem from 94 different countries/regions, with Figure 1.2 illustrating the distribution of publications per country/region. Table 1.2 provides statistical data for the top 30 countries/regions in terms of overall contributions to the field. Leadership is held by the USA, which boasts the highest number of publications at 1,882 (42.60%), closely followed by the UK with 487 (11.02%). Together, these nations represent over 53% of the total publications, highlighting their significant influence in the

Table 1.2 Top most prolific countries/regions ranked by total number of publications

Rank	*Name*	*TP (%)*	*TC*	*H*	*>=300*	*>=100*	*>=50*	*2004–2013*		*2014–2023*	
								TP (%)	*TC*	*TP (%)*	*TC*
1	USA	1882 (42.60)	58891	111	13	123	198	493 (57.53)	35321	1351 (44.19)	23570
2	UK	487 (11.02)	15016	56	6	28	37	108 (12.60)	9954	336 (10.99)	5062
3	China	336 (7.61)	7072	45	2	22	29	56 (6.53)	2691	178 (5.82)	4381
4	Australia	291 (6.59)	5420	39	0	9	16	33 (3.85)	3290	134 (4.38)	2130
5	Canada	184 (4.16)	5553	39	2	13	13	20 (2.33)	3636	140 (4.58)	1917
6	Spain	156 (3.53)	2983	32	0	4	13	11 (1.28)	1673	120 (3.93)	1310
7	Sweden	143 (3.24)	2016	23	0	2	6	18 (2.10)	1083	86 (2.81)	933
8	Taiwan	115 (2.60)	2939	32	0	5	13	11 (1.28)	1069	81 (2.65)	1870
9	South Korea	103 (2.33)	1437	21	1	0	5	5 (0.58)	672	85 (2.78)	765
10	Norway	97 (2.20)	853	16	0	0	2	6 (0.70)	185	83 (2.72)	668
11	Finland	91 (2.06)	1158	19	0	0	4	4 (0.47)	342	77 (2.52)	816
12	Germany	89 (2.01)	2614	25	2	3	5	16 (1.87)	1487	63 (2.06)	1127
13	Turkey	86 (1.95)	1141	19	0	1	4	12 (1.40)	405	66 (2.16)	736
14	Japan	85 (1.92)	1313	18	0	3	3	16 (1.87)	668	56 (1.83)	645
15	Netherlands	82 (1.86)	1285	19	0	1	7	5 (0.58)	410	66 (2.16)	875
16	Israel	78 (1.77)	1175	18	0	2	3	12 (1.40)	492	52 (1.70)	683
17	New Zealand	74 (1.67)	1344	20	0	3	6	18 (2.10)	453	45 (1.47)	891
18	Singapore	70 (1.58)	2018	21	2	3	6	8 (0.93)	1536	46 (1.50)	482
19	South Africa	69 (1.56)	994	17	0	3	1	8 (0.93)	679	36 (1.18)	315
20	Iran	53 (1.20)	873	17	0	1	4	3 (0.35)	93	37 (1.21)	780
21	Chile	43 (0.97)	755	13	0	1	3	1 (0.12)	173	27 (0.88)	582
22	Italy	26 (0.59)	313	8	0	0	1	9 (1.05)	115	18 (0.59)	198
23	Cyprus	26 (0.59)	295	9	0	0	1	3 (0.35)	161	23 (0.75)	134
24	Denmark	25 (0.57)	320	6	0	0	2	6 (0.70)	119	18 (0.59)	201
25	France	24 (0.54)	262	6	0	1	0	0 (0.00)	227	24 (0.79)	35
26	Switzerland	22 (0.50)	388	8	0	1	0	3 (0.35)	285	20 (0.65)	103
27	Mexico	21 (0.48)	138	4	0	0	1	7 (0.82)	98	15 (0.49)	40
28	Belgium	20 (0.45)	392	8	0	1	1	0 (0.00)	0	22 (0.72)	392
29	Brazil	19 (0.43)	728	8	1	1	0	2 (0.23)	675	17 (0.56)	53
30	Ireland	19 (0.43)	296	6	0	1	0	5 (0.58)	194	14 (0.46)	102

Abbreviations: TP (%): publication count and percentage; TC: total citations; H: H-index of a country/region; >=300, >=100, >=50: publication counts of publications with more than 300, 100, or 50 citations.

research domain. The USA also holds the highest H-index of 111, a testament to its leading role not only in terms of quantity but also in academic impact within the field. The top three countries/regions remain consistent when ranked based on Total Publications (TP), Total Citations (TC), or H-index (H). The surge in published studies can be attributed to a rise in research efforts from non-English speaking countries/regions such as China and Singapore, as well as to substantial contributions from scholars in the USA and the UK. The USA's substantial output, particularly since 2012, is underscored by its presence in five of the ten most productive institutions and having the most prolific authors, signifying its overriding position.

The data reveal that 1,782 institutions across the globe have contributed to research aligned with the published studies. In Table 1.3, the 30 institutions with the most extensive contributions to the field from 2014 to 2023 are highlighted. Notably, 22 of these leading institutions are based in the United States, further underscoring the nation's preeminence in this area of research. Among the top 30, the University of Cambridge stands out with the highest Total productiveness (TP) at 48 from 2014 to 2023. And, the University of Cambridge has the highest Total Citation (TC) count at 3,417, suggesting that its contributions are both high in quality and impactful in the scholarly community.

Main themes and their evolution

The top 20 keywords ranked by frequency are shown in Table 1.4. The keyword 'classroom' is ranked first with a frequency of 725. Other widespread keywords include 'discourse' (585), 'student' (482), and 'education' (451). The evaluation of the keywords in terms of frequency with respect to particular periods of time is compared. As regards the subject matter, science and literacy have been given more focus than other subjects. Understanding knowledge and learning achievement serve as more concerns for dialogic research as scholars have determined to testify whether or not classroom dialogue helps with learning. Over these periods of time, most keywords have demonstrated a growth in frequency.

As shown in Figures 1.3–1.6, throughout the analysed periods, several keywords recurred frequently, representing broad thematic categories. The term 'classroom' consistently appeared as the most prominent keyword across the four periods, suggesting a prevalent focus on the application of dialogic methods within this setting. Moreover, the terminology used was varied, with 'discourse', 'talk', 'dialogue', and 'discussion' regularly seen, with 'discourse' being the most commonly used term. While reflecting conceptual nuances, this variety of terms may contribute to a lack of a universally accepted definition among researchers for these key concepts, which could lead to ambiguity. As highlighted by Howe and Mercer (2017), there is a need for the field to establish common analytical frameworks to facilitate comparison across an expanding body of research. A majority of the studies were also cantered on interactions between teachers and students, while research focusing on student group work without teacher involvement was less prevalent. Science education has been a consistent focus over the past two decades, with 'science' ranking among the top ten most frequently used keywords, likely due to the communicative

Table 1.3 Top institutions ranked by total number of publications

Institution	*Country*	*2014–2023*		*2004–2013*		*2004–2023*						*ARWU 2023*	*QS 2023*
		TP	*TC*	*TP*	*TC*	*TP*	*TC*	*H*	*>=300*	*>=100*	*>=50*		
University of Cambridge	UK	48	1461	15	1956	63	3417	27	3	8	8	4	2
The University of Hong Kong	China	45	1608	30	105	75	1713	22	1	1	8	88	26
The Ohio State University	USA	40	678	30	1163	70	1841	19	0	6	5	101–150	151
University College London	UK	38	564	45	1008	83	1572	17	1	5	2	17	9
Pennsylvania State University	USA	31	452	20	892	51	1344	20	0	3	8	101–150	83
University of Jyvaskyla	Finland	31	473	8	164	39	637	14	0	0	3	701–800	446
Michigan State University	USA	30	529	38	936	68	1465	19	0	2	10	151–200	136
Nanyang Technological University	Singapore	30	235	24	1414	54	1649	17	2	2	4	93	26
Arizona State University	USA	28	829	20	512	48	1341	19	0	3	7	101–150	179
University of North Carolina at Chapel Hill	USA	28	222	32	536	60	758	14	0	2	2	30	132
The University of Queensland	Australia	27	269	7	618	34	887	16	0	1	5	51	43
University of Oslo	Norway	26	383	16	153	42	536	12	0	0	2	73	117
University of Pittsburgh	USA	26	519	20	978	46	1497	19	0	5	6	83	222
University of Colorado at Boulder	USA	25	730	8	247	33	977	8	0	0	4	57	264
University of Virginia	USA	24	1101	8	196	32	1297	9	0	5	1	201–300	260
Florida State University	USA	24	756	9	28	33	784	15	0	1	5	201–300	461
University of Texas at Austin	USA	23	722	11	359	34	1081	16	1	1	4	43	58
Vanderbilt University	USA	22	444	7	364	29	808	12	0	5	1	66	261
University of Michigan, Ann Arbor	USA	22	494	20	1659	42	2153	15	1	2	7	26	33
University of Washington	USA	21	583	30	839	51	1422	16	1	2	7	18	63
University of Georgia	USA	20	678	7	116	27	585	10	0	2	3	301–400	514
University of Illinois, Champaign Urbana	USA	20	314	24	886	44	1200	18	0	2	6	52	64
University of Melbourne	Australia	20	141	15	645	35	786	11	0	3	0	35	14
University of Wisconsin–Madison	USA	20	215	16	712	36	927	13	0	5	2	35	102
Purdue University	USA	19	327	9	182	28	509	13	0	1	2	96	99
University of California, Davis	USA	18	234	10	461	28	695	12	0	2	2	101–150	118
Columbia University	USA	17	119	17	562	34	761	6	1	1	0	8	23
Boston University	USA	17	330	14	611	31	941	8	0	3	3	101–150	93
University of California, Los Angeles	USA	16	448	12	355	28	803	6	0	2	5	13	29
University of Maryland, College Park	USA	15	242	12	343	27	443	12	0	0	2	50	169

Abbreviations: TP: publication count; TC: total citations; H: H-index of a country/region; >=300, >=100, >=50: publication counts of publications with more than 300, 100, or 50 citations; ARWU: The 2023 Academic Ranking of World Universities; QS Rank: QS World University Rankings 2023.

Table 1.4 Top 20 keywords ranked by total frequency for different periods of time

Keyword	*2004–2023*		*2004–2008*		*2009–2013*		*2014–2018*		*2019–2023*	
	R (TP)	*%*	*R (TP)*	*%*	*R (TP)*	*%*	*R (TP)*	*%*	*R (TP)*	*%*
Classroom	1 (725)	16.41	1 (47)	7.83	1 (104)	10.05	1 (217)	14.14	1 (357)	23.26
Discourse	2 (585)	13.24	2 (33)	5.50	4 (71)	6.86	2 (158)	10.29	2 (323)	21.04
Student	3 (482)	10.91	3 (32)	5.33	3 (78)	7.54	5 (133)	8.66	3 (239)	15.57
Education	4 (451)	10.21	5 (22)	3.67	5 (59)	5.70	4 (140)	9.12	4 (230)	14.98
Knowledge	5 (388)	8.78	6 (20)	3.33	6 (53)	5.12	3 (150)	9.77	6 (165)	10.75
Language	6 (350)	7.92	4 (31)	5.17	2 (79)	7.63	6 (96)	6.25	9 (144)	9.38
Instruction	7 (318)	7.20	9 (16)	2.67	14 (32)	3.09	9 (89)	5.80	5 (181)	11.79
Science	8 (284)	6.43	8 (17)	2.83	9 (38)	3.67	11 (75)	4.89	7 (154)	10.03
Teacher	9 (275)	6.23	15 (10)	1.67	10 (38)	3.67	10 (76)	4.95	8 (151)	9.84
School	10 (251)	5.68	16 (9)	1.50	40 (13)	1.26	7 (92)	5.99	10 (137)	8.93
Achievement	11 (231)	5.23	13 (10)	1.67	21 (24)	2.32	8 (90)	5.86	12 (107)	6.97
Literacy	12 (215)	4.87	12 (13)	2.17	17 (30)	2.90	13 (65)	4.23	13 (107)	6.97
Collaborative learning	13 (199)	4.51	22 (8)	1.33	31 (16)	1.55	14 (63)	4.10	11 (112)	7.30
Talk	14 (195)	4.41	11 (14)	2.33	18 (30)	2.90	12 (75)	4.89	18 (76)	4.95
Children	15 (192)	4.35	7 (18)	3.00	12 (33)	3.19	16 (58)	3.78	17 (83)	5.41
Classroom discourse	16 (182)	4.12	27 (7)	1.17	8 (40)	3.86	15 (62)	4.04	20 (73)	4.87
Performance	17 (174)	3.94	37 (5)	0.83	23 (20)	1.93	21 (47)	3.06	14 (102)	6.46
Motivation	18 (165)	3.74	39 (5)	0.83	45 (12)	1.16	17 (55)	3.52	16 (93)	6.06
Computer mediated communication	19 (162)	3.67	34 (5)	0.83	33 (16)	1.55	18 (48)	3.13	15 (93)	6.06
Communication	20 (156)	3.53	31 (6)	1.00	25 (19)	1.84	22 (47)	3.06	22 (84)	5.56

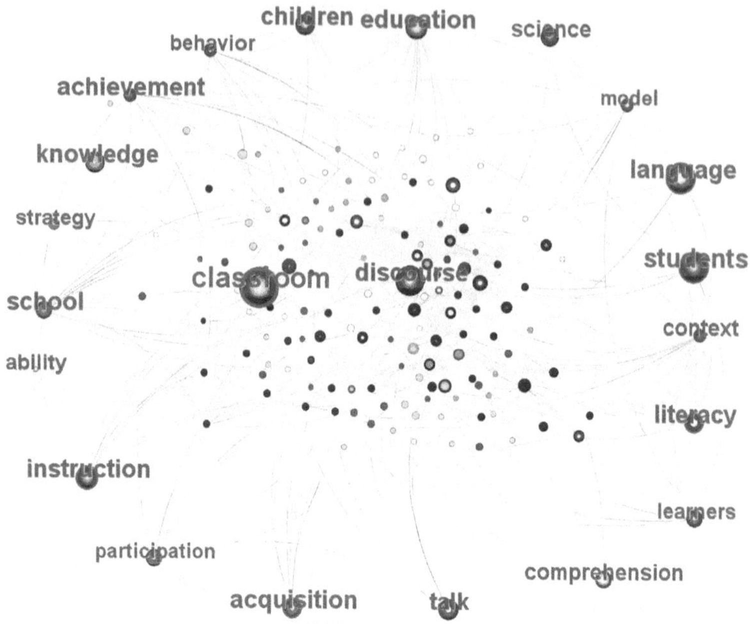

Figure 1.3 The visualization of keyword evolution during 2004–2008

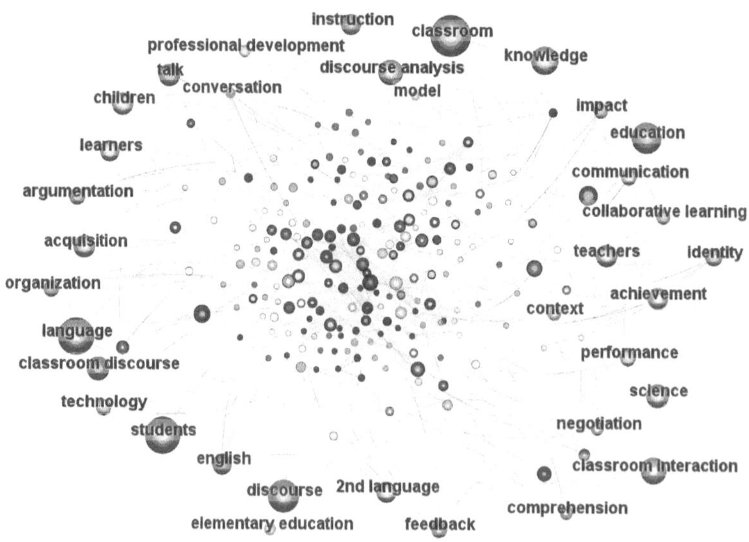

Figure 1.4 The visualization of keyword evolution during 2009–2013

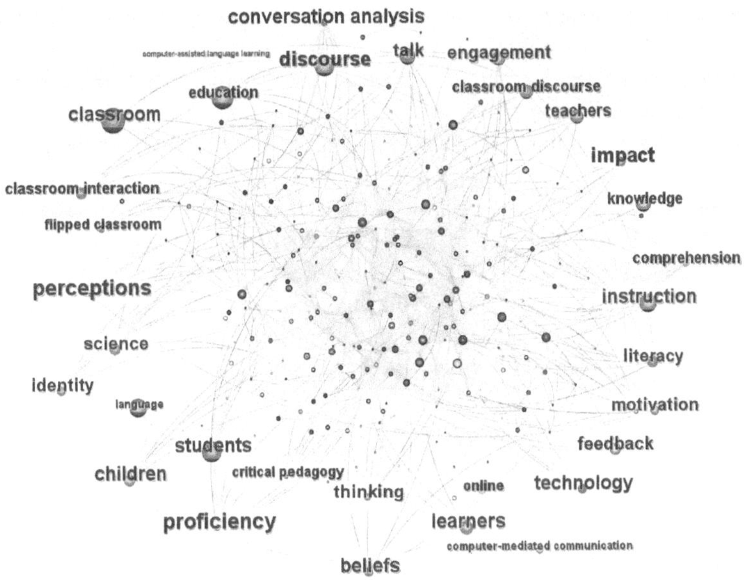

Figure 1.5 The visualization of keyword evolution during 2014–2018

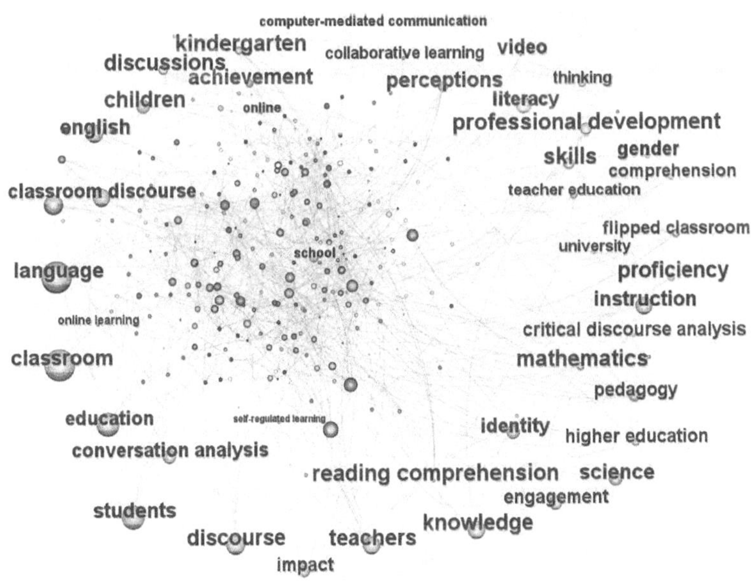

Figure 1.6 The visualization of keyword evolution during 2019–2023

and negotiation processes that aid in reasoning and thinking, which are particularly crucial in scientific learning (McNeill et al., 2017). Additionally, there was a notable interest in mathematics and language learning. The importance of language was underscored, with 'language' being among the top ten most frequently occurring keywords, acknowledging its role as a means of transferring knowledge (Littleton & Mercer, 2013). The study frequently examined linguistic features related to vocabulary, grammar, and rhetoric, while aspects such as gestures, verbal fluency, and clarity received less attention. Lastly, the publications predominantly concentrated on school-based education, as most studies have been based in primary and secondary school contexts. However, during the latest years, classroom dialogue in early childhood education and higher education has been more frequently studied, as indicated by the keyword frequencies for 'school', 'preschool', 'university', and 'kindergarten'.

The text describes how the importance of specific keywords in academic discourse has evolved over time, indicating shifts in the field. Initially, the appearance of keywords like 'computer-mediated communication' and 'technology' in 2004–2008, and their subsequent rise, signifies a growing focus among scholars on computer-facilitated communication and the role of media and technologies in knowledge construction. According to Zawacki-Richter and Latchem (2018), digital tools are not just instruments but active participants in the cognitive process of knowledge creation, which can be utilized both within and outside educational institutions. Within the realm of educational research, the integration of information and communication technologies (ICT) and digital media in school settings has emerged as a significant area of inquiry over the past decade. For instance, González-Howard et al. (2018) discussed a technology toolkit that facilitated argumentation in science classrooms. The research indicates that the development of an interactive, authentic hypermedia environment is instrumental in fostering dialogic pedagogies, which, in turn, can enhance learning outcomes. Additionally, the study of dialogues has increasingly embraced online learning platforms and web-based systems, as indicated by keywords such as 'flipped classroom' and 'online'. For example, Epp et al. (2010) examined patterns of interaction between students and instructors in online scientific discussions. The integration of digital tools in dialogic instruction and learning will likely continue to feature prominently in future research on classroom dialogue, further underscoring its significance as an area of focus.

The impact of classroom dialogue on student accomplishments has long been a focus of scholarly interest. Between 2004 and 2013, the dominant themes in this discourse were 'knowledge', and 'achievement', though since 2014, 'creativity', 'thinking', 'comprehension', and 'outcome' have also become prominent. This evolution reflects a shift from a broad concern with academic success to a more nuanced interest in the specific benefits of dialogue-based learning. Concurrently, the literature has emphasized the role of educators in fostering dialogue quality, as seen in the rise of studies on teacher professional development from 2009 to 2013 and its continued growth after that. Such development programmes aim to promote dialogic teaching methods and assist teachers in their implementation (e.g. Howe et al., 2015;

van der Veen et al., 2017). Research has also highlighted the importance of student engagement in classroom dialogue and the influence of individual characteristics, such as gender, on dialogic performance. However, the latter has seen a decrease in attention in recent years.

This analysis, utilizing bibliometric techniques, provides a panoramic view of the scholarly output on classroom dialogue from 2004 to 2023. It offers insight into the research trends and evolution of the field over two decades, helping researchers identify key areas of interest as they choose their research foci. Notably, the integration of digital technology into the study and application of classroom dialogue has emerged as a significant new direction.

Classroom dialogue: its affordance and challenges

Potential benefits for learning

Being a learning method, the ultimate goal of involvement in classroom dialogue is that it should help with learning. The relationship between participation in classroom dialogue and learning outcomes is probably one of the most popular topics in the educational field. It is essential for the advancement of evidence-based academic understanding and the innovation of classroom practices (van der Veen & van Oers, 2017). Scholars' conclusions regarding whether and how these two variables are related are rather varied (see Howe & Abedin, 2013; Resnick et al., 2010; Rocca, 2010). One widely acknowledged proposal is that classroom dialogue has a positive effect on learning (D'Ambrosio et al., 1995; Koichu et al., 2007; Resnick et al., 2015). Talk is often regarded as crucial for pedagogy to be effective (van der Veen & van Oers, 2017), and students are expected to gain access to diverse ideas, gain practice in critical thinking, and deepen understanding (Mercer & Dawes, 2014). This may consequently be beneficial in terms of achieving satisfactory learning outcomes (Dallimore et al., 2010; Resnick et al., 2015). This effectiveness is undeniable in tasks that reflect higher-order thinking and complex cognitive abilities (Mercer & Dawes, 2014).

Many scholars have put forward persuasive arguments for the importance of classroom dialogue in developing students' reasoning and thinking, and in understanding curriculum subjects, especially mathematics and science (e.g. Alexander, 2001; Mortimer & Scott, 2003; Resnick et al., 2015). It is considered that the more a student talks in public, the better he/she will learn, while, on the contrary, students who play a less active role in classroom talk will have a lower level of learning (Bonwell & Eison, 1991; Dallimore et al., 2010; Nystrand, 1997). It is explained that through dialogue, students not only embrace diverse ideas but also 'gain practice in thinking through problems and organizing concepts, formulating arguments and counter-arguments, and responding thoughtfully and critically to diverse points of view' (Mercer & Dawes, 2014). This is assumed to facilitate learning achievement (Handelsman et al., 2005; Weaver & Qi, 2005). In particular, verbal participation, that is talk, has been highlighted as a key medium in the development of thinking and knowledge acquisition, as cited in Littleton and Mercer (2013, p. 98):

> Language plays an important role, as it is a medium for transmitting knowledge from one mind to another. . . . Individuals in a group can also gain new levels of understanding through co-construction, if they jointly construct new explanations with their partners. . . . It will promote their metacognitive awareness of how they talk and reason together.

There is empirical evidence that participation in classroom dialogue is associated with gains in learning outcomes in terms of both specific learning skills and general academic achievement (see Resnick et al., 2015). A few notable studies have been demonstrated, as follows. The work of Palincsar and Brown (1989) was a significant early contribution to the above claim, showing a positive relationship between talk and increases in a specific learning skill, reading comprehension. The study was conducted in a primary school, and the teachers adopted a reciprocal teaching method, which aimed to encourage students to participate, that is, talk actively and critically in class; in particular, students were prompted to contribute more by questioning, clarifying, summarizing, and predicting. Brown and Palincsar designed a series of specific dialogic strategies for both teachers and students. Results indicated that students made expressive gains in reading comprehension, and students who achieved a higher level of talk were more likely to understand reading content better.

Leach et al. (2003) conducted an ESRC-sponsored project, 'Evidence-based practices in science education'. The team worked with science teachers in nine local secondary schools in the design of three short teaching interventions, which were aimed primarily at students aged between 11 and 14 years. The interventions helped teachers adopt a dialogic teaching approach, including leaving time for students to express their ideas, helping them clarify ideas, extending their ideas, and assisting them in exploration. They chose a number of classes in which to conduct the intervention, while others were used for comparison. Students' learning outcomes were measured through diagnostic tests. The team found that students in the classes in which the intervention took place, namely those in which students were supported to talk more in class, generally had higher learning outcomes, particularly in relation to questions probing understanding.

A study conducted by Nystrand (1997) provides further positive evidence. Nystrand collected data from students aged about 16 years and then analysed these data qualitatively. He found that there was a close association between high-quality dialogue and student achievement. He noted that the talk that facilitated learning did not simply consist of a statement of facts or recall of information but involved those aspects that could improve understanding and thinking, such as explanation or hypothesis, which, in his view, constituted high-quality talk. A study carried out by Dallimore et al. (2010) with university students obtained similar results. Dallimore et al. collected data during 14 sections of an accounting course specially designed for university undergraduates. Participation referred only to verbal contributions and was assessed through the use of questionnaires, in which a 5-point Likert-type self-evaluation ranging from 'absent' to 'making outstanding comments' was used to grade students' participation performance. Course grades were collected from the lecturers afterward. Dallimore et al. reported significant positive associations between participation frequency and learning outcomes.

An intervention reported by Mercer and Littleton (2007) is seen as one of the most convincing studies supporting Vygotsky's sociocultural theory and showing that participating in classroom talk enhances learning outcomes. The project lasted a few months, targeting students between 7 and 11 years of age. Researchers working with teachers planned the intervention, aiming to engage more students in classroom dialogue, particularly through exploratory talk. Exploratory talk refers to a specific kind of dialogue in which speakers share relevant knowledge, challenge ideas, evaluate evidence, consider options, and try to reach agreement in an equitable manner. The intervention was then implemented in British primary schools. Students in the experimental schools were matched with those of the same age in other local schools, which taught the same curriculum using established methods. In the experimental classes, students were scaffolded to share information, challenge ideas, evaluate opinions, and explore knowledge. In order to investigate whether participation in classroom dialogue helps with reasoning and mastery of course content, researchers assessed learning outcomes using both Raven's Progressive Matrices test and standard academic tests. Results showed that students in the experimental classes used more exploratory talk than those in the control classes. Groups who contributed more and a higher level of talk solved Raven's problems more successfully, indicating that reasoning ability can be improved through classroom participation. Moreover, students in the experimental classes obtained higher scores on the science and mathematics tests. The researchers then concluded that participating in classroom dialogue facilitated learning. Effective as it may be, it should be acknowledged that this kind of dialogic teaching is exceedingly rare in classrooms (Cazden, 2001; O'Connor et al., 2017).

More recently, Webb et al. (2017) indicate that verbal exchanges that make explicit explanations are likely to facilitate learning gains. Research has shown improvements in science, mathematics, and language scores when classroom discussion is employed in school-level science and mathematics classes. They noted that such discussions led to better scores in these subjects. Furthermore, engaging students in exploratory talk was shown to significantly improve their reasoning skills as assessed by Raven's Standard Progressive Matrices test. Although these findings suggested effective transfer of learning, some dialogue-intensive studies yielded little positive results, only demonstrated delayed transfer, or faced criticism regarding methodology, sample size, or small effect sizes. However, within Barnett and Ceci's taxonomy of transfer, a selected set of studies focusing on exploratory talk and reasoning abilities using methodologically robust designs provided compelling evidence for the occurrence of far transfer. This research aims to delve into the connection between exploratory talk, argumentation, and critical areas of the science of learning to account for the observed far-transfer effects.

Howe et al. (2019) conducted a large-scale study on British pupils, which offered encouraging outcomes. Most prior research suggesting a link between talk and learning had been experimental or involved interventions with specifically designed dialogic teaching. However, there was a lack of evidence regarding the impact of everyday classroom discussions on learning outcomes. To address this gap, the study focused on two lessons – in mathematics and science – recorded on video in 72 classrooms representing a diverse demographic (with students aged 10–11 years). The teacher-student dialogue was examined in relation to six indices of student performance, covering curriculum understanding, reasoning, and relevant attitudes. The researchers took into account prior academic performance and attitudes, as well as other variables such as student demographics and aspects of classroom dynamics that could influence the dialogue-outcome relationship. They discovered that when students participated extensively and engaged in elaborate and inquisitive dialogue, it positively correlated with mastery of the curriculum and reasoning abilities.

To summarize, there is evidence that talking in classroom dialogue helps with learning. Scholars examine how specific modes of classroom dialogue might contribute to students' learning outcomes, such as an interactional configuration based on exchanges among students and teachers that go beyond the predominantly monologic approaches of classroom talk. In each of their contributions, different types of learning outcomes were studied as a result of specific ways of orchestrating classroom dialogue. All in all, these studies provide evidence for the plausibility of the assumption that dialogic orchestrations of classroom talk are likely to produce various desired learning and developmental outcomes in students, depending on what outcomes we want to articulate and how they are assessed. Due to the potentially more significant opportunity for achieving good outcomes, many scholars (e.g. Dallimore et al., 2010; Mercer, 2000; Weaver & Qi, 2005) have advocated that students should participate actively and, in particular, make more effective contributions in classroom dialogue. It is suggested that to support all students' learning equitably, teachers should encourage students to talk (see O'Connor et al., 2017). Ideally, contributions should be equalized across the student body, and students who play a less active role in talking probably should be given a chance by teachers (Howe & Abedin, 2013).

Challenges for implementing classroom dialogue

In practice, challenges exist to establishing classroom dialogue and bringing its role into full play. Several studies suggest that enhancing dialogic inquiry and genuine student engagement in productive interactions is a highly demanding task (Kumpulainen & Lipponen, 2010). Research further indicates that productive dialogic interactions are not commonly observed in classrooms and that teachers' awareness of how communicative practices unfold and their constitutive role in the process is limited (Nystrand et al., 2003). Due to the rapid pace of lessons and soliciting of correct answers, full sharing and exploration of ideas are less commonly observed (Mercer et al., 2010; Nystrand, 1997).

Educators frequently encounter challenges in utilizing classroom dialogue to accomplish their instructional objectives. According to Jacobs and colleagues (2022), many educators are unaware of the critical role that dialogue plays in the learning process. Several constraints hinder the effectiveness of dialogic instruction. Initially, educators often overlook the essential benchmarks for evaluating the success of dialogic instruction. Despite the existence of numerous evaluation tools proposed by educational researchers, these options can overwhelm teachers and obscure the essence of dialogic pedagogy, as noted by Howe and associates (2019). Furthermore, while teachers aim to enhance interaction through questioning, they may inadvertently overlook the deeper purposes of dialogue, as highlighted by Wilkinson and colleagues (2023). Specific forms of conversation are identified as pivotal to the richness of educational dialogue.

Moreover, the nature of classroom discussion is frequently fragmented, with exchanges being brief and disjointed (Lehesvuori & Ametller, 2021). Crafting a comprehension of dialogues as a shared, dynamic process where both educators and students contribute meaningfully is a formidable task for teachers, as reported by Parker and Bickmore (2020). Finally, while efforts have been made to integrate dialogic methods through professional development, the feedback loop for educators remains protracted due to the intricacies and time requirements of manual coding, as described by Song and colleagues (2021).

To address these barriers, it is imperative to devise more efficient and effective strategies for integrating classroom dialogue. Advancing dialogic education requires the exploration of innovative approaches and technologies. Breakthroughs in artificial intelligence technology hold the potential to significantly bolster both the research and application of classroom dialogue. By offering tools that facilitate interaction, encourage collaboration, and cater to individualized learning, AI can empower educators to make data-informed decisions. This can enhance the quality and depth of educational discussions and promote a more robust learning environment.

2 Educational use of artificial intelligence

Introduction of artificial intelligence

Artificial intelligence (AI) is a vast and dynamic field of computer science that endeavours to develop machines capable of executing tasks that would typically necessitate human intelligence. These tasks encompass a range of activities, such as speech recognition, decision-making, problem-solving, learning, and comprehending intricate data. The term 'artificial intelligence' was officially introduced in 1956 during a two-month colloquium at Dartmouth Conference. This event brought together scholars to engage in discussions about machine intelligence. During this meeting, McCarthy proposed the formal adoption of the term 'artificial intelligence', thereby establishing it as a distinct academic discipline. As a result of his seminal contributions, McCarthy is renowned as the father of artificial intelligence. The fundamental areas of research within artificial intelligence include:

1. *Data Mining and Knowledge Representation*: This involves transforming human knowledge into a formal or model-based structure. The goal of data mining is to uncover meaningful patterns within databases, using various methods such as rules, clustering, decision trees, and network-based techniques.
2. *Machine Perception*: This aims to endow machines with human-like perception capabilities, particularly computers. Machine vision and machine hearing are two primary aspects of this, where machines replace human eyes and ears for measurement and evaluation purposes.
3. *Machine Learning*: This field of research focuses on developing algorithms that enable computers to learn and acquire knowledge in a manner similar to humans. This empowers computers to automatically learn and improve from experience, without being explicitly programmed for specific tasks.

There are a few key concepts of AI area and their relationships can be viewed in Figure 2.1. Machine learning (ML) is a crucial component of AI that empowers systems to autonomously learn from datasets, recognize patterns, and render decisions with minimal human involvement. ML algorithms grant computers the capacity to glean insights from historical data, enhancing their proficiency in

DOI: 10.4324/9781003543039-2

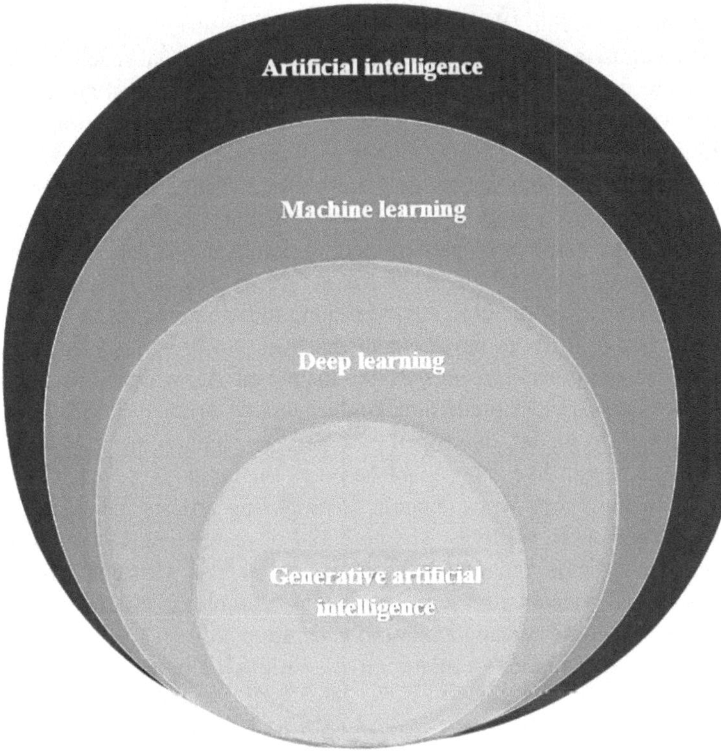

Figure 2.1 The relationships between basic concepts of artificial intelligence

performing specific tasks continuously. This advancement is accomplished through training models on extensive datasets, enabling algorithms to pinpoint and decipher patterns and connections that can subsequently be employed for forecasting or decision-making purposes. ML technology enables computers to acquire knowledge independently, without the need for explicit programming. The two primary categories of machine learning models are supervised and unsupervised learning models. The fundamental disparity between these two types is that supervised models utilize data with pre-existing labels, which are essentially tags such as names, categories, or numbers attached to the data. On the other hand, unsupervised problems involve examining unlabelled data to determine if it naturally clusters into distinct groups.

Deep learning (DL) is a focused area of machine learning that utilizes neural networks with multiple layers, earning it the name 'deep'. These neural networks aim to mimic the functions of the human brain, though in a simplified version, enabling the system to identify patterns and feature hierarchies. Composed of billions of interconnected nodes or neurons, these networks can learn tasks through data processing and prediction. DL models, with their numerous layers of neurons, are capable of recognizing more intricate patterns than traditional machine learning models. This technology has caused substantial progress in several domains, such as computer vision, natural language processing, and speech recognition.

Generative artificial intelligence, a branch of deep learning, is capable of producing novel content by drawing on learnt information from existing material. This type of AI is engineered to generate new information, such as text, images, or videos, through the analysis of patterns within a substantial dataset. Generative AI operates by employing ML algorithms to scrutinize extensive data to pinpoint underlying patterns and structures. After grasping these patterns, it can utilize that acquired knowledge to forge new content that was not previously encountered. This is distinct from other forms of AI, like diagnostic AI, which aims to discern patterns within data to make predictions or decisions. A prime example of generative AI is the GPT-4 model, developed by OpenAI, which is adept at producing text that mimics human-like expressions based on the input it receives. GPT-4 has been applied in numerous ways, including composing articles, generating code, and even building entire websites. The potential of generative AI to transform a broad spectrum of fields, including education, is immense. However, its deployment raises ethical concerns. As with any potent technology, it is crucial to consider the appropriate use and application of generative AI.

Regarding the AI technique's relation to classroom dialogue, natural language processing (NLP) has an excellent role to play. NLP is one of the main areas of research in artificial intelligence. It cares about how to make computers understand, interpret, and generate human natural language. It is the transition from natural language to machine internalization, enabling the machine to perform certain linguistic functions expected by humans. Important applications of NLP include: (1) *Question answering*: the computer correctly answers relevant questions entered in natural language. (2) *Text generation*: the machine is able to produce a summary of the input text. (3) *Paraphrasing*: the machine is able to paraphrase the input natural language information using different words and sentence patterns. (4) *Translation*: the machine is able to translate from one language to another. (5) *Sentiment Analysis*: Determining the attitude – positive, negative, or neutral – of the speaker or writer in a given text. (6) *Text Classification:* Assigning texts to predefined categories based on their content. In recent years, NLP has seen rapid progress due to the availability of large amounts of data, computational power, and sophisticated generative AI algorithms. It continues to be an active area of research and application, with new models and techniques constantly developed.

The rapid development of artificial intelligence, especially the NLP technique, provides practical tools and means to promote the advancement of the field of classroom dialogue. Deep learning methods have advanced from simple language imitation to information storage. Instead, it helps to learn the intrinsic laws of dialogic data and is able to tap into the reasoning chain, track knowledge construction, and facilitate problem exploration. AI techniques also provide valuable insights for teachers and students to reflect on their dialogic contributions and make improvements in a more personalized way. AI technique is releasing its potential in research and practice of classroom dialogue.

Main application scenarios of artificial intelligence in education

The application of Artificial Intelligence in Education (AIED) has seen significant advancements in recent times. It is crucial to comprehend the direction and progress of AIED research to foster innovation and integration in educational settings. A study employing bibliometric analysis from Web of Science and Scopus revealed that China, the United States, India, Spain, and Germany are at the forefront of AIED production (Guo et al., 2024). AIED research has predominantly utilized technologies such as machine learning, generative AI, deep learning, speech recognition, and computer vision. Upon examining AIED research, it is evident that several critical aspects have garnered substantial interest and attention.

Automated feedback systems

Automated feedback systems (AFS) can deliver real-time, personalized feedback to students, allowing for support at any location and time. They have been developed across multiple fields and are designed with unique approaches to address varied educational objectives (Pardo et al., 2019). Gupta and Jain (2017) noted that technology's role in education ensures accessible, high-quality learning opportunities for students globally. AFS collects data to construct learner profiles and models, customizing the learning material to individual needs and progress. Educators and researchers can leverage these datasets to anticipate students' performance and potential challenges (Godwin-Jones, 2019). Automated Writing Evaluation (AWE) is one of the AFS tools that supports educational assessment, providing immediate feedback to students on their writing, often accompanying Automated Essay Scoring to aid in revision and enhancement (Wilson & Roscoe, 2020; Grimes & Warschauer, 2010). AWE aims to alleviate teacher workload associated with grading, allowing them to offer more frequent writing practice and targeted feedback on advanced writing skills (Wilson & Czik, 2016). Studies indicate that AWE improves students' writing quality, motivation, and self-efficacy related to writing (e.g. Knight et al., 2020; Wilson & Roscoe, 2020). Computer-based evaluation system works not only for multiple-choice questions but also on proper evaluation systems for grading essays and short answers. Many researchers have been working on automated essay grading for a few decades and can assess an essay by considering parameters like the relevance of the content to the prompt, development of ideas, cohesion, and coherence. Additionally, AI methods are proficient in accurately predicting student outcomes. As the number of teachers' student ratio is gradually increasing, the manual evaluation process becomes complicated. The drawback of manual evaluation is that it is time-consuming and lacks reliability. Typical uses of such AI predictions include forecasting academic results, engagement levels, knowledge retention, dropout rates, and the early identification of learning difficulties (Luan & Tsai, 2021).

Intelligent tutoring system

Advancements in technology have made it possible to create diverse computer-based tutoring systems (ITS). ITS are advanced computer programs engineered to offer customized learning experiences tailored to each student's needs (Sani & Aris, 2014). These systems replicate the interaction that takes place between a human tutor and learner, falling under the domain of computer-assisted learning and drawing heavily on cognitive science theories (Yang, 2011). ITS are applicable across numerous subjects and educational stages, ranging from early childhood education through to higher education. Notable aspects and the advantages of ITS in educational settings include: firstly, ITS accommodates students' individual learning preferences and speeds, offering appropriate guidance such as explanations, clues, or illustrations depending on their progress and requirements (Klašnja-Milićević et al., 2011). Secondly, by integrating various multimedia tools like videos, simulations, and interactive games, ITS fosters dynamic and captivating learning environments, maintaining student motivation and involvement (Delen et al., 2014). These systems evaluate a spectrum of learner attributes and educational needs, often with superb granularity, adjusting the teaching approach in alignment with established learning principles. Due to these capabilities and robust empirical evidence, ITS has gained widespread adoption across diverse educational contexts to bolster student learning (Guo et al., 2024). Additionally, they serve as robust platforms for advancing research in learning sciences and artificial intelligence. For example, VanLehn's (2011) analysis of tutoring methodologies revealed that the effectiveness of human tutoring and ITS was almost equivalent, with respective effect sizes of $d = .79$ and $d = .76$. In a meta-analysis conducted by Ma et al. (2014), ITS was demonstrated to deliver significant educational benefits over traditional teacher-led lessons, group instructions, non-ITS computer-based training, and printed materials. These advantages were validated across different educational levels and disciplines. The iSTART program (McNamara et al., 2004), an ITS focusing on reading comprehension that coaches the application of self-explanatory strategies, has proven particularly effective for students with below-average abilities, as evidenced by the research of Jackson et al. (2010).

Educational use of AI agents

AI agents are entities capable of executing intelligent tasks through reasoning, learning, and some degree of self-expression. These agents come in various forms, such as humanoid and cartoon, as noted by Randall (2019). They can also be categorized based on their visibility – embodied or disembodied – with the former including physical robots and virtual agents (e.g. Randall, 2019; Van den Berghe et al., 2019) and the latter typically being invisible and utilized through smart devices like Google Assistant and Amazon's Alexa (e.g. Dizon, 2020; Moussalli & Cardoso, 2020). AI agents, including robots and virtual assistants, are increasingly being integrated into educational settings to aid in the learning process across different subjects. For example, Chen et al. (2020) looked into how second-language learners at varying English proficiency levels perceived the utility of Google Assistant for language learning. Initial findings from surveys and interviews suggested that these learners found interactions with Google Assistant engaging and believed it could enhance their speaking and listening skills, suggesting its educational potential. Jeon (2022) further explored the educational benefits of AI chatbots for English as a Foreign Language (EFL) learning by analysing primary school students' interviews and interaction logs with the chatbots. The analysis revealed the chatbots' pedagogical, technological, and social affordances, which are opportunities for students to engage in interactive learning. Research by Lee and Jeon (2022) has shown that AI agents are beneficial in enhancing students' linguistic abilities, including areas like vocabulary, listening, and speaking.

Using chatbots for students' learning

Chatbots that utilize AI have the capacity to create more engaging and adaptable educational tools through the use of machine learning (Colace et al., 2018). In recent times, AI-driven chatbots such as ChatGPT and Bing Chat have received a surge in global interest. According to Huang et al. (2022), educational chatbots fall into three primary categories of development. First, the cognitive chatbots are designed to foster students' cognitive growth. This approach stemmed from AutoTutor (Graesser et al., 1999), which was widely employed to assist students in gaining in-depth knowledge of various subjects. Countless studies along this line provide guidance for practice, suggesting that students engage in specific cognitive activities to accomplish certain learning objectives. These may include posing questions to students or responding to their queries (Fryer et al., 2019; Lin & Chang, 2020; Mazzoni & Benvenuti, 2015). In mathematics, chatbots help guide students' focus on intended instructional elements (Mohammadhasani et al., 2018) or prompt them to respond to questions (Konijn & Hoorn, 2020). Research has validated the beneficial impact of chatbot interaction on learning outcomes. Datta et al. (2021) introduced chatbots as learnable agents instead of teaching agents, which can potentially engage learners more actively than previous methods. The second kind of chatbot is the meta-cognitive variety, which encourages students to contemplate meta-cognitive issues. For instance, Song and Kim's (2021) chatbot acts as a facilitator for self-regulated learning, demonstrating that meta-cognitive questions can boost the level of self-regulated learning. Additionally, Kautzmann and Jaques' (2019) chatbot prompts students to reflect on their own knowledge, while Tegos and Demetriadis (2017) encourage students to evaluate their concepts and connect them to overarching domain principles. These studies have shown that meta-cognitive questions can enhance meta-cognitive performance during the learning process. The third category is social chatbots. These are particularly beneficial in open learning settings where students can explore freely. Social chatbots' main role is not to provide cognitive support but to accompany students and offer emotional encouragement to facilitate active learning (Huang et al., 2022). Social robots play a crucial role in keeping students emotionally engaged to sustain their interest in learning. Laeeq and Memon's (2019) research supports the idea that social chatbots can increase students' motivation to complete tasks within a learning management system. In Fryer et al.'s (2017) study, a chatbot was used to accompany students during learning, and the results indicated that the chatbot helped students maintain initial interest in tasks, similar to human interaction. However, it did not have a lasting effect.

Educational use of virtual reality

Virtual reality (VR) technology serves as a bridge between the real and digital spheres, merging features of augmented reality (AR), mixed reality (MR), and digital humanities. This interdisciplinary approach can enrich learning through immersive, interactive experiences. The integration of generative AI has further enhanced VR's capacity for intelligent and adaptable user interaction, leading to the creation of more tailored and precise content delivery (Kasneci et al., 2023). VR, AR, and MR are distinguished by their high level of interactivity and ability to simulate environments closely resembling reality. This has significant implications for teacher training and the advancement of teaching methodologies (Vertemati et al., 2019). By integrating the real and virtual worlds, these technologies offer teachers the opportunity to engage in realistic teaching exercises, surpassing the limitations of real-life classrooms and facilitating the repeated practice of teaching skills (Bradley & Kendall, 2014). Extensive research shows that VR, AR, and MR significantly contribute to the development of teaching skills and professional growth. For instance, the University of Central Florida developed TeachLivE, a mixed-reality simulation that duplicates various classroom scenarios, enabling pre-service teachers to refine their skills repeatedly (Paul et al., 2020). Dawson and colleagues (2017) utilized a Technology-Enhanced Learning Environment (TLE) to provide structured feedback and repetitive practice, enhancing the delivery of feedback and error correction. Lamb and Etopio (2020) confirmed the transferability of skills developed in virtual settings to real-life classrooms. Lee and Wu (2024) suggested that virtual teaching environments encourage teachers to reflect on interactions with students, fostering better questioning, listening, and understanding, thereby improving teaching strategies. Chen et al. (2021) found that using Interactive Spherical Video-Based Virtual Reality in teaching can enhance conceptual understanding, encourage educational technology integration, and bolster teachers' technological proficiency.

Recommender systems with educational sources

Recommender systems, which are types of software designed to supply users with Digital resource suggestions that could be beneficial, assist individuals in managing the vast array of alternatives available to them (Klašnja-Milićević et al., 2015). These systems help learners, educators, and other education stakeholders by lessening information overload and guiding them towards relevant resources, such as web pages, scholarly articles, educational materials, and more (Dhahri & Khribi, 2021).

In educational settings, intelligent recommender systems have several significant uses:

1. *Educational Pathway and Curriculum Suggestions*: These systems can evaluate a student's academic record, preferences, and learning styles to propose fitting courses and curricula, aiding students in choosing paths that align with their aspirations and leading to improved academic engagement and outcomes (Klašnja-Milićević et al., 2011).
2. *Educational Content and Resources*: Recommender systems can suggest educational materials tailored to a student's learning preferences, existing knowledge, and academic requirements, enriching the learning experience and providing additional resources to aid comprehension (Ezaldeen et al., 2022).
3. *Personalized Learning Journeys*: By assessing a student's progress and learning needs, these systems can recommend customized learning paths, tutorials, and interventions, thus supporting students with diverse needs and enhancing learning achievements (Lin et al., 2013).
4. *Professional Development for Educators*: Intelligent recommender systems can identify suitable professional development resources and communities for teachers based on their field of expertise, teaching experience, and professional curiosity, promoting ongoing professional development and better teaching methodologies (Dascalu et al., 2016). For instance, a study conducted by Shelton et al. (2010) examined the effectiveness of an educational recommender system, 'Folksemantic', which aids teachers in discovering Learning Resources (LRs). Their analysis of user interaction logs revealed that 11% of the recommendations were selected for further exploration. However, the study noted that interaction did not necessarily imply that the suggested LRs were found to meet the teachers' needs.

Exploring usages of artificial intelligence in the field of classroom dialogue

Transforming the way classroom dialogue is tracked

Traditionally, data collection for assessing educational achievement is a manual process that involves creating and distributing questionnaires and test papers to collect specific information from students, teachers, and other staff members. AI technology has revolutionized this process by enabling the automatic compilation of comprehensive data from the learning and teaching experience. This allows for continuous assessment of educational activities. The advent of intelligent recording and broadcasting systems, wearable technology, and interactive whiteboards has made data collection concurrent, automatic, and multimodal. These technologies can accurately capture the speech and interaction dynamics during classroom dialogue. They can also reflect students' and teachers' psychological states, attention levels, stress levels, and cognitive patterns through natural language processing and facial and gesture recognition. This provides educators and researchers with valuable insights into the dialogic process, allowing them to tailor educational strategies to meet the needs of students better. AI enables the comprehensive assessment of the dialogic process in classroom settings, providing valuable data that can be used to improve educational outcomes.

AI enhances the understanding of the complex dynamics involved in dialogue processes

Traditional methods of assessing classroom instruction, such as questionnaires and static data analysis using quantitative statistical methods, fail to capture the intricacies and evolving nature of dialogic education. In contrast, AI is capable of detecting the fine details of verbal exchanges through machine learning-based automatic annotation. This helps in understanding the essence of classroom dialogue. AI technology goes beyond manual coding by offering superior scalability and efficiency, revealing the implicit construction of knowledge, cognitive development, and skill enhancement that are crucial for effective classroom engagement. It can also encode and shape new teaching methodologies, dissect the pedagogical ecosystem, and articulate the interactive patterns within inquiry-based and heuristic instructional approaches. AI enables the digitalization of complex relationships, such as sequential and cause-and-effect linkages, taking classroom process computability to a deeper level. This computational approach empowers educators to identify the profound rules of engagement, refine exemplary teaching models, support the proliferation of innovative teaching practices, and establish efficient learning environments. Furthermore, AI improves the precision of the evaluation of classroom dialogue. Technologies like graph neural networks excel in extracting relational and spatial data features, helping to capture the dynamic and patterned features of classroom interaction. As a result, AI technology offers a path to accurate teaching evaluation, aiding teachers in understanding their effectiveness, informing decisions, and providing an effective tool for overseeing educational quality.

Optimizing strategies for dialogic pedagogy in a personalized and scalable way

High-calibre and effective dialogue in the classroom serves as a critical pathway for enhancing the standards of talent development. The challenge now lies in providing tailored and prompt optimization strategies to educators, which has emerged as a pivotal aspect of superior teaching quality. AI technique can optimize dialogic strategies in a personalized and scalable manner, which involves adapting and tailoring the teaching methods to suit individual needs while also ensuring that these strategies can be effectively implemented on a larger scale. By harnessing the capabilities of generative artificial intelligence in natural language understanding and content creation, intelligent agents, such as virtual teaching assistants, can be developed to diversify strategies for dialogic contribution. It eliminates the limitations of time and space and bolsters the levels of scalability and personalization. This, in turn, fosters the transformation and evolution of educational paradigms and teaching methodologies. These AI assistants autonomously craft teaching strategies and chart improvement paths for educators, assisting in enriching and broadening the scope of dialogic content, establishing comprehensive knowledge frameworks, refining instructional structures, and planning operationalized teaching approaches. They offer targeted guidance and data-driven insights on dialogic pedagogy, thereby enhancing teaching effectiveness and augmenting the cultivation of innovative talent.

3 Automatic assessment of classroom dialogue using machine learning technique

One common method for examining classroom dialogue is to segment a transcribed conversation into a set of features based on coding categories. Coding is primarily manual and labour-intensive, typically taking several times longer than the recorded lesson to process a transcript. Participants in dialogue, especially teachers, lack timely feedback about the conversation's progression, which has been identified as a crucial factor contributing to low-quality classroom dialogue. Therefore, automatic classification of transcribed classroom dialogue is urgently needed. In this chapter, we introduce two methods for automatic dialogic coding. One approach is a discriminate approach, with a hybrid CNN-BiLSTM model introduced. The other approach is retrieval augmented generation, which can combine the benefits of the traditional deep learning model with generative artificial intelligence. After training, these machine learning techniques can comprehend the semantic content of the dialogue and assist humans in coding. Timely feedback for teachers and students about dialogic performance can then be provided. The efficiency of detecting productive forms of dialogue should significantly improve. Teachers can use the data from productive dialogue to understand how well students understand the material and adjust their teaching strategies accordingly. This can lead to more effective classroom instruction.

Importance of automatic coding to classroom dialogue research

To illustrate the dialogic process and examine its relationships with other variables, systematic observation is widely used. This method offers the advantage of reducing dialogue transcript data into a specific set of features (Mercer, 2010). Coding involves developing categories based on their relevance to research questions and then classifying dialogue accordingly. Examples of frequently used codes for classroom settings include elaboration, teachers' raising questions, and subjective expression. Trained observers/coders typically sit in classrooms or work with conversation transcripts, assigning dialogue segments to appropriate categories. Several computer-based text analysis software applications, such as NVivo, have been designed to assist humans in coding (Mercer & Dawes, 2014). This software can assist human researchers in identifying patterns of language use and the occurrence of specific words, aiding in both qualitative and quantitative analyses

DOI: 10.4324/9781003543039-3

of dialogue. However, even with such assistance, coding classroom dialogue relies heavily on manual work (Blanchard et al., 2015). Training eligible coders can be time-consuming, and reliability between coders may be challenging due to differences in their ability to understand episodes (Webb et al., 2019). Furthermore, coding is a time-consuming task, and participants must wait for substantial periods before receiving feedback on their actual performance in dialogic teaching and learning (Wang et al., 2014).

It is rational to assume that timely feedback is more effective than delayed feedback, as memories of class performance may be overridden by subsequent experiences and become inaccurate (Murphy et al., 2009). Formative feedback plays a crucial role in enhancing the quality of dialogic instruction and students' learning achievements (Steen-Utheim & Wittek, 2017). Researchers often struggle with the decision to provide detailed accounts of the dialogic process for a few classes or to survey the dialogue's nature in a large sample of classrooms in a more general manner. For instance, Hennessy and her team (2016) proposed a coding scheme for classroom dialogue using explicit categories, which were later condensed into a smaller number for greater implementation in large-scale observations (Howe et al., 2019). The question of whether it is possible to process a large number of dialogic transcripts while providing prompt feedback is crucial. A viable solution would be to develop a model that can automatically and rapidly classify classroom dialogue into suitable categories.

Automatic classification refers to a technique that enables machines to operate independently in classifying data into predefined categories (Dorofeyuk, 1971). In comparison to manual classification, automatic classification is faster and more cost-effective. A broad spectrum of classification tasks can be performed, including text classification, image recognition, and more. Text classification has garnered increasing attention in recent years as a research topic in natural language processing. It involves assigning predefined categories to texts based on their extracted features and content (Dalal & Zaveri, 2011). A variety of methods have been developed for text categorization, with the rule-based approach being one of the earliest and most utilized (Sigaud & Wilson, 2007). Rule-based methods heavily depend on a set of manually crafted linguistic rules, but creating these rules is time-consuming and often incomplete (Varadarajan et al., 2003). This approach is less effective in identifying the categories to which new texts belong, based on a training set containing texts with known categories. In such cases, machine learning and language representation methods are employed. By using pre-labelled text as a training dataset, machines can learn semantically relevant elements and associations between text content, enabling them to identify relevant categories based on learnt features (Olsson, 2009). For example, da Silva et al. (2014) proposed a technique for automated detection of Twitter sentiment using classifier ensembles consisting of random forest, logistic regression, support vector machine, and multinomial naive Bayes. As natural language processing tasks have become more complex, deep learning techniques have been developed and applied to text classification (Pouyanfar et al., 2018). Deep learning approaches are better at learning semantic information at more profound levels by utilizing neural networks, making them efficient for various text classification tasks such as intent detection, sentiment analysis, and news classification (Young et al., 2018). For instance, Chen (2015) proposed a convolutional neural network for sentence distinction. Liu et al. (2016) presented a recurrent neural network for text classification. These deep learning-based models have brought about significant improvements in various text classification tasks.

Recently, some studies that combine large language models (LLMs) and natural language processing tasks have shown new promise. Based on the input of massive data, the machine is capable of automatically generating various forms of response like textual answers. The ability of LLMs has significantly enhanced in terms of understanding context, learning from feedback, and promoting the generation of coherent, logical, and precise responses (Min et al., 2023). However, despite the significant advances in LLMs, their use, as previously mentioned, still presents several challenges. Notably, in specialized vertical domains, these models often exhibit the phenomenon of hallucination, which can severely impact the accuracy of their results (Raiaan et al., 2024). Retrieval-augmented generation techniques can help mitigate such issues by leveraging domain-specific databases, enhancing the application effectiveness and information accuracy of large language models (Radeva et al., 2024). This technology has demonstrated promising results in other fields. For instance, GeneGPT employs the National Center for Biotechnology Information (NCBI) web application programming interface to answer genomics questions and incorporates these answers into crafted prompts before querying the large language model Codex. This approach significantly outperforms large biomedical language models and GPT-3 on the GeneTuring test set. Chat-Orthopaedist retrieves information from a knowledge base containing AIS diseases and treatment options to augment the response capabilities of large language models like ChatGPT, effectively reducing the risk of unrealistic outputs and enhancing model transparency (Shi et al., 2023). However, in the realm of classroom dialogue research, the use of retrieval-augmented generation techniques with large language models has not yet been explored, and the substantial potential of this technology in the educational field remains untapped.

Existing research has investigated the potential of using machines to aid manual labour by automatically coding classroom conversations. Ford and his team (2008) designed a Language Environment Analysis (LENA) system to record and automatically identify information about the language environment of young children. Weisleder and Fernald (2013) recorded dialogic interactions between children and their parents with LENA's assistance, discovering that children with more dialogic interactions showed faster language development. Wang et al. (2014) automatically categorized dialogue activities into teacher lectures, whole-class discussions, and small-group conversations using LENA, employing a random forest technique for machine training. The reliability of the machine classification was found to be comparable to that of human coders. Blanchard et al. (2015) automated the coding of questions and answers (Q&A) in classroom conversations. They developed a model to detect Q&A segments using a 90-second time window, achieving an area under the receiver operating characteristic curve (AUC) of 0.78 for generalizing to new classes. Suresh et al. (2022) investigated the feasibility of using enriched contextual cues to improve model performance. They applied state-of-the-art deep learning approaches for Natural Language Processing (NLP) to classify teacher talk moves. Shin et al. (2023) employed computational linguistic tools and natural language processing (NLP) to classify educators' language choices. Variations in language choices, as signified by discourse markers, were examined through a K-means clustering approach. The resulting 17 clusters were grouped into interpersonal, structural, and cognitive pedagogic functions.

These studies represented critical initial steps in automating classroom dialogue classification, yet they were primarily preliminary and failed to address the core attributes of dialogue thoroughly. These techniques distinguish between general dialogue forms, such as activities or Q&A, but few can code semantic content or dialogue quality automatically. Typically, detecting such forms of classroom dialogue cannot accurately reflect learners' proficiency levels or demonstrate how they contribute to knowledge construction and thinking development (Howe et al., 2019). Categories related to productive classroom dialogue, such as elaboration and coordination, are less considered. Scholars have identified these limitations but have not yet provided viable solutions (see Blanchard et al, 2015; Wang et al., 2014).

To address these constraints, this chapter will introduce the development of a coding framework, the Coding Instrument for Productive Classroom Dialogue (CI-PCD). Moreover, automatic classification and evaluation of the semantic content of classroom dialogue into categories will be introduced. Two approaches of machine learning methods for assisting humans in assessing dialogue quality have been proposed, along with validation. The primary aspects of this chapter's development include:

1. Development and introduction of an assessment instrument for classroom dialogue. This instrument aims to cater to the needs of intelligent classroom dialogue analysis and automatic assessment and is designed to be measurable and operational.
2. Development of automatic coding techniques for classroom dialogue based on audio-video transcription text. According to the evaluation system, a mixed neural network will be used to automatically label and efficiently extract key characteristics involving thinking cultivation in classroom teaching, which is a crucial step in achieving large-scale analysis.
3. Testing the feasibility of the coding instrument and machine learning models using data from authentic classroom settings.

Coding instrument for classroom dialogue

The development of coding instruments is essential for assessing classroom dialogue performance. It serves as the basis for applying artificial intelligence technology to classroom teaching analysis and enables precise machine labelling. Furthermore, it is a critical step in converting abstract thinking cultivation objectives into quantifiable and evaluable indicators. Numerous coding categories and frameworks have been proposed for classroom dialogue, but there is a lack of consensus among them, and occasionally, different terminologies are used to express similar meanings (Hennessy et al., 2016). Over the past 20 years, the number of publications on classroom dialogue has skyrocketed, and there has been growing interest in research and practical applications of classroom dialogue worldwide (Song et al., 2019). When examining dialogue, scholars typically utilize codes derived from specific scripts or design a framework tailored to their research interests. A multitude of coding frameworks, instruments, and specific codes have been developed, making cross-study comparisons challenging and hindering the field's impact on policy and practice (Hennessy et al., 2016). Consequently, a systematic review of the coding frameworks used in assessing classroom dialogue is desperately needed to facilitate the emergence of typical themes and forms across frameworks. This would enable scholars and practitioners to become more proficient in designing or selecting frameworks.

Data selection

'Classroom' and its two associated terms 'whole-class' and 'small-group' were taken as one set of keywords and 'dialogue' and associated terms, 'dialogic', 'discourse', 'conversation', 'discussion', 'language', 'interaction', 'talk', 'communication', and 'speaking' acted as the other set of keywords in the literature search. Publications were retrieved from the most important bibliometric database, Web of Science (WoS) (Cobo et al., 2015), and 3,914 publications were filtered after computer retrieval and artificial preprocessing. We checked these publications and retained the ones showing complete parts of coding frameworks, which resulted in 51 articles remaining for reviewing. The following information was systematically reviewed: name of instruments, contexts of the use of instruments (i.e. educational contexts and cultural contexts), coding domains, specific codes, and evaluation of frameworks (i.e. reliability and validity). A summary of the main coding domains is listed in Figure 3.1.

The demonstration of coding framework themes

As indicated in Howe et al. (2019), classroom dialogue should exhibit certain characteristics in order to optimize student outcomes. The review of publications indicates that there are six themes that a dialogic framework should encapsulate in its categories (see Table 3.1). Firstly, there should be categories that take account of prior-known information, which includes standard-referenced knowledge, rule-governed answers, and repetition of previous knowledge (see, e.g. Alexander, 2017; Chinn et al., 2000; Ruiz-Primo, 2011). Standard-referenced knowledge is that which can be judged right or wrong with reference to textbooks or knowledge that teachers have taught before; rule-governed dialogue is concerned with culturally recognized explanations and solutions to a problem of an algorithmic kind, which student(s) is expected to know or should be able to compute; repetition of previous knowledge refers to the dialogue narrating or describing previous

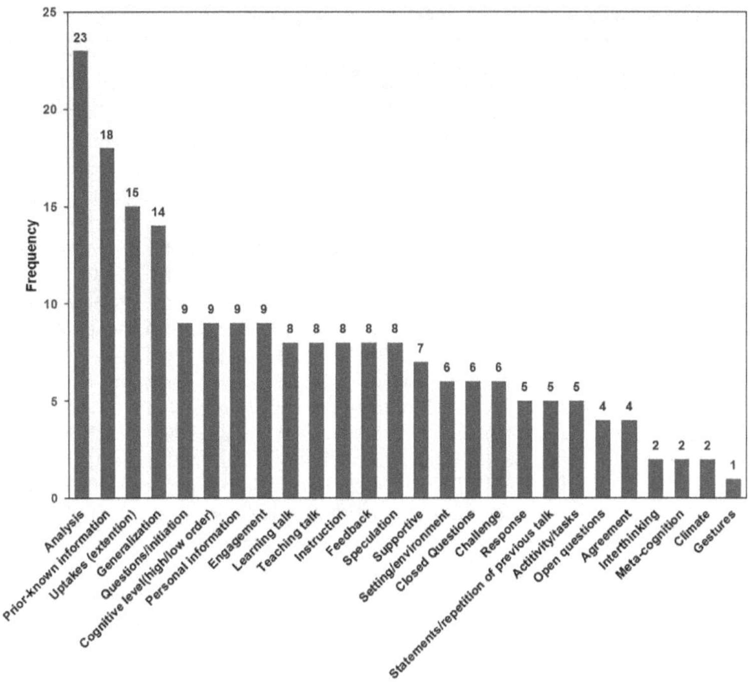

Figure 3.1 Frequencies for the coding domains in the frameworks

contributions made by other students or teachers. It usually only requires recitation to contribute to this kind of dialogue and does not involve a complicated process of thinking, which is recognized as a low cognitive level (Chin, 2006). Dialogue in this theme aims to help students obtain information, concepts, basic knowledge, and facts, and to learn basic methods and ground rules.

The second theme deals with personal information, which is further divided into the categories of personal experience, imagination, subjective opinions, and feelings/emotions (see, e.g. Boyd & Markarian, 2011; Fisher, 2007; Galton et al., 1999; Hennessy et al., 2016). Dialogue coded as personal experience is an invitation or providing events in the speaker's life that are not assumed to be known to other participants; imagination is the personal response of an imaginative kind to a situation or work of art; subjective opinions are what the speaker personally believes about a topic or situation of personal concern; feelings/emotions invites or describe affective and sensitive states. This kind of dialogue aims to help students express individual thoughts, emotions, opinions, and feelings.

The third theme shown in coding frameworks is concerned with elaboration, which can further be found in evaluation, explanation/justification and exemplification (see, e.g. Boyd & Markarian, 2011; Dolin et al., 2018; Hennessy et al., 2016;

Table 3.1 Themes emerged from a review of dialogic frameworks

Themes	*Codes in the dialogic frameworks*
Prior-known information	Narrate, rote, recitation, exposition (Alexander, 2017); closed questions, direct speaker nominations, didactic statements, revoicing of student language, direct prompting (Boyd & Markarian, 2011); repetitions (Chinn et al., 2000); provides background information (Dwyer et al., 2016); precise question, leading question, something missing (Ellegaard et al., 2018); sharing previous knowledge or experience (Fisher, 2007); recasts, repetition, introduce authoritative perspective (Hennessy et al., 2016); recall facts, providing information, offer ideas and solutions (closed) (Jay et al., 2017); factual questions, personal connection (Jie et al., 2016); knowledge (Lee & Irving, 2018); direct, closed questions (Lefstein et al., 2015); factual (Muhonen et al., 2017); fact, rule-governed answer, report of public event (Nassaji & Wells, 2000); teaching social rule, teaching academic skill (National Institute of Child Health and Human Development Early Child Care Research Network, 2002); learning basic skills (Nichd & Bonnie, 2005); describing processes or reactions, definitions, stating laws, principles, terms, models, symbols, knowledge from everyday life (Podschuweit, Bernholt, & Brückmann, 2016); recitation, revoice, rephrase/repeat (Alexander, 2018); tapping into diverse types of knowledge, type of information asked in the question (Ruiz-Priomo, 2011); linking concepts (Smith et al., 2013); reviewing, rote recall, previous conversation, memory/prior knowledge, fact, rule-governed answer (Wells & Arauz, 2006)
Personal Information/ Subjective expression	Everyday talk, imagine (Alexander, 2017); open questions, inauthentic questions (Boyd & Markarian, 2011); sharing experience, imagining and seeing things in the mind's eye (Fisher, 2007); offer ideas and solutions (open) (Galton et al., 1999); invite opinions/ beliefs/ideas (Hennessy et al., 2016); imagine (Jay et al., 2017); open questions, presentation (Lefstein et al., 2015); experiential, imaginative, affectional, view (Muhonen et al., 2017); experience, imagination, opinion (Nassaji & Wells, 2000); negative with peers, positive/neutral with peers, positive/neutral with teacher, negative with teacher (Nichd & Bonnie, 2005); emotional engagement, emotional support (Pöysä et al., 2018); imagination, personal opinion, opinion (Wells & Arauz, 2006)

(Continued)

Table 3.1 (Continued)

Themes	*Codes in the dialogic frameworks*
Elaboration	Explain, analyse, evaluate, justify, discuss, reasoning (Alexander, 2017); explications (Boyd & Markarian, 2011); precise valuing, precise correction (Dolin et al., 2018); facilitates reasoning, encourages students to provide evidence from text (Dwyer et al., 2016); wondering question (Ellegaard et al., 2018); giving examples (Fisher, 2007); generative mechanisms, reasoning activities, acknowledgement, frames, forestall/secure, forestall/remove (Harney, Hogan, & Quinn, 2017); ask for explanation or justification of another's contribution, invite building on/elaboration/(dis)agreement/evaluation of another's contribution or view, ask for explanation or justification, ask for elaboration or clarification, explain or justify another's contribution, explain or justify own contribution (Hennessy et al., 2016); elaboration, reasoning, elaboration of previous contributions, reasoned discussion of competing viewpoints (Howe et al., 2019); asking for clarifications (Hulsman & Vloodt, 2015); why question, explain, evaluate, justify (Jay et al., 2017); comments (Jie et al., 2016); explanation/examples (Lee & Irving, 2018); explain, elaborated feedback, explain, elaborated feedback (Lefstein et al., 2015); argumentational, expositional (Muhonen et al., 2017); conventional explanation, explanation, amplification, justification (Nassaji & Wells, 2000); learning analysis/inference (Nichd & Bonnie, 2005); level of evaluation (Nystrand et al., 2003); analysis and inquiry (Pianta, Hamre, & Allen, 2012); describing and justifying arrays of causes, giving reasons for linear chains of causes and effects or reaction schemes, justifying results or steps within a process, justifying factors of influence, deductive reasoning, calculations with multiple steps (Podschuweit et al., 2016); explain, analyse, evaluate, evidence of reasoning (Alexander, 2018); analysis of the interaction, analysis of the discourse, analysis of problem-solving (Rojas-Drummod et al., 2003); offering explanations, elaborating, offering explanations (Ruiz-Priomo, 2011); elaborated explanations, reasoning words (Soter et al., 2008); analysis/explanation, commenting (Wells & Arauz, 2006); teacher explanation (Xie & Cao, 2010)
Coordination	Summarizing (Dolin et al., 2018); prompts students to make text-to-self connections, draws out students' knowledge and experience, synthesizes/summarizes (Dwyer et al., 2016); making connections and seeking relationships (Fisher, 2007); synthesize ideas, compare/evaluate alternative views, link learning to wider contexts (Hennessy et al., 2016); simple coordination, Reasoned coordination, linkage and coordination across contributions (Howe et al., 2019); summarizing (Hulsman & Vloodt, 2015); summing up and refocusing (Jie et al., 2016); asking children to sum up, summing up (Jadallah et al., 2011); connection, summarize (Nassaji & Wells, 2000); describing or completing commonalities and differences (Podschuweit et al., 2016); summarizing (Ruiz-Priomo, 2011); relating a student's response to another student's response, promoting students' questions and comments about a student's contribution, comparing and contrasting students' ideas/contributions (Ruiz-Priomo, 2011); connection (Wells & Arauz, 2006)

(Continued)

Table 3.1 (Continued)

Themes	*Codes in the dialogic frameworks*
Speculation	Speculate (Alexander, 2017); speculate (Jay et al., 2017); invite possibility thinking based on another's contribution, invite possibility thinking or prediction, speculate or predict on the basis of another's contribution, speculate or predict, propose resolution (Hennessy et al., 2016); extrapolation (Mortimer & Scott, 2003; Aguiar, Mortimer, & Scott, 2010); hypothetical (Muhonen et al., 2017); conjecture, prediction (Nassaji & Wells, 2000); speculate (Alexander, 2018); speculation, prediction, conjecture (Yanfen & Yuqin, 2010)
Construction	Expand, clarify thinking (Alexander, 2017); explore, dialogue (Alexander, 2017); inter-thinking, redirecting, tie-ins (Boyd & Markarian, 2011); extension by responsive questioning, focusing and Zooming (Chin, 2006); uptake (Dolin et al., 2018); clarifies students' ideas (Dwyer et al., 2016); explicit correction, clarification requests, repair, needs-repair (Heift, 2004); build on/clarify others' contributions, clarify/elaborate own contribution (Hennessy et al., 2016); asking for clarification (Jadallah et al., 2011); expand question (Jay et al., 2017); asking for clarification, fostering independence (Jie et al., 2016); uptake questions, repeat or repair question (Lefstein et al., 2015); uptake, repair, recast, translation, clarification request, metalinguistic feedback, elicitation, explicit correction, repetition (Lyster & Ranta, 1997); accepts or clarifies student comments (Macgregor & Atkinson, 2002); continuation (Mortimer & Scott, 2003; Aguiar et al., 2010); uptake (Nystrand & Gamoran, 1991); uptake (Nystrand et al., 2003); rephrasing, clarifying, elaborating, summarizing, and repeating help to verify students' responses, debugging (Ruiz-Priomo, 2011); clarifying, relating a student's response to another student's response, comparing and contrasting students' ideas/contributions, connecting the discussion (conversation) to the learning goal (Ruiz-Priomo, 2011); teacher invites students to expand on an utterance (Rojas-Drummond et al., 2013); uptake (Soter et al., 2008); clarification request, accept plus uptake (Wells & Arauz, 2006)

Note: To save space, we include only the first author followed by et al. in the text citations.

Nystrand et al., 2003). Evaluation is used to request or provide an opinion about how valuable or appropriate another person's contribution (in words or action) has been; explanation/justification refers to an argument to support a preceding contribution or to show that it was reasonable or appropriate; exemplification requests more information, including examples, to supplement existing, relatively simple information or to illustrate a point that has just been made. Dialogue of this kind involves using deductive reasoning to make knowledge explicit and easy to understand. The setting of codes in this theme aims to support students in digging deeper into their ideas and reasoning, and abstractly separate a whole into its constituent parts in order to study the parts and their relationships.

The fourth theme is that coding should show the coordination of information, and summarization, comparison, and connection are its main specific embodiments (see Alexander, 2008; Kumpulainen & Lipponen, 2014; Mercer & Littleton, 2007; Reznitskaya & Gregory, 2013). Summarization is a condensed statement of what has been said by one or more participants or the provision of only the main information; comparison refers to dialogue examining similarities or differences in knowledge and information; connection assesses whether dialogue builds and explores the relationships between things and information. This type of dialogue assists students in concentrating, connecting, coordinating, and reflecting, ultimately fostering deep learning. It is a process of formulating general concepts by reasoning from detailed facts and involves inductive reasoning and the development of ideas.

The fifth theme concerns speculation, which refers to dialogue that considers possibilities, going beyond the current state of knowledge but with a theoretical or factual basis (see, e.g. Chin, 2006; Mortimer & Scott, 2003; Nystrand, 1997; Ruiz-Primo, 2011). This kind of dialogue supports students' generation of new ideas and develops creative abilities.

The sixth theme is that categories should be able to assess how teachers and students use construction (see, e.g. Mortimer & Scott, 2003; Ruiz-Primo, 2011; Wells & Arauz, 2006). The issue at hand relates to how someone's previous response is received by others. Uptake can be demonstrated through a comment that explicitly acknowledges the previous response and expands on it in some manner. Alternatively, it can be shown through a question that prompts the previous respondent to elaborate on what they have said. Extension of talk provides a constructive supplement based on previous talk, rather than simply a repetition of a previous articulation (see, e.g. Alexander, 2008; Nystrand, 1997; O'Connor et al., 2015; Rojas-Drummond et al., 2010). The inclusion of this theme aims to encourage students to listen carefully to their peers' ideas to build on, think, and reason with others.

Coding Instrument for Productive Classroom Dialogue

Based on the review mentioned earlier, a comprehensive assessment tool, CI-PCD was developed. The CI-PCD proposes nine primary coding dimensions to evaluate the quality of classroom conversations, including elaboration, coordination, speculation, construction, prior-known knowledge, personal information, agreement, querying, and guidance. These dimensions, particularly elaboration, coordination, speculation, and construction, reflect high-level thinking as they involve complex information processing methods (Pehmer et al., 2015). These dimensions were discussed in Chapter 1 as indicators of dialogue productiveness. The remaining dimensions were included considering their consistent presence in classroom conversations, which are likely to be initiations or follow-ups related to productive dialogue forms (Song et al., 2022). These dialogues generally exhibit a lower level of thinking associated with rote learning, simple information retrieval, and procedural instruction following. They involve minimal reflection and analysis, relying on pre-existing knowledge and basic cognitive skills (Sychev et al., 2021). To illustrate reciprocal exchanges between teachers and students, the first six dimensions were further divided to incorporate dialogic forms, namely initiation and response. It is worth noting that the dialogic form 'feedback' often occurs alongside new initiation turns, making its addition less reliable (Hennessy et al., 2020). Consequently, feedback forms were excluded; see also the work of the Cambridge team (Howe et al., 2019; Hennessy et al., 2020). Table 3.2 illustrates the coding dimensions, their categories, descriptors, functions, and examples.

Coding objects and units

Several frameworks focus solely on teacher talk (e.g. Fisher, 2007) or student talk (e.g. Norman, 1992; Mercer, 2000; Mercer et al., 2004). Others include all teacher and student utterances, which appear to be a more recent trend (e.g. Howe et al., 2019; Hennessy et al., 2016). We favour the latter approach because teachers' and students' talk often influence each other. Although student talk is crucial due to its role in shaping thinking, learning, and understanding, it is primarily through teacher talk that student talk is facilitated, mediated, probed, and extended – or, conversely, inhibited (Hennessy et al., 2016; Kumpulainen & Wray, 2003). Teacher initiations and feedback are effective only when tailored to students' needs and based on student dialogue (Gillies & Baffour, 2017).

The unit of coding and analysis varies among studies. Dialogue can be coded at the level of a single word, a sentence, or sentences with identifiable characterizations or functions (Chin, 2006; Wells & Arauz, 2006). Some frameworks focus on specific dialogic strategies or knowledge-building techniques (e.g. Alexander, 2017; Hennessy et al., 2016), while others assess broader dialogic activities or interactive behaviours during teaching and learning (e.g. Galton et al., 1999; Jay et al., 2017; Mortimer & Scott, 2003). Different levels of coding can be applied, ranging from macro to micro levels, to elicit multi-dimensional information. Researchers like Saville-Troike (2003) and Hennessy et al. (2016) use an ethnography of communication, establishing a hierarchical system of analysis with micro-level 'communicative acts' (CA) embedded within meso-level 'communicative events' (CE), which are part of macro-level 'communicative situations' (CS). Others such as Wells and Arauz (2006) and Nystrand et al. (2003) propose a five-level coding scheme with episodes, sequences, exchanges, moves, and acts at different levels from macro to micro. Howe et al. (2019) differentiate between turn-level coding and lesson-level ratings for measuring dialogue.

The choice of unit and levels of coding depends on research interests and is influenced by methodological choices (Mercer, 2010; O'Connor et al., 2015). A broad, macro-level coding is suitable for large-sample studies and quantitative analysis (Howe et al., 2019). Using a detailed, micro-level coding framework can be time-consuming and costly due to data collection and analysis (Gillies & Nichols, 2015). Scholars often employ qualitative research methods and work with a small number of students and teachers, resulting in findings that may not be

Table 3.2 Introduction of CI-PCD

Coding dimensions	*Coding categories*	*Descriptives*	*Functions*	*Examples*
Elaboration	Initiating elaboration (Ie) Elaboration response (El)	Splitting information, explaining, analysing, evaluating, etc. Teachers guide students to analyse complex and abstract knowledge and turn it into specific and easy-to-understand content.	Encourages students to analyse problems in-depth, enhances their deductive thinking ability, and strengthens their understanding.	Teacher: Please explain us how you obtained this answer. Show us the steps. Student A: That's -$\sqrt{3}$, because $180°-120° = 60°$, which is exactly the opposite of the one above.
Coordination	Initiating coordination (Ic) Coordination response (Co)	Summarizing information, comparing information, and establishing connections. Teachers use dialogue and questioning methods to guide students to reason and generalize methods and rules to solve certain types of problems from complex knowledge.	Develops students' abilities to comprehensively view issues, enhance their global thinking, and discover the rules of things through comparison and connection.	When we put these three sets of equations together, can we discover their common characteristics?
Speculation	Initiating speculation (Is) Speculation response (Sp)	Using existing knowledge to infer and solve unknown problems, predict the direction of things based on evidence, and explore the unknown and innovate on the basis of existing information.	Supports students in developing innovative thinking and enhancing transferable skills.	Imagine you were an astronaut. What kinds of experiments do you like to testify in the space station?
Uptakes/ Construction	Initiating uptakes/ construction (Iu) Uptakes/ Construction(Up)	Further discussing the content of the previous dialogue, deepening the analysis, and proposing opposing opinions. Teachers guide students to discuss a certain issue in depth and further analyse and explore different opinions on the basis of previous comments made by others.	Encourages students to make construction and extension, collaborate with others, and enhances self-reflection.	Good. He just used abdication method to calculate. Does anybody use another different method?

(Continued)

Table 3.2 (Continued)

Coding dimensions	*Coding categories*	*Descriptives*	*Functions*	*Examples*
Prior-known knowledge	Initiating prior-known knowledge (Ipk) Prior-known knowledge response (Pk)	Memorization-based learning includes factual knowledge, standard answers, common practices, traditions, and repeating dialogue or content. Teachers can refer to textbooks or existing knowledge to judge whether the dialogue is right or wrong, and the questions can be answered by memorization.	Helps students acquire information, concepts, basic knowledge, and facts, and learn basic methods and rules.	The textbook indicates that 'put forward' has a similar meaning to 'suggest'.
Personal information	Initiating personal information (Ipi) Personal information (Pi)	Experience-based learning includes personal experiences and subjective opinions without any evidence. Teachers can ask questions to understand students' personal experiences and allow them to freely express their views and opinions without any evidence.	Encourages students to express their own thoughts, emotions, and opinions.	Please share with us your experience to the seaside. How do you feel when you watch the sea?
Agreement	Agreement (Ag)	Confirming, accepting, or agreeing with a certain statement as evidence that the answer or question meets the prescribed requirements or reaches a higher level.	Encourages listening and promotes communication and thinking.	Yeah, it's good.
Querying	Querying(Qu)	Questioning or disagreeing with a certain statement, questioning its reasonableness, and denying a statement.	Conducive to the cultivation of critical thinking, it is a manifestation of active participation in classroom learning and a means of inspiring exploration and innovation.	That seems not correct. Please reconsider and see if other classmates have different ideas.
Guidance	Guide (Gu)	Giving instructions to others, requiring them to respond appropriately, and teaching, guiding, and directing.	Teachers provide targeted support and guidance based on students' learning progress and cognitive level.	Let's turn to page 9 and read the second paragraph.

generalizable or comparable to other contexts (Gillies & Baffour, 2017). However, this approach allows for a deeper understanding of classroom dynamics by moving beyond mere frequency descriptions or modelling (Bakeman & Gottman, 1997) and tracking collaborative knowledge construction over time (Mercer & Dawes, 2014). There appears to be a tension between the varied levels of coding, which may be reconciled with the development of methodological technology (e.g. AI), enabling multi-level and unit coding for large samples. Dialogue research can benefit from interdisciplinary research methods.

The dialogic transcripts were coded at a turn level identified through the speaker switch for our research. For each turn, multiple coding categories could be attached. For example, a turn 'The diagram in the textbook is of a sphere, just like the football at in gyms. It's shaped like this because it can roll, and it doesn't have any sharp edges' demonstrated knowledge learnt in textbooks, made a link to daily life and showed analytical process. Categories prior-known knowledge, personal information, and elaboration were therefore coded simultaneously. This way of coding is recommended as it can be fairly reliably distinguished and detected by coders (Hennessy et al., 2021).

Introducing discriminate model to automatically code classroom dialogue

In the last chapter, I have introduced a few basic concepts of artificial intelligence. Within the area of AI, deep learning becomes a popular one and can be used to cope with complicated tasks because neural network has been brought in. A neural network technique is a computing method inspired by the structure and function of the human brain. It entails creating a network of interconnected nodes, known as artificial neurons, to process and analyse data. There are two main research approaches within the field of deep learning techniques: one is the discriminate approach, and the other one is the generative approach. Discriminate models are used to classify or predict. They are typically trained on vast amounts of data, enabling them to learn and make predictions or decisions based on the input they receive. They learn the relationship between features of data and labels. Generative models not only can classify text but also can generate new data. They work by exploring patterns from raw data and finding out how data naturally fall/cluster into groups. A large language model is a type of generative AI that is specifically trained on large datasets of text to understand and generate human-like language.

My team started to work on the automatic coding of classroom dialogue in 2019, and the discriminate approach was dominant at that time. The discriminate approach is extensively used in extracting deep information about text data in classification tasks, especially before the launch of GPT-3. Convolutional neural networks (CNNs) and recurrent neural networks (RNNs) are two fundamental types of neural networks, with the former focusing on extracting local feature information and the latter capable of extracting global feature information. A Bi-LSTM is a variant of an RNN that not only acquires past context information but can also capture future context information (Young et al., 2018). To merge the benefits of these different types of networks, my team employed a neural network-based model called CNN-BiLSTM. This was a text classification model that utilized a CNN and a Bi-LSTM network in its training to automate the classification of dialogue content.

Model description

The model comprised three layers: an embedding layer, a CNN layer, and a Bi-LSTM layer. The embedding layer was employed to learn the relationships between words extracted from dialogue sentences in a dense vector space. Before the model could be trained, it was crucial to convert the dialogue text into the format required by the model. To transform the dialogue text into a mathematical format, BERT, a pretrained language model, was used to encode sentences of classroom dialogue text into fixed vectors in the embedding layer. The transformed data were then fed into the CNN layer. A CNN was utilized to learn the local semantic information of the dialogue text. The convolutional filters of the CNN were used to extract specific features from these sentences and add them to the final sentence representations. To capture global information about long-distance semantic dependencies, a Bi-LSTM network was employed to learn the global context information of the classroom dialogue text in the third layer. The long short-term memory (LSTM) network is a special type of recurrent neural network that can emulate the human memory system to uncover hidden semantic information in classroom dialogue. In addition to capturing bidirectional semantic dependencies, the network also captures both past and future information using forward and backward networks.

The training of the model involves a series of procedures: forecasting the current state of the model, calculating the error degree of the prediction, and then updating the weights or parameters of the network. These procedures are repeated until the model converges and stops learning. Finally, the model outputs the probability distribution for each category, selecting the category with the highest probability as the final category. The model's architecture is depicted in Figure 3.2. The trained model is capable of automatic classification of new classroom dialogue text based on the information learnt from the previous training dataset.

We introduced three metrics to assess the efficiency of the classification model. In the realm of text classification, precision, recall, and F1 score are extensively employed as performance evaluation metrics for classification models (Sokolova & Lapalme, 2009). For a coding record with a category annotated by a human coder, a true positive (TP) refers to the number of assessments made to verify if the category predicted by the model aligns with the actual category. In contrast, a false negative (FN) occurs when the model predicts the record to belong to other categories instead of the actual one. For coding records with categories annotated by the human coder, a false positive (FP) represents an outcome where the model's predicted category does not match any of the actual categories in the record. Precision is calculated as the ratio of instances of correctly predicted categories among those assigned to their respective categories, while recall is the proportion of correctly

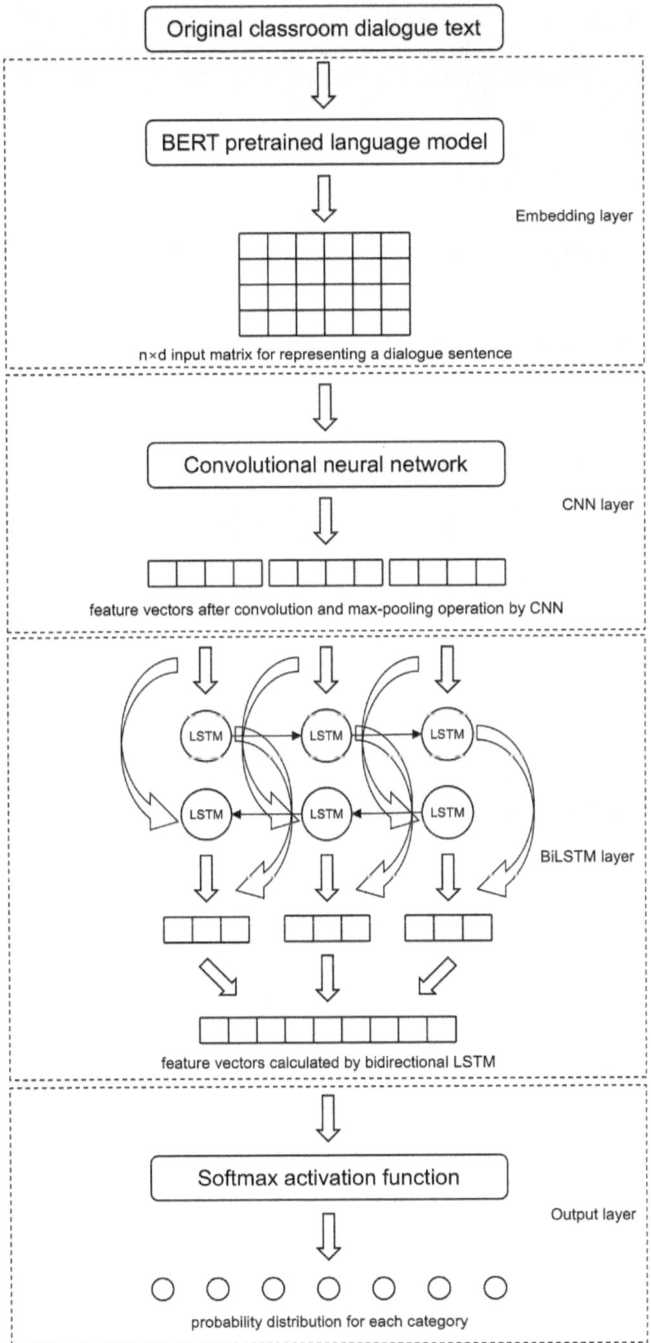

Figure 3.2 Architecture of the neural network model

predicted instances among the coding records (Tasche, 2018). The F1 score is a comprehensive measure that integrates precision and recall, serving as the harmonic mean of both. The evaluation metrics are defined as follows:

$$Precision = \frac{TP}{TP + FP} \tag{1}$$

$$Recall = \frac{TP}{TP + FN} \tag{2}$$

$$F1 = \frac{2 \times Precision \times Recall}{Precision + Recall} \tag{3}$$

Model performance

We worked with 310 recorded lessons (of length 40 minutes each), of which 148 took place in primary schools and 162 in secondary schools. The subjects of mathematics, science (primary schools), physics (secondary schools), and literacy were selected to allow for a comparison with other studies due to their popularity worldwide (Howe & Abedin, 2013). The recorded lessons covered a wide range of grades (grades 1 to 9) and regions, and were downloaded from a free-access website, the National Education Resources Public Service Platform (http://1s1k.eduyun.cn/portal/html/1s1k/index/1.html#). This platform stores and provides videos of lessons from all over China at primary and secondary levels, thus facilitating the sharing of educational resources. Teachers typically record their lessons with the assistance of an intelligent recording and broadcasting (IRB) system and then upload the videos to the platform after obtaining permission from their students. IRB systems are a powerful means of providing HD audio and videos. Given the rapid development of educational informalization, most schools in China are equipped with at least one IRB system. With the broad range of accessible resources, the lessons on this platform are an optimal choice for implementing dialogic classification. However, although these videos clearly show whole-class dialogue, dialogue within small groups was difficult to capture and distinguish. Many studies suggest that small-group dialogue is hard to track (Mercer et al., 2017), and whole-class dialogue was the focus of the current chapter.

The videos were transcribed using a speech recognition software called iFLYTEK Translator, and the transcripts in text form were then manually checked and corrected by researchers. Two trained researchers worked with the transcripts and coded the 155 lessons independently. The inter-rater reliability was high (kappa=.94), and inconsistent cases were fully discussed before reaching a consensus. One source of confusion was the distinction between speculation and personal information, since one aspect of personal information is personal imagination, and these two categories both involve possibilities that might happen in the future. We therefore supplemented the descriptions of these categories. We clarified that speculation should be seen as a kind of dialogue based on theoretical or factual grounds, while personal information did not need this basis. Another source of disagreement was which types of talk should be coded as uptake. One coder regarded the kind of talk that merely repeated the previous talk as uptake. In contrast, the other coder disagreed, since students who contributed to this type of talk did not build or construct knowledge. In order to eliminate misunderstandings, the definition of uptake was refined to mean that an extension of talk should make a constructive addition. After some discussion, they reached an agreement on the semantics of each coding category, and the coded records were formed into a good template for machine learning.

They utilized a deep learning-based method to classify the dataset into categories automatically. This method involved four steps: data preprocessing, feature extraction, model training, and model evaluation. First, we deleted duplicate coding records with the same text and labels, converted the dialogue texts from sentences to words, and removed all punctuation. Following this, dialogue texts were pre-processed as sequence vectors for the deep learning model. A BERT model of pre-training language representation was used to transform each text into numerical format, in the form of a vector that captured the relationships and similarities between words within the dialogue text corpus. The third step came with model training. Model training is the process of teaching a machine learning model how to predict outcomes based on given input data. It involves using an algorithm to adjust the model's internal parameters to minimize the difference between the predicted outcomes and the actual outcomes. This is done by feeding the model a large dataset that contains input features and corresponding target values (labels). During training, the model learns from the data by identifying patterns, relationships, and trends. It generalizes from the training data to unseen data, allowing it to make accurate predictions on new, unseen examples. In our work, a model consisting of a convolutional neural network and a bi-directional long short-term memory network (Bi-LSTM) was applied to capture the local features and main characteristics of the training data, respectively, to represent the semantic content of the dialogue text. The final step is model evaluation. Model evaluation is the process of assessing the performance of a trained machine learning model. The goal is to determine how well the model will generalize to new, unseen data. Evaluation involves using a separate dataset, called the test dataset, that the model has not seen during training. The model analysed the semantics of new dialogue texts and predicted their categories. There are several metrics to evaluate the performance of a machine learning model, depending on the problem at hand. Some common metrics include accuracy, precision, recall, and F1 score.

The classroom dialogue dataset contained 15,167 manual coding records, of which 12,134 (80%) were randomly chosen as the training dataset and the other 3033 (20%) were used as the testing dataset. The training dataset was utilized to train the classification model, while the testing dataset was used to evaluate the performance of the model. The classification model underwent training using the training dataset for multiple epochs, and the performance of the trained model was then evaluated using the testing dataset. The performance of the classification model for different categories is shown in Table 3.3, which is the final training result of the model. The values of precision for speculation, prior-known knowledge,

Table 3.3 Performance of the proposed classification model for different categories

Coding category	*Precision*	*Recall*	*F1 score*
Elaboration/analysis	0.692	0.767	0.728
Coordination	0.579	0.620	0.598
Speculation	0.850	0.347	0.493
Construction/uptake	0.584	0.404	0.478
Prior-known knowledge	0.798	0.875	0.835
Agreement	0.792	0.864	0.826
Querying	0.438	0.250	0.318
Overall	0.688	0.690	0.680

and agreement were 0.8500, 0.7982, and 0.7917, respectively, making these the top four categories, followed by elaboration, construction, and coordination with values of 0.692, 0.584, and 0.579, respectively. Querying obtained the lowest precision of 0.438. The overall precision for all categories was 0.688. In terms of recall, the top three categories were prior-known knowledge, agreement, and elaboration, with values of 0.8750, 0.8636, and 0.7668, respectively, followed by coordination, construction, speculation, and querying, with 0.620, 0.404, 0.347, and 0.250, respectively. The overall recall for all categories was 0.690. In terms of F1 score, prior-known knowledge, agreement, and elaboration, they achieved the top three scores of 0.8349, 0.8261, and 0.7276, respectively, while coordination, speculation, construction, and querying obtained F1 scores of 0.598, 0.493, 0.478, and 0.318, respectively. The overall F1 score for all categories was 0.680. Prior-known knowledge and agreement performed the best in all categories, and the results showed that 87.5% and 86.4% of categories of coding records predicted correctly respectively. In summary, the results indicate that our classification model was capable of recognizing most of the classroom dialogue text with high satisfactory precision and reliability.

After the model had been trained, new dialogic texts were given to the model to predict their categories. To clarify this process for the reader, an example of automatic classification by the model is shown in Figure 3.3. An episode of dialogue containing the words 'the reason for this phenomenon is . . .' was input into the trained classification model, which analysed the semantic content of the dialogue based on the information previously learnt from the training dataset, and then automatically output the relevant category with the highest probability. The output indicated that this episode was most likely to be analytical rather than uptake or querying, and this result was consistent with the judgment of the researchers based on the use of the word 'reason'. We found that the performance of this model was generally acceptable and comparable to that of human coders. The results indicate that this model can assist human beings in automatic dialogue coding.

The consistency between human coders and the model varied across categories, with high agreement in prior-known knowledge, agreement, analysis, and coordination (up to .80). In contrast, lower agreement was observed for querying, uptake, and speculation (below 0.50). This discrepancy may be due to the number of

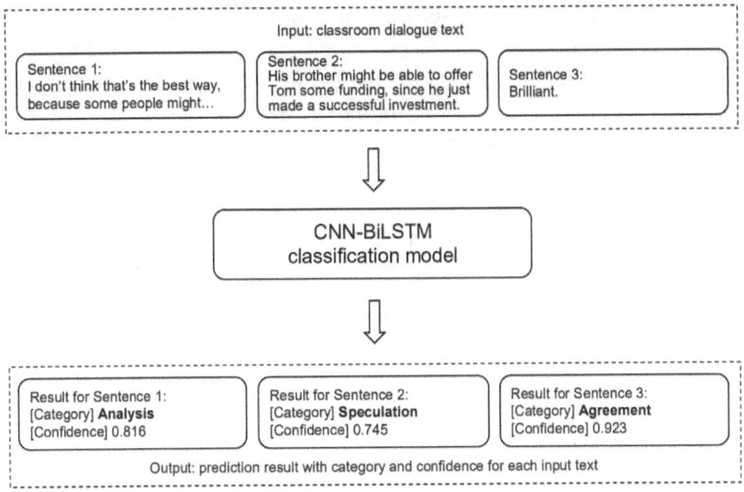

Figure 3.3 Examples of automatic coding results by neural network technique

records, as categories with better performance contained significantly more records than those with unsatisfactory performance. Using a limited corpus, it's challenging for the model to grasp the deep relationships between texts and explore various contexts for word usage. During the automatic classification process, querying, uptake, and speculation were often misassigned as analysis or coordination, which might be a linguistic issue. Lexical components of language and semantic expressions for these categories tend to be similar, sometimes even confusing human coders (see Howe et al., 2019). Addressing these issues may require new techniques, which may lead to the following technical approach.

Retrieval augmented generation and its usage in classroom dialogue

To cope with the above limitation, a new approach making use of both discriminate and generative models is introduced, which is called Retrieval augmented generation (RAG). RAG is a powerful pre-trained language model that combines retrieval and generation mechanisms to enhance the performance of language models on various downstream tasks (Radeva et al., 2024). The main idea behind RAG is to use a retrieval-based approach to enhance the model's generation capabilities. Specifically, RAG uses a retrieval mechanism to fetch relevant chunks of text from a large corpus during the training process, which are combined with the input sequence to generate a more accurate and coherent output (Siriwardhana et al., 2023). By incorporating retrieved text chunks into the generation process, RAG can leverage the contextual information from the corpus to improve the quality of the generated text. At the same time, it could cope with the problem of hallucinations, which are words or phrases generated by LLMs that are often nonsensical or grammatically incorrect (Sartori & Orrù, 2023).

We propose an **L**LM and **R**AG-based **U**niversal **F**ramework (LRUF) to enhance the semantic content classification tasks for classroom dialogue. The framework is divided into three sections: pre-works, retrieval module, and generation module. Figure 3.4 shows the workflow of our proposed framework with the use of LLMs and RAG. The pre-works involve two phases: data preprocessing and embedding. My team's previous work on building up a database of coded transcripts of classroom dialogue makes it likely for the use of the RAG technique. These coded transcripts were split into text chunks to enhance the knowledge scope of the LLMs. After that, the embedding model is used to convert text chunks into numerical vector representations and to store them in a vector database. The retrieval module of the framework is designed to use the embedding model to transform a task query (e.g. Please identify coordinated dialogue from the following dialogue transcripts) into vectors. Then, the machine conducts similarity searches from our database to

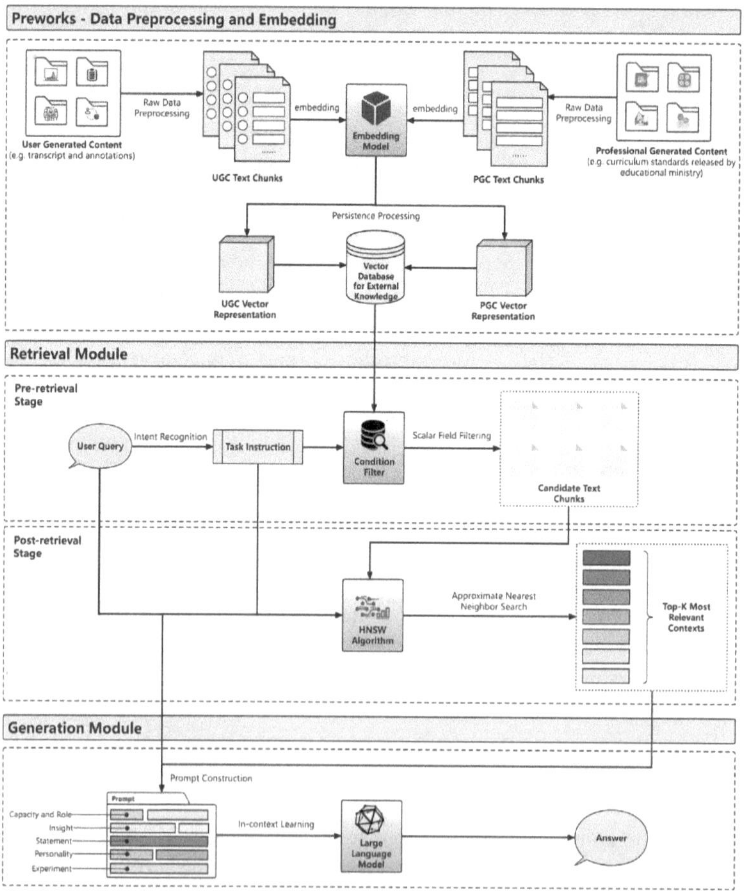

Figure 3.4 The architecture of the proposed framework based on LLMs and RAG

provide the Top-K results relevant to that query. These results are combined with the original query to create a prompt that provides a comprehensive context for the LLMs. Finally, the generation module is used to amplify the retrieval capabilities of the LLMs. RAG augments the user input by adding the relevant retrieved data in context. This step uses prompt engineering techniques to communicate effectively with the LLMs. The augmented prompt allows the LLMs to answer the user query accurately.

In order to demonstrate the feasibility and effectiveness of our proposed framework, we conducted several experiments to evaluate its performance for semantic content classification and teaching evaluation tasks using a self-built dataset. The dataset contained approximately 20,000 dialogue turns generated by random sampling from over 250 lessons, covering various subjects, including literacy, mathematics, and science.

The overall comparison results of semantic content classification are presented in Table 3.4. The experiment results are evaluated by precision, recall, and F1-score. It can be observed that our proposed framework significantly outperforms other baseline methods, with a precision of 0.913, a recall of 0.911, and an F1-score of 0.908. Our proposed framework obtains remarkable improvements of 0.357 and 0.494 compared to the FastText and TextCNN, respectively, demonstrating that the framework achieves superior performance with the support of LLMs and RAG.

We proceeded to conduct experiments to assess the performance of our proposed framework on each subject and each category. The experiment results are reported in Tables 3.5 and 3.6, respectively. It is noteworthy that our proposed framework achieved a remarkable performance on the Literacy corpus, reaching a precision of 0.938 and an F1-score of 0.924. In terms of the Mathematics corpus, our framework attained a recall of 0.923. For the Science corpus, our framework

Table 3.4 The overall performance of our proposed framework against other baseline methods in semantic content classification task

Methods	*Precision*	*Recall*	*F1-score*
TextCNN	0.419	0.106	0.118
TextRNN	0.321	0.151	0.180
FastText	0.556	0.101	0.106
BERT	0.032	0.065	0.038
LRUF	0.913	0.911	0.908

Table 3.5 The performance of our proposed framework for each subject in semantic content classification task

Subject	*Precision*	*Recall*	*F1-score*
Literacy	0.938	0.922	0.924
Mathematics	0.934	0.923	0.923
Science	0.866	0.920	0.888

Table 3.6 The performance of our proposed framework for each category in semantic content classification task

Category	*Precision*	*Recall*	*F1-score*
Invite prior-known knowledge	0.977	0.929	0.952
Prior-known knowledge	0.978	0.885	0.929
Invite subjective expression	0.981	0.905	0.941
Subjective expression	0.943	0.934	0.938
Invite elaboration	0.981	0.968	0.974
Elaboration	0.926	1.000	0.962
Invite coordination	0.913	0.905	0.909
Coordination	0.965	0.986	0.975
Invite speculation	0.967	1.000	0.983
Speculation	0.990	0.621	0.763
Invite uptake/construction	0.951	0.933	0.942
Uptake/construction	0.967	0.986	0.976
Agreement	0.803	0.949	0.870
Querying	0.545	0.968	0.698
Guide	0.684	0.948	0.795

achieved a recall of 0.920, indicating a similar performance to the results on other subjects.

According to the experiment results for each category, it can be observed that 'Speculation', 'Invite subjective expression', and 'Invite elaboration' achieved high precision values of more than 0.98. Notably, 'Elaboration' and 'Invite speculation' obtained full scores in terms of recall, and 'Invite speculation' also achieved the highest F1-score compared to the other categories. Meanwhile, 'Invite elaboration', 'Coordination', and 'Uptake/construction' performed better than the other categories in terms of F1-score. To summarize, 'Invite speculation', 'Invite elaboration', and 'Uptake/construction' offer a good balance between precision and recall, as indicated by their higher F1-scores.

The above results indicate that our LRUF framework not only showcases the outstanding capabilities of LLMs in terms of deep semantic analysis and complex context understanding but also leads to more comprehensive and targeted outcomes for teaching evaluation and improves generalization and adaptability when dealing with multilingual corpora. Experiment results indicate that our proposed framework provides a significant performance improvement compared to previous methods, achieving an F1-score of over 91% in semantic content classification, proving the feasibility and effectiveness of the framework.

Conclusion and contributions

The present chapter elucidates how classroom dialogue can be automatically coded and assessed with the aid of artificial intelligence, thereby introducing a novel coding tool, CI-PCD, for assessing the productiveness of classroom interactions.

Furthermore, a hybrid discriminate model, CNN-Bi-LSTM, was developed to identify and differentiate the semantics of dialogic text. The model's performance rivals that of human coders, as evidenced by precision, recall, and F1 score metrics. More recently, the LURF framework based on the idea of retrieval augmented generation has been proposed. It addresses the limitations of conventional neural network-based models for the tasks of semantic content classification and teaching evaluation for classroom dialogue. The human coding and model classification have been highly consistent. My team's empirical exploration achieves new milestones for educational dialogue analysis and processing by leveraging LLMs and RAG. For future work, we aim to consider how to improve the classification performance on a broader corpus and various coding schemes through the chain of thought of LLMs and the design of a retrieval strategy for RAG.

Automated coding methods significantly reduce manual coding labour and enhance the efficiency of detecting productive dialogue forms. Automatic coding is inherently more cost-effective and accessible than its human counterpart. Theoretically, machines can be trained to encode dialogue content with great detail or work with various languages, provided sufficient sample data is available. This enables a comprehensive presentation of the dialogic process while handling large-scale data. With automated coding, large-scale studies, international comparisons of lessons, and dialogic teaching have become feasible. Automatic coding also offers timely feedback for teachers and students, helping them grasp their performance in dialogic interactions. This feedback can be utilized in professional teacher development, providing insights that enhance facilitative dialogue abilities and classroom management skills. Formative feedback can also assist students in comprehending the role of dialogue in enhancing their thinking and learning, as well as their contributions to the dialogic process. This may increase student engagement and ultimately lead to better learning outcomes through productive dialogue.

4 Exploring the collective process of classroom dialogue using sequential pattern mining technique

The importance of understanding sequential patterns of classroom dialogue

Classroom dialogue is valued for its collaborative nature, where educators and learners interact to develop concepts, reason collectively, and build understanding (Mercer et al., 2017). This exchange is facilitated by acknowledging and refining each other's inputs (van der Veen & van Oers, 2017), with the aim of synergistically and cooperatively addressing challenges (Alexander, 2017). According to Alexander (2017), five key principles underpin high-quality dialogic pedagogy: collective, reciprocal, supportive, cumulative, and purposeful. Among these, the cumulative principle stands out as particularly demanding, necessitating teachers to be attuned to the evolving contributions and equipped with strategies to guide the dialogue effectively (Alexander, 2018).

From a sociocultural viewpoint, engaging in classroom dialogue significantly impacts the quality of instruction and learning. Profitable dialogue within the classroom setting fosters profound comprehension, critical thinking, and academic success (Howe et al., 2019). Participants engage in the mutual sharing of thoughts and reasoning, constructing arguments and considering counterarguments while responding critically to various perspectives (Mercer & Dawes, 2014). This collaborative exploration leads to the emergence of meaning and the construction of knowledge (Rojas-Drummond et al., 2013). Such interactions also facilitate the development of social communication skills, reasoning abilities, and learning potential (Chesnais, 2021). Teachers' proficiency in managing discussions and strategically employing various dialogic approaches, known as dialogic pedagogy, significantly correlates with their teaching productivity and students' cognitive development (Kim & Wilkinson, 2019; Wilmes & Siry, 2021). This pedagogical approach, which is advanced by the Organization for Economic Co-operation and Development (OECD), is highlighted in the 2030 Learning Compass as essential for nurturing twenty-first-century skills, including critical thinking and creativity (OECD, 2019). There is a growing call for enhancing teachers' skills in employing dialogic pedagogy and motivating student engagement in classroom discussions (Parker & Bickmore, 2020).

DOI: 10.4324/9781003543039-4

In actual practice, classroom dialogue frequently stays at a superficial level, with students' responses not indicating profound reflection and not effectively building upon one another (Tang et al., 2021). Educators often lack both recognition of the importance and the strategies required to foster a fruitful dialogic approach (Blanchard et al., 2015). Many lessons are overly focused on asking numerous questions, lacking both collaborative and constructive elements (Howe et al., 2019). Additionally, there exists a lack of clear guidelines or templates for teachers on how to implement dialogic teaching methods. It is imperative to instruct teachers on enhancing the quality of classroom discussions and to illuminate the pathways that lead to productive interactions. Furthermore, the subject matter significantly influences classroom dialogue (Muhonen et al., 2018). Dialogic patterns can differ depending on the subject and educational level, with what benefits one subject/level not necessarily profiting another. For instance, Hennessy et al. (2020) noted that dialogue in English classes was typically longer than in math classes, yet math classes exhibited more reasoning. This indicates that the sequence of dialogic inputs within a subject and their construction may vary. Thus, it's essential to demonstrate how productive classroom dialogue can be fostered.

Scholars have established a variety of methods to study the attributes of classroom dialogue. A widespread technique is transcribing recorded dialogues and then manually or computer-assisted coding. Subsequently, studies are categorized based on their approach to analysing these coded transcripts, either qualitative or traditional quantitative (Mercer, 2008). Qualitative analysis typically focuses on brief excerpts from dialogic transcripts selected to align with research goals, allowing examination of utterance changes and the process of co-constructing knowledge, although this method is time-consuming and doesn't facilitate generalization or comparisons across studies (Hennessy et al., 2020). Traditional quantitative analysis, on the other hand, simplifies abundant data into categorizable items that can be counted and compared numerically across studies, yet it doesn't adequately show how talk's structure and content evolve over a lesson or how individual contributions shape shared understanding (Lefstein et al., 2015). Measuring sequential patterns in classroom dialogue is intricate and challenging (Hennessy et al., 2020). Consequently, relying solely on traditional methods isn't sufficient, calling for new techniques and methods that specialize in capturing data stream pathways.

To harness the potential of classroom dialogue and enhance the efficacy of dialogic pedagogy, this chapter endeavoured to expose common characteristics and sequential patterns found in dialogic interactions within whole-class contexts. It extracts evolutionary patterns of classroom dialogue from diverse lessons and compares them across different subjects, teaching levels, and educational stages. This approach promises to be significant in the study of classroom dialogue by offering a novel way to inspect classroom instruction and learning, distinct from traditional qualitative or quantitative methods. These identified patterns can be utilized for pedagogical advancement and professional teacher development. They will enable teachers and students to become more conscious of productive dialogic processes and follow the extracted patterns to construct knowledge collectively and think collaboratively, thereby facilitating more effective dialogue that supports in-depth learning and reasoning.

Data mining technique and its applications in educational field

Data mining is a process of discovering patterns, relationships, and insights from large datasets using statistical methods, machine learning algorithms, and artificial intelligence techniques (Song et al., 2022). It is a branch of computer science and statistics that focuses on the development of methods for analysing large amounts of data. The main usages of data mining include: association rule learning, which discovers relationships between variables; clustering, which groups similar data points together to identify natural structures or segments within a dataset; classification, which refers to building models that classify data into predefined categories based on the features or attributes of the data; and regression, which involves predicting continuous outcomes based on historical data. Data mining is widely used in the educational field. For example, the technique can be used to predict student performance and tailor interventions to improve outcomes (Song et al., 2023). By analysing historical data on student performance, educators can identify patterns and factors that are associated with success or failure and use this information to make informed decisions about teaching strategies and support services. Data mining techniques can also be used to evaluate the effectiveness of teaching methods and interventions (Roy & Garg, 2017). By identifying what works best for different groups of students, educators can make informed decisions about how to improve instruction and support student learning.

Sequential pattern mining, a branch of data mining, serves as a robust mechanism for tracking sequences of actions or behavioural elements (He et al., 2021). This method is instrumental in identifying trends within relational and procedural data streams (Gupta & Kumar, 2020). It involves the examination of graphs or networks that mirror the interconnections among entities, such as tasks, organizations, or dialogue corpora (Le et al., 2021). By evaluating patterns based on data processing and graphical architecture, this approach can unveil essential features of complex tasks (Cooper & Shallice, 2006; Vista et al., 2016). This analytical method employs diverse metrics to highlight recurrent and pivotal sequences, demonstrate sequence lengths, and detect commonalities across extensive datasets (Kolahkaj et al., 2020). Sequential pattern mining stands out as a promising solution as it may reveal the directional relationships that various types of classroom dialogue have with one another. The intricacies of dialogic interactions in educational settings are compounded by the diverse contributions from participants, leading to diverse sequences (Hennessy et al., 2020). This technique is valuable in managing the complexity of classroom dialogue and extracting shared attributes and structures across many high-quality sessions (Vista et al., 2016). It can uncover underlying cognitive and knowledge-building processes that are not immediately apparent (Vista et al., 2016). It also highlights dialogic successions linked to advanced thinking and profound comprehension.

While the exploration of sequential patterns is a nascent method in educational research, some studies have demonstrated its utility. For instance, Yang et al. (2016) utilized lag sequential analysis to pinpoint student behaviours in an online learning environment, identifying 14 significant pathways. Vista et al. (2016) applied sequential pattern mining to dissect interactions in a defined educational exercise involving olive oil measurement by two collaborating learners, visualizing directed pathways with Gephi. Poon et al. (2017) employed sequential mining techniques to derive behavioural features within a learning management system. Wong et al. (2019) adopted sequential data mining from learning analytics to analyse learning activity sequences in online MOOCs, noting distinguishable patterns between self-regulated and non-self-regulated learners. He et al. (2021) detected behavioural patterns in a computer-based problem-solving assessment. In summary, sequence mining has been predominantly applied to data from online courses or limited activities for path discovery. However, few studies have effectively used this method to reveal the ensemble process of classroom dialogue in authentic educational settings. Its usage is mostly experimental, and it is yet to be proficient in managing the vast amount of process data generated in whole-class contexts (He et al., 2021; Paquette et al., 2020). Xu et al. (2023) used data mining to trace collaborative patterns in computer programming education. Given the multifaceted nature of pair programming due to students' discourse, behaviour, and socio-emotional factors, it is crucial to examine their collaborative patterns from a comprehensive, multifaceted, dynamic viewpoint. The study revealed four collaborative patterns associated with varying levels of process and summative performance. Ouyang and colleagues (2023) leveraged sequential pattern mining to inspect students' collaborative knowledge construction, showcasing the method's capacity to represent the intricacies and dynamics of knowledge development.

Revealing patterns of classroom dialogue across different subjects, educational sections, and quality levels

Engaging in dialogue within educational settings yields numerous advantages. Enhancing the productiveness of dialogic instruction and student engagement is an urgent concern for both academic researchers and educational professionals. Analysing classroom dialogue is an intricate task due to its extensive data, numerous coding categories, and vague developmental trajectories, which heighten the challenge of assessing the sequential nuances involved. Traditional analytical approaches are insufficient in depicting the dynamic structure of how successive speech exchanges develop and interlock. Sequential pattern mining, a method that has not been widely applied to the study of classroom conversation, holds potential in this context. The manner in which different types of dialogues mutate into one another and the prevalent sequences or models through which dialogic interactions unfold remain largely unexplored.

In this segment, we employed various sequential pattern mining strategies to delve into the evolving patterns present in classroom dialogue, aiming to illuminate how collective contributions evolve over the course of a lesson. We aimed to address several specific questions: What are the distinctive sequential patterns exhibited in classroom dialogue? How do these patterns differ across various subject areas? How do the patterns differ when conducted by preliminary, intermediate, and expert teachers? How do the patterns vary between different stages of school lessons? The insights gained from this series of research will deepen our comprehension of the essential aspects of classroom communication. They could potentially enhance the quality of dialogic interactions and bolster educators' proficiency in conducting productive dialogic lessons.

Dataset

Video-recorded lessons were downloaded from a public open-access platform, the National Cloud Platform for Educational Resources and Public Service (NCP-ERPS). The platform is provided and managed by a top Chinese educational council. It serves as a hub for educators across the nation to exchange their teaching materials and experiences, thereby facilitating their instructional proficiency and professional growth. It assembles a collection of instructional videos from primary and middle schools nationwide, encompassing diverse subjects and educational levels. After securing consent from students and relevant parties, teachers upload their videos to the platform. Fuelled by educational technology innovation and government encouragement, over 90% of Chinese primary and secondary schools now own at least one intelligent recording and broadcasting system (IRB). This technology simplifies the recording, management, and sharing of audio-visual materials, commonly utilized for effective handling of real-time or stored observations, lectures, or discussions. The IRB system ensures a crisp recording of classroom interaction and is regularly utilized in daily teaching activities in China. The local educators and students have grown familiar with its usage, which aids in reviewing teaching and learning experiences. Our research concentrated on classroom discussions involving the entire class, where both the teacher and students participated actively, excluding small-group discussions. This approach is based on empirical findings that whole-class discussions tend to be more organized, promoting more effective learning outcomes than small-group conversations (Kutnick & Blatchford, 2014; Mercer et al., 2017). Additionally, we aimed to enhance teachers' understanding and proficiency in dialogic pedagogy, making whole-class interactions, where the teacher is engaged, more relevant. Moreover, using the IRB system to track student discussions in small groups can be challenging.

As regards subject matter, mathematics, science, and literacy lessons were selected for analysis (100 lessons per subject) as these subjects are widely acknowledged as important worldwide and are often selected for assessment, for example, in the Programme for International Student Assessment (PISA). The three subjects are those most likely to be chosen for study in the field of classroom dialogue, and using them here allows for comparison between studies (Howe & Abedin, 2013). The samples included were lessons in which new content knowledge was being taught. The selections were generally average across grades in primary and secondary schools. Classroom size ranged from 35 to 40 students, and all classes were mixed gender, with little difference in the number of male and female students. Lesson samples selected for subject comparison were from high-level conducted by expert teachers (see explanation in the next paragraph). This was because we expected the examination would provide useful strategies for teachers to improve their dialogic pedagogy.

As regards dialogic patterns across lessons in different quality levels, 300 lessons were selected, covering preliminary, intermediate, and high-level lessons (100 lessons each). Lessons uploaded to the NCP-ERPS platform are assessed at three different levels, preliminary, intermediate, and high, by a professional committee specializing in curriculum and pedagogy. Teachers who conduct these lessons are recognized as preliminary, intermediate, and expert. The assessment criteria encompass several general principles: (1) emphasizing the construction of knowledge and understanding through inquiry while still attending to standard procedures and skills; (2) fostering classrooms that are inclusive, equitable, interactive, caring, and conducive to intellectual growth; (3) promoting interaction between teachers and students, valuing dialogue-based instruction over traditional transmission of knowledge; (4) enhancing student engagement and the integration of the whole person (physical, mental, emotional, and behavioural aspects); and (5) promoting in-depth comprehension, critical thinking, and cognitive skill development, with a focus on innovation and practical skills. These principles align closely with those promoted in many developed nations, such as the United States, the United Kingdom, Singapore, and Australia. It is inferred that high-level lessons are more indicative of effective classroom dialogue and more reflective of dialogic pedagogical approaches than are preliminary or intermediate lessons.

Concerning the variations in dialogue across different educational stages, we selected 300 advanced mathematics lessons from the NCP-ERPS platform for examination. One hundred lessons each were chosen from primary (ages 7–12), secondary (ages 13–15), and high school (ages 16–18) levels. Mathematics instruction was chosen for comparison across educational stages due to its significance in the benefits of classroom dialogue (Erath et al., 2018), particularly in the context of mathematics education (Diez-Palomar et al., 2021; Morgan et al., 2014). The content and curriculum objectives vary for mathematics education at different stages of education, requiring distinctive approaches to classroom dialogue appropriate to each level (OECD, 2019). There has been limited research on classroom dialogue at all three educational stages, necessitating an examination of the distinct patterns of mathematical discussion specific to each level (Corriveau & Bednarz, 2017). Additionally, there is no uniformity globally regarding the scope of course content for science and literacy across educational stages, prompting the exclusion of these disciplines from the study of dialogic patterns across educational stages.

Methods

This study used the CI-PCD for dialogue coding, which is introduced in detail in Chapter 3. To help readers understand our research, we briefly review its main components. The CI-PCD comprises nine main categories: prior-known knowledge, personal information, elaboration, coordination, uptakes/construction, speculation, agreement, querying, and guidance. Studies based on the coding categories have proved valid for capturing the main aspects of dialogue (see Hennessy et al., 2020; Howe et al., 2019; Song et al., 2020). 'Prior-known knowledge' is used to assess whether dialogue helps students obtain information and facts, and learn basic methods and rules; 'personal information' is related to the expression of personal thoughts, feelings and views; dialogue in the category of 'elaboration' is used to elaborate in-depth thinking, show deductive reasoning and increase understanding; 'coordination' dialogue involves contributions that understand problems comprehensively, improve overall thinking, and identify the operating laws through comparison and connection; 'speculation' refers to dialogue that supports students in developing innovative consciousness and improving innovative ability; the 'uptakes/construction' category shows how contributions build on each other; 'agreement' is dialogue that acknowledges the contributions of others and is important in prompting communication; and 'querying' challenges previous talk and is open to diverse ideas; and 'guidance' is the targeted support and direction provided by teachers during classroom instruction, tailored to students' learning progress and cognitive levels. Each of the first six categories is further divided into initiating dialogue and giving responses. For example, the 'elaboration' category will produce two sub-categories, inviting elaboration (Ie) and giving an elaborate response (El).

The video-recorded lessons were transcribed into text forms on the turn level. A large number of transcripts of classroom dialogue were then reduced to a set of manageable features through coding (Mercer, 2008). The transcripts of classroom dialogue were coded with reference to the CI-PCD. Automatic coding was used first, using the hybrid neural network introduced in Chapter 3. Given the good performance of our model, the transcripts were classified automatically by the model and gave a quick output of coding results. Results with indexical scores above 0.90 were used directly, while results with scores below 0.90 were checked and corrected by human researchers.

The subsequent data analysis was conducted on coded transcripts, which was a structured kind of data format suitable for data mining. In these studies, a variety of data mining techniques have been selected and developed to use with classroom dialogue datasets.

1. *Dialogue transformation*. Adjacency matrixes were generated to show how pairs of dialogue categories were converted. An adjacency matrix, sometimes also referred to as a connection matrix, is a square matrix with rows and columns to indicate whether and how a finite set of vertices/nodes is adjacent in the graph (Amiri et al., 2020). The matrix appears as a square array in which each row represents the out-nodes of a graph and each column represents the in-nodes (Baghipur et al., 2021). In our research, categories of classroom dialogue acted as the nodes of the matrix. The per cent of transformations from one dialogic category to another was calculated. For example, number 20 fits into the matrix with the category 'Ie' in the row and 'El' in the column, and this can be interpreted as meaning that there are 20 contributions that are converted from inviting elaboration to giving elaborate responses.

2. *Evolution pattern of classroom dialogue.* Lag sequential analysis was conducted to determine the sequential patterns in the collective process of classroom dialogue. Lag sequence analysis (LSA) (Pohl et al., 2016) is an important statistical technique of sequence analysis, which is utilized to analyse the causal relationship of the event and visualize its sequence pattern. This method is beneficial in terms of exploring significant event flows in complex interaction sequences. The Z value was generated using GSEQ software by dividing the raw residuals (or the difference between the observed counts and expected counts) by an estimate of the standard error (García-Fariña et al., 2018). The association is considered significant if the Z value is greater than a certain threshold (usually 1.96). Accordingly, we drew graphs to show the significant sequences, which consisted of a set of vertices and edges. Vertices are nodes representing dialogue categories, and edges, shown as directed paths, are used to describe relationships between vertices (Amiri et al., 2020).

3. *Long sequences of dialogue and clusters.* We explored long sequences of classroom dialogue in order to discover the longest path in a given graph. A common belief is that productive classroom dialogue should be a collective process where contributions build on each other to generate long chains of interaction (Howe & Abedin, 2013). It is assumed that a long sequence of dialogue is preferable to a short sequence as it will embody more diverse functions in terms of thinking and knowledge building. This analysis was done to extract valuable long sequences embedded in these high-quality lessons. An extended Dijkstra algorithm was adapted to mine long sequential paths of classroom dialogue. This algorithm can dynamically forward search nodes furthest from a starting node, and the termination condition was to traverse all categories of dialogue (Rosita et al., 2019). We produced characteristic paths that connected communities of dialogue categories by using spectral clustering analysis. Spectral clustering is an exploratory technique that can reduce complex datasets into a small number of groups based on their uniqueness (Sharma & Seal, 2021). The method uses a connectivity approach for clustering, while communities of nodes that are connected or immediately next to each other are captured (Affeldt et al., 2020). This analysis indicated that communities of classroom dialogue are more likely to appear together. Then, we used the following formula to filter prominent paths between groups of dialogue categories.

$$E = \{e_{ij} \mid i, j \in V \wedge W_{ij} > \lambda_i \wedge i \neq j\}$$

In the formula, V is the set of nodes, W is the weight of the edge, λ is a set of hyper-parameters (i.e. thresholds) to control the number of prominent edges selected, and λi is the hyper-parameter (threshold) of the weight of all edges starting from node i. This analysis showed the sequence between communities of classroom dialogue, which can yield possibly valuable insight as it is an important break between distinctly different communities of behaviours (Vista et al., 2016). The detailed algorithmic process for detecting long sequential paths is illustrated in Table 4.1.

Table 4.1 Algorithms for long sequential mining and spectral clustering

Algorithm for detecting long sequential paths
Input: The starting node of dialogue Vs The classroom dialogue graph G=(V, E) The weight threshold t Output: The long dialogue path Pv 1: Initialize the long path sequence Pv = {} 2: Vb = Vs; Pv={Vb}; select start node Vs as the base node 3: Repeat 4: Vi = NextNeiborNode(G, Pv, Vb, t); select a node with a higher level type Vi from the adjacent nodes as the next base node Vb and WVi->Vb is greater than t 5: Pv = Pv U {Vb}; update long path sequence Pv 6: Until all nodes are traversed or no next node meets the search conditions 7: Return Pv Algorithm for spectral clustering analysis Input: Similarity matrix $S \in R^{n \times n}$ The number k of clusters Output: Clusters $A_1, A_2, \ldots A_k$ with $Ai = \{j \mid y_j \in C_i\}$ 1: Construct a similarity graph. Let W be its weighted adjacency matrix 2: Compute the normalized Laplacian L_{sym} 3: Compute the first k eigenvectors $u_1, \ldots, u_k$ of L_{sym} 4: Let $U \in R^{n \times k}$ be the matrix containing the vectors $u_1, \ldots, u_k$ as columns 5: Form the matrix $T \in R^n$ from U by normalizing the rows to norm 1, that is set $t_{ij} = u_{ij} / \left(\sum_k u_{ik^2}\right)^{1/2}$ 6: For i = 1, . . ., n, let y_i R be the vector corresponding to the i-th row of T 7: Cluster the points $(y_i)_{i=1,\ldots,n}$ with the k-means algorithms into clusters $C_1, \ldots, C_k$

Patterns of classroom dialogue in mathematics, science, and literacy

The primary objective of this section was to show the evolutionary patterns of dialogue across different subjects. Using a set of data mining techniques, the results were able to illustrate the collective process of dialogic contributions and capture the evolving structure of productive dialogic lessons. The transformation between initiations and responses facilitates an understanding of the interaction between teachers and students. It also provides information about the kinds of questions leading to responses at a high cognitive level, and contributions from students that triggered productive feedback. Elaborate, coordinated, and speculated contributions are representative of classroom dialogue at a high cognitive level, and usually require complicated ways of processing and suggesting in-depth thought (Hennessy et al., 2016). This kind of talk is, therefore, the focus of the following demonstration.

- **Dialogue transformation in different subjects**

Tables 4.2–4.4 reveal the transformation patterns of classroom dialogue exchanges across mathematics, science, and literacy instruction. The first datum in each cell

Table 4.2 Transformations of pairs of classroom dialogue in mathematics lessons

	Ipk	Pk	Ipi	Pi	Ie	El	Ic	Co	Is	Sp	Iu	Up	Ag	Qu	Gu
Ipk	2.06 (2.38)	7.92 (35.39)	0.65 (−6.0)	0.34 (−6.21)	0.6 (−3.93)	0.57 (−9.87)	0.28 (−3.58)	0.06 (−6.1)	0.03 (−2.32)	0.02 (−2.7)	0.08 (−4.82)	0.02 (−4.32)	0.08 (−6.67)	0.09 (−2.24)	0.32 (−1.19)
Pk	4.52 (14.02)	3.51 (2.67)	1.78 (−0.87)	0.45 (−7.37)	1.27 (−0.99)	1.64 (−6.56)	0.3 (0.21)	0.63 (−1.58)	0.11 (−1.28)	0.05 (−2.62)	0.45 (−1.63)	0.12 (−3.58)	1.44 (4.61)	0.12 (−2.64)	0.53 (−0.26)
Ipi	1.22 (−1.64)	0.49 (−9.59)	2.09 (7.33)	4.42 (33.73)	0.42 (−4.36)	0.76 (−6.93)	0.2 (−3.62)	0.15 (−4.23)	0.09 (−0.32)	0.05 (−1.55)	0.14 (−3.28)	0.06 (−3.02)	0.28 (−3.59)	0.12 (−1.07)	0.45 (1.55)
Pi	0.76 (−2.54)	0.6 (−6.16)	2.06 (11.24)	0.87 (2.51)	0.9 (2.82)	0.76 (−4.16)	0.34 (−0.27)	0.17 (−2.73)	0.09 (0.5)	0.02 (−1.86)	0.31 (0.66)	0.14 (−0.59)	0.46 (0.4)	0.22 (2.08)	0.29 (0.74)
Ie	0.29 (−6.64)	0.68 (−5.58)	0.28 (−5.68)	0.31 (−3.61)	1.27 (6.83)	4.05 (22.48)	0.12 (−3.38)	0.15 (−2.97)	0.03 (−1.39)	0.08 (0.02)	0.2 (−1.13)	0.03 (−2.84)	0.26 (−2.25)	0.12 (−0.12)	0.12 (−2.17)
El	1.48 (−3.92)	1.76 (−5.85)	1.36 (−2.69)	0.37 (−7.29)	1.52 (1.95)	4.53 (12.01)	0.34 (1.26)	0.87 (1.52)	0.12 (−0.65)	0.12 (−0.65)	0.85 (3.82)	0.23 (−1.57)	1.35 (4.67)	0.32 (1.2)	0.19 (−3.96)
Ic	0.32 (−3.05)	0.26 (−5.33)	0.25 (−3.05)	0.36 (−0.05)	0.29 (−0.95)	0.42 (−3.17)	0.82 (11.54)	1.3 (20.42)	0.08 (1.36)	0.03 (−0.49)	0.11 (−0.93)	0.02 (−2.14)	0.06 (−3.12)	0.09 (0.63)	0.09 (−1.08)
Co	0.39 (−2.36)	0.51 (−2.82)	0.46 (−0.38)	0.08 (−4.05)	0.36 (−0.09)	0.79 (0.74)	0.43 (4.29)	0.6 (7.42)	0.06 (0.74)	0.03 (−0.49)	0.14 (−0.28)	0.05 (−1.31)	0.36 (1.89)	0.06 (−0.33)	0.2 (1.32)
Is	0.03 (−2.32)	0.02 (−3.3)	0.05 (−1.55)	0.03 (−1.39)	0.09 (0.49)	0.06 (−2.05)	0.05 (0.13)	0 (−1.72)	0.15 (12.32)	0.4 (33.27)	0 (−1.48)	0 (−1.16)	0.02 (−1.33)	0.02 (0.0)	0.05 (0.77)
Sp	0.08 (−1.18)	0.05 (−2.62)	0.09 (−0.32)	0.03 (−1.39)	0.08 (0.02)	0.17 (0.59)	0.03 (−0.49)	0.03 (−0.5)	0.12 (9.7)	0.14 (11.01)	0.02 (−0.77)	0.03 (0.62)	0.05 (−0.21)	0.03 (1.02)	0.02 (−0.69)
Iu	0.15 (−3.8)	0.22 (−4.35)	0.12 (−3.5)	0.22 (−0.86)	0.2 (−1.13)	0.73 (2.32)	0.05 (−2.26)	0.12 (−0.62)	0 (−1.48)	0 (−1.48)	0.25 (3.3)	1.16 (33.81)	0.08 (−2.08)	0.06 (0.27)	0.02 (−2.31)
Up	0.2 (−1.24)	0.23 (−1.99)	0.23 (0.03)	0.03 (−2.83)	0.2 (0.67)	0.2 (−2.05)	0.11 (0.37)	0.03 (−1.73)	0.02 (−0.27)	0 (−1.16)	0.34 (8.36)	0.15 (4.31)	0.22 (2.53)	0.08 (1.94)	0.06 (−0.13)
Ag	1.08 (3.9)	0.57 (−3.49)	0.49 (−1.13)	0.2 (−3.04)	0.42 (−0.23)	0.73 (−1.33)	0.25 (0.05)	0.34 (1.51)	0.02 (−1.33)	0 (−1.9)	0.39 (4.0)	0.08 (−0.91)	0.53 (3.62)	0.08 (−0.28)	0.26 (1.88)
Qu	0.11 (−1.94)	0.11 (−2.9)	0.2 (0.51)	0.17 (0.98)	0.2 (1.7)	0.28 (0.39)	0.08 (0.15)	0.03 (−1.29)	0.02 (0.0)	0.02 (0.0)	0.11 (1.91)	0.02 (−0.82)	0.09 (0.15)	0.19 (8.11)	0 (−1.85)
Gu	0.42 (0.05)	0.48 (−0.85)	0.84 (7.21)	0.11 (−2.44)	0.2 (−0.88)	0.23 (−3.4)	0.11 (−0.75)	0.03 (−2.48)	0.02 (−0.7)	0.02 (−0.7)	0 (−2.71)	0 (−2.13)	0.17 (−0.02)	0 (−1.86)	0.54 (11.67)

Table 4.3 Transformations of pairs of classroom dialogue in science lessons

	Ipk	*Pk*	*Ipi*	*Pi*	*Ie*	*El*	*Ic*	*Co*	*Is*	*Sp*	*Iu*	*Up*	*Ag*	*Qu*	*Gu*
Ipk	1.18 (−1.42)	8.17 (36.26)	0.32 (−6.25)	0.19 (−7.74)	0.47 (−4.34)	0.3 (−8.05)	0.15 (−3.35)	0.2 (−5.28)	0.02 (−4.16)	0.02 (−4.24)	0.07 (−3.54)	0.1 (−2.97)	0.17 (−4.32)	0.02 (−0.68)	0.34 (−3.09)
Pk	4.97 (16.74)	4.24 (3.1)	1.47 (−1.89)	0.44 (−9.41)	1.38 (−1.41)	0.88 (−8.4)	0.52 (−1.51)	0.86 (−2.74)	0.39 (−0.95)	0.12 (−4.51)	0.59 (1.23)	0.39 (−1.17)	1.65 (7.02)	0.08 (1.25)	1.06 (0.37)
Ipi	0.32 (−6.25)	0.4 (−9.12)	1.11 (2.52)	4.87 (35.7)	0.51 (−2.47)	0.47 (−5.09)	0.2 (−1.71)	0.19 (−4.31)	0.05 (−2.98)	0.19 (−0.76)	0.07 (−2.84)	0.1 (−2.22)	0.29 (−1.82)	0 (−1.27)	0.4 (−1.02)
Pi	0.62 (−4.21)	1.6 (−1.74)	1.65 (6.78)	0.76 (−1.74)	0.86 (0.44)	1.16 (0.0)	0.24 (−1.49)	0.49 (−1.36)	0.22 (−0.31)	0.22 (−0.44)	0.54 (4.7)	0.44 (3.15)	0.47 (0.15)	0.03 (0.37)	0.49 (−0.41)
Ie	0.27 (−6.1)	0.44 (−8.13)	0.32 (−4.26)	0.45 (−3.36)	1.3 (6.15)	4.46 (30.02)	0.34 (0.72)	0.2 (−3.69)	0.12 (−1.51)	0.12 (−1.61)	0.02 (−3.47)	0.07 (−2.53)	0.05 (−4.48)	0 (−1.21)	0.15 (−3.63)
El	1.13 (−1.93)	0.99 (−7.69)	1.04 (−0.36)	0.71 (−3.64)	1.7 (6.18)	2.43 (7.48)	0.64 (2.94)	0.96 (2.08)	0.25 (−0.55)	0.12 (−2.74)	0.35 (0.72)	0.25 (−0.72)	0.77 (2.44)	0.03 (0.08)	0.49 (−1.56)
Ic	0.24 (−2.25)	0.13 (−5.66)	0.2 (−1.71)	0.22 (−1.73)	0.17 (−1.84)	0.29 (−1.66)	0.37 (5.7)	1.41 (20.67)	0.15 (1.83)	0.02 (−1.9)	0.05 (−1.04)	0 (−2.36)	0.13 (−0.58)	0 (−0.76)	0.1 (−1.6)
Co	0.66 (−0.79)	0.64 (−4.52)	0.71 (1.43)	0.29 (−3.52)	0.51 (−0.2)	0.76 (0.1)	0.37 (2.61)	0.81 (5.38)	0.35 (4.14)	0.12 (−0.81)	0.25 (1.81)	0.22 (1.21)	0.27 (−0.4)	0.02 (−0.01)	0.34 (−0.01)
Is	0.05 (−3.64)	0.05 (−5.25)	0.12 (−1.81)	0.1 (−2.3)	0.13 (−1.21)	0.13 (−2.37)	0.03 (−1.39)	0.08 (−1.41)	0.22 (5.22)	1.35 (41.21)	0.02 (−1.44)	0 (−1.96)	0.05 (−1.5)	0 (−0.63)	0.08 (−1.02)
Sp	0.1 (−2.95)	0.29 (−2.4)	0.19 (−0.76)	0.15 (−1.56)	0.29 (1.39)	0.15 (−2.23)	0.25 (4.44)	0.24 (1.58)	0.39 (10.46)	0.13 (2.26)	0.03 (−0.96)	0.02 (−1.46)	0.19 (1.57)	0.02 (0.96)	0.08 (−1.1)
Iu	0.2 (−1.5)	0.3 (−2.32)	0.22 (−0.29)	0.4 (2.49)	0.13 (−1.4)	0.17 (−2.07)	0.07 (−0.6)	0.17 (0.12)	0.02 (−1.44)	0 (−2.01)	0.08 (0.55)	0.74 (20.95)	0.03 (−2.01)	0 (−0.65)	0.03 (−2.25)
Up	0.32 (0.37)	0.4 (−0.96)	0.27 (0.65)	0.32 (1.2)	0.19 (−0.44)	0.1 (−3.02)	0.05 (−1.0)	0.17 (0.19)	0.07 (0.2)	0 (−1.99)	0.22 (4.77)	0.08 (0.64)	0.2 (1.94)	0.02 (0.95)	0.12 (−0.38)
Ag	0.72 (1.97)	0.69 (−1.89)	0.4 (−0.33)	0.4 (−0.68)	0.29 (−1.37)	0.27 (−3.25)	0.1 (−1.25)	0.35 (0.87)	0.1 (−0.3)	0.1 (−0.39)	0.25 (3.02)	0.08 (−0.8)	0.34 (2.0)	0.03 (1.48)	0.56 (4.92)
Qu	0.02 (−0.68)	0.07 (0.61)	0.02 (−0.4)	0.05 (1.21)	0.02 (−0.3)	0.05 (0.85)	0 (−0.76)	0 (−1.04)	0.02 (1.0)	0 (−0.64)	0.02 (0.93)	0.02 (0.95)	0 (−0.89)	0 (−0.21)	0 (−0.95)
Gu	0.91 (2.98)	0.62 (−3.48)	1.13 (7.54)	0.44 (−1.01)	0.37 (−0.93)	0.25 (−4.07)	0.15 (−0.66)	0.17 (−2.39)	0.07 (−1.4)	0 (−2.58)	0.02 (−2.62)	0.02 (−2.59)	0.08 (−2.72)	0.02 (0.16)	1.11 (12.51)

Table 4.4 Transformations of pairs of classroom dialogue in literacy lessons

	Ipk	*Pk*	*Ipi*	*Pi*	*Ie*	*El*	*Ic*	*Co*	*Is*	*Sp*	*Iu*	*Up*	*Ag*	*Qu*	*Gu*
Ipk	1.14 (0.77)	7.15 (24.64)	0.39 (−4.35)	0.11 (−8.03)	0.36 (−2.34)	0.15 (−7.39)	0.16 (−0.45)	0.1 (−5.13)	0 (−1.31)	0.02 (−1.45)	0.05 (−4.09)	0.19 (−2.46)	0.02 (−7.2)	0 (−2.15)	0.55 (−1.65)
Pk	3.62 (4.34)	9.07 (5.23)	2.3 (0.65)	0.99 (−10.75)	1.02 (−3.48)	2.19 (−2.76)	0.42 (−1.04)	1.09 (−2.53)	0.1 (1.06)	0.1 (−1.41)	0.83 (−0.52)	0.7 (−2.89)	3.07 (7.4)	0.11 (−1.46)	2.22 (2.42)
Ipi	0.42 (−4.05)	0.58 (−10.46)	0.88 (2.94)	4.8 (38.67)	0.26 (−2.04)	0.16 (−5.88)	0.11 (−0.62)	0.08 (−4.17)	0 (−1.13)	0.05 (0.15)	0.05 (−3.34)	0.16 (−1.92)	0.06 (−5.63)	0.02 (−1.27)	0.23 (−3.54)
Pi	0.58 (−4.02)	1.52 (−7.75)	1.31 (5.03)	1.62 (4.46)	0.86 (4.07)	1.01 (0.33)	0.16 (−0.44)	0.41 (−1.06)	0.02 (−0.46)	0.03 (−0.89)	0.5 (2.64)	0.37 (0.03)	1.27 (5.39)	0.11 (1.52)	0.45 (−2.45)
Ie	0.23 (−3.84)	0.71 (−5.9)	0.1 (−3.93)	0.31 (−2.5)	0.78 (8.13)	2.5 (23.94)	0.06 (−0.79)	0.18 (−1.36)	0 (−0.91)	0.02 (−0.64)	0.1 (−1.39)	0.03 (−3.28)	0.13 (−3.36)	0.02 (−0.79)	0.08 (−3.85)
El	1.01 (0.29)	1.35 (−7.78)	0.63 (−1.06)	0.5 (−4.09)	0.62 (1.31)	1.91 (9.12)	0.16 (−0.21)	0.7 (2.69)	0.03 (0.49)	0 (−1.93)	0.47 (2.54)	0.34 (−0.1)	1.17 (5.02)	0.13 (2.24)	0.5 (−1.54)
Ic	0.08 (−2.03)	0.18 (−4.25)	0.08 (−1.33)	0.18 (−0.12)	0.13 (0.92)	0.1 (−1.52)	0.16 (5.76)	0.79 (9.14)	0 (−0.53)	0 (−0.8)	0.03 (−0.83)	0.02 (−1.55)	0.02 (−2.57)	0 (−0.86)	0.03 (−2.1)
Co	0.6 (0.86)	0.78 (−4.85)	0.42 (0.42)	0.36 (−1.81)	0.31 (0.75)	0.36 (−1.47)	0.11 (0.66)	0.83 (9.64)	0 (−0.89)	0 (−1.36)	0.32 (3.46)	0.16 (−0.34)	0.39 (0.5)	0.02 (−0.72)	0.32 (−0.15)
Is	0.02 (−0.46)	0 (−2.41)	0.02 (−0.17)	0 (−1.31)	0.02 (0.24)	0.03 (0.49)	0 (−0.53)	0.02 (0.3)	0 (−0.19)	0.11 (23.79)	0 (−0.7)	0 (−0.75)	0 (−1.07)	0 (−0.31)	0.03 (1.02)
Sp	0.06 (0.22)	0.08 (−1.79)	0.05 (0.15)	0.02 (−1.45)	0 (−1.4)	0.03 (−0.78)	0.02 (0.47)	0 (−1.36)	0.02 (3.15)	0.05 (6.32)	0.05 (1.83)	0.03 (0.67)	0.1 (2.31)	0 (−0.48)	0.06 (1.11)
Iu	0.29 (−0.5)	0.47 (−4.1)	0.29 (0.72)	0.29 (−0.48)	0.08 (−1.72)	0.21 (−1.41)	0.03 (−0.83)	0.05 (−2.25)	0 (−0.7)	0.03 (0.86)	0.19 (2.42)	1.15 (24.92)	0.02 (−3.65)	0 (−1.15)	0.05 (−2.95)
Up	0.42 (0.68)	0.78 (−2.13)	0.29 (0.11)	0.26 (−1.54)	0.21 (0.38)	0.26 (−1.25)	0.05 (−0.52)	0.28 (1.85)	0 (−0.75)	0.03 (0.67)	0.24 (3.1)	0.26 (2.9)	0.31 (0.83)	0.06 (1.32)	0.18 (−1.1)
Ag	1.12 (3.87)	1.77 (−1.44)	0.73 (1.92)	0.49 (−2.45)	0.39 (0.19)	0.36 (−3.39)	0.15 (0.41)	0.39 (0.49)	0.02 (−0.07)	0.11 (2.97)	0.29 (1.16)	0.15 (−1.83)	0.39 (−1.4)	0.06 (0.71)	0.71 (2.84)
Qu	0.06 (−0.58)	0.06 (−2.52)	0 (−1.85)	0.11 (1.52)	0 (−1.5)	0.05 (−0.45)	0.06 (3.91)	0.02 (−0.72)	0 (−0.31)	0 (−0.48)	0.03 (0.67)	0.05 (1.32)	0.03 (−0.52)	0.13 (15.29)	0.05 (0.19)
Gu	0.71 (0.02)	3.31 (10.01)	0.36 (−2.02)	0.19 (−5.13)	0.21 (−2.03)	0.23 (−4.47)	0.13 (0.19)	0.08 (−3.67)	0.06 (3.08)	0.02 (−0.92)	0 (−3.82)	0.02 (−3.82)	0.16 (−3.87)	0 (−1.71)	1.28 (10.31)

is the progressive percentage between two types of dialogue; a large number indicates a higher level of probability that one type of dialogue appears after another. The second datum is the adjusted residual parameter of associations (Z value), and it indicates the associations that reach a significant level, which are highlighted in the tables. The dialogic categories listed are source nodes, namely, the type of dialogue that showed first. The categories listed in the first row are target nodes, namely, the type of dialogue following a preliminary type of dialogue. The target categories of classroom dialogue were often treated as a response to or feedback on, the source categories. For instance, figure 7.92 (35.39) from the top left corner suggests that 7.92% of invitations related to prior-known knowledge in math classes were frequently followed by responses about foundational knowledge, a pattern significantly prevalent in dialogic interactions. Dialogue focusing on prior-known knowledge (e.g. Ipk, Pk), personal information (e.g. Ipi, Pi), and elaboration (e.g. Ie, El) occurred more frequently than other dialogue types. Across all subjects, a specific initiation type (categories starting with 'I') often led to a response of the same type or to further inquiries about that dialogue type. For non-initiation types (those not starting with 'I'), similar feedback or questions were commonly elicited.

Subject-specific patterns also emerged: in math classes, expressions of personal opinion (Pi) often prompted invitations for elaboration (Ie), and elaborate dialogue (El) tended to lead to invitations involving uptakes/construction (Iu). This may be due to the fact that when students were asked for their personal opinions, they typically provided evidence or justification for their ideas. Additionally, when students were encouraged to challenge or extend classmates' contributions, they had to clarify and explain mathematical problems. In science classes, elaborate talk (El) frequently transitioned into coordination-related contributions (Ic/Co) and coordinated talk often led to speculative invitations (Co→Is). This is likely because both types of talk require the reasoning process and often involve questions like 'why', 'how', or 'in what way'. After critically engaging with perspectives and problems, teachers might evaluate them by comparing and critiquing them. Coordination-creating responses could then inspire feedback on speculation, possibly because hypothesis formulation and prediction in science often rely on an understanding of summarized principles. In literacy classes, coordination and speculative contributions were relatively rare and less likely to prompt further questions. Invitations for uptakes/construction (Pi/El/Co→Iu) were common after personal opinions, elaborate talk, and coordinated talk. Agreement was often linked to prior-known knowledge, elaboration, and uptakes/construction, while questioning was related to personal information in math and to elaboration in literacy. This suggests that teachers seek further justification or elaboration, or request a connection to previous comments, to enhance the reasoning process. The findings suggest that certain dialogue invitations are more effective at prompting high-quality responses, and specific student contributions lead to in-depth feedback. In math, teachers should encourage students to express personal views and explain their thought processes. Students should also clarify their contributions to foster deeper understanding. In science, more strategic and frequent use of questions and responses concerning elaboration and coordination should be encouraged. Literacy classes would benefit from inviting students to build upon previous discussions, leading to more productive dialogue exchanges. This understanding can help teachers manage questioning and student participation more skilfully.

The three subjects featured similar dialogue sequences while maintaining their distinct features. Graph analysis results, presented in Figures 4.1–4.3, display the sequential patterns of dialogue involvement. Different types of dialogue are represented by nodes, with the direction of edges or paths indicating the progression through dialogic categories. These subjects exhibited a shared sequential structure, which commenced with a dialogue about prior-known knowledge (Ipk), followed by a response based on that knowledge (Pk), and concluded with an agreement (Ag). The dialogue about prior-known knowledge (Ipk, Pk) and elaboration (El) emerged as crucial nodes in the network, frequently serving as starting points or transitions within the dialogue. These dialogues were pivotal in triggering or responding to other types of dialogue across the subjects. Despite the common structure, each subject had its unique sequential patterns. In mathematics classes, a distinctive sequence began with guidance (Gu), continued through invitations and provision of personal information (Ipi, Pi), expanded into elaboration-related contributions (Ie, El), and concluded with some dialogues evolving into uptakes/construction (Iu) or agreements (Ag). Science classroom discussions followed a characteristic sequence, where all dialogue categories demonstrated a high cognitive level, progressing from requesting elaboration (Ie) to providing elaboration (El), seeking coordination (Ic) to offering coordination (Co), and from initiation of speculation (Is) to providing speculative content (Sp). In literacy lessons, two distinctive pathways were identified: one began with personal information contributions (Ipi, Pi), moved through elaborate dialogues (Ie, El), and culminated in uptakes/construction contributions (Iu, Up); the other transitioned into questioning (Qu) after elaboration (El), followed a route through coordinated dialogue (Ic, Co) to reach uptakes/construction (Iu, Up).

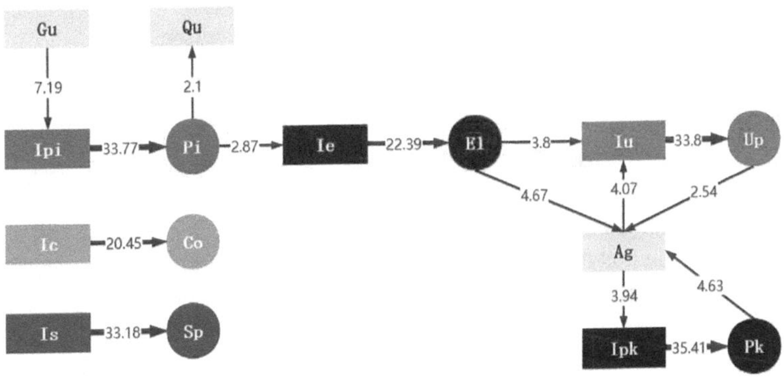

Figure 4.1 Sequence graphs for classroom dialogue in mathematics lessons

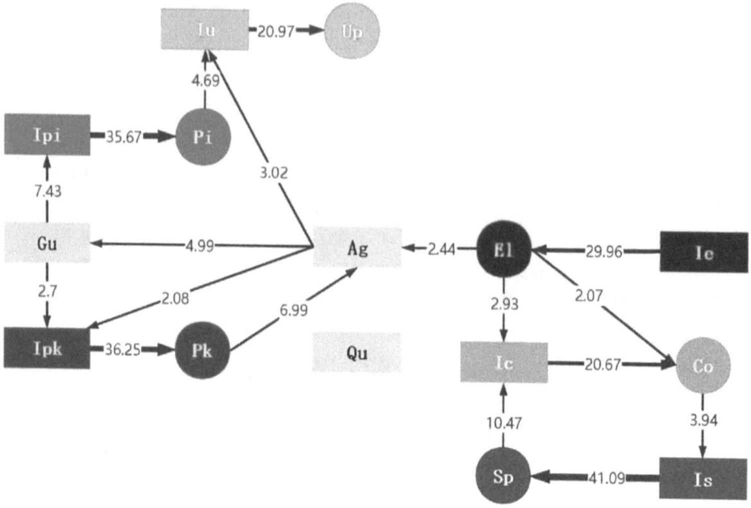

Figure 4.2 Sequence graphs for classroom dialogue in science lessons

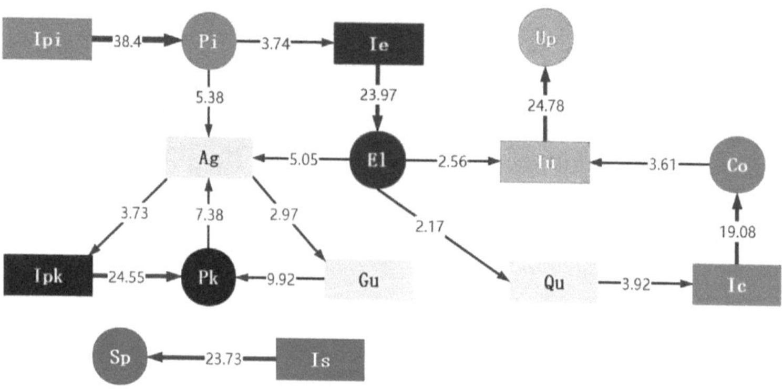

Figure 4.3 Sequence graphs for classroom dialogue in literacy lessons

The clustering results are shown in Figures 4.4–4.6, in which categories of classroom dialogue clusters are circles and edges whose weights are greater than the threshold. For example, only one edge, namely, Ipk → Pk, embodied a weight greater than the threshold λIpk (we set Ipk → Pk) among edges starting from category Ipk, which is marked in the graph. We use the Rand index to measure the clustering effect/result. The Rand index score was highest when categories were clustered into three groups for mathematics and science lessons. In contrast, the highest score appeared in the four-group division in a literacy lesson. For the three subjects, the prior-known knowledge and personal information categories were clustered in one group, and the topics of coordination, speculation, and uptakes/

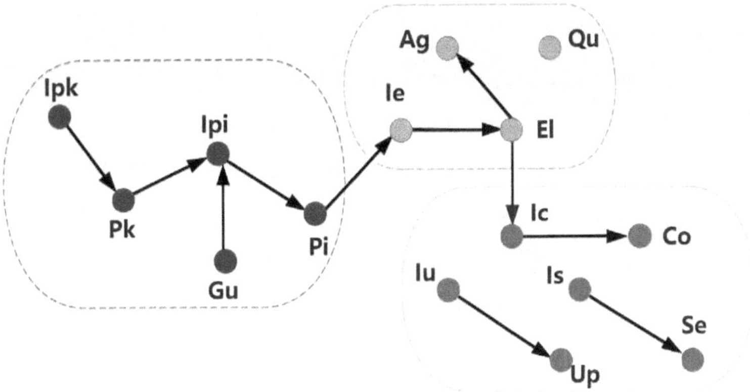

Figure 4.4 Sequences of clustered classroom dialogue in mathematics lessons

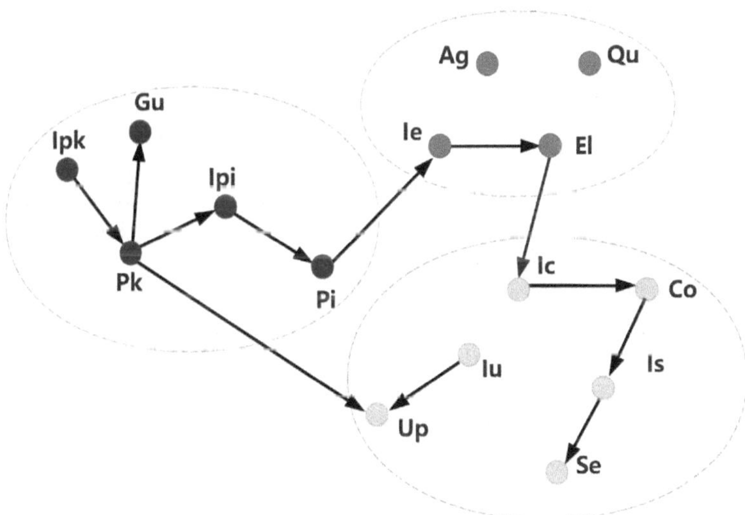

Figure 4.5 Sequences of clustered classroom dialogue in science lessons

construction were clustered as a community. In mathematics and science lessons, invitation to elaboration and giving elaborate responses, querying, and agreement emerged together. In literacy lessons, the elaborate talk was grouped separately; agreement tended to appear together with guidance while querying was clustered in the yellow group. As regards the edge between groups, Pi→Ie and El→Ic were channels for the three communities of classroom dialogue in mathematics lessons; Pi→Ie, El→Ic, and Pk→Up were channels for the three communities of classroom dialogue in science lessons, while Pi→El, El→Co, and Pk→Ag were channels for the three communities of classroom dialogue in literacy lessons.

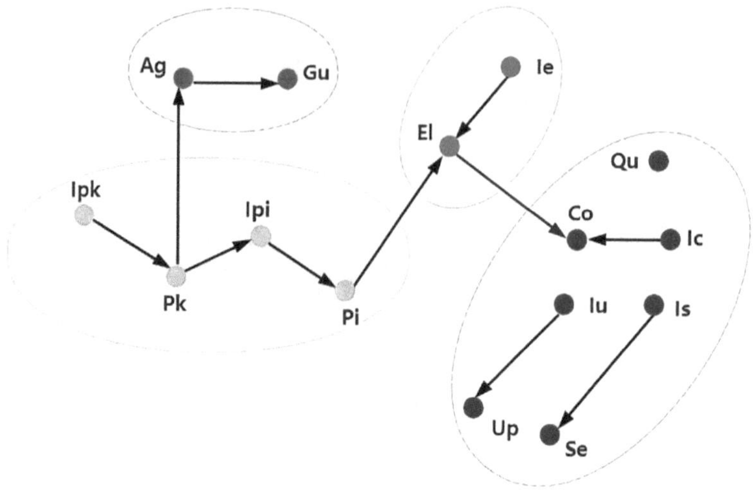

Figure 4.6 Sequences of clustered classroom dialogue in literacy lessons

Dialogue concerning prior-known knowledge and personal information tended to emerge together. This community of group often acted as a springboard for the evolution of long sequences of classroom dialogue. Dialogue concerning prior-known knowledge is somehow often accorded less attention when scholars select productive kinds of dialogue (see Hennessy et al., 2016). However, our empirical evidence indicates that contributions to basic knowledge play an essential role in the process of classroom dialogue. The findings align with those of Maldonado-Mahauad et al.'s (2018) study, which shows that learners who followed the sequential structure of the course materials designed by the instructor tended to perform well. Basic knowledge (e.g. principles, formulae, poetry) is the essence of research and exploration. Familiarity with subject content is the starting point for reasoning and lays a good foundation for the development of complex cognition. Teachers and students can probably start their verbal interaction by inviting talk based on previously learnt knowledge, and build on their utterances towards analysing problems. Verbal contributions comprising coordination, speculation, and uptakes/construction were often clustered as a group, which was mostly positioned at the back during the succession of dialogic contributions. This result is logical, as the former group involves a lower level of thinking and cognition, usually referring to memory or sometimes not even needing to contribute this kind of dialogue (Nystrand et al., 2003), while the latter group usually relies on a complicated process of thinking (Hennessy et al., 2020). Paths of Pi→Ie and El→Ic were connections between groups of classroom dialogue and can be treated as indications of upgrades during the process of classroom dialogue. The elaborate talk was an essential intermediary point and channelled the dialogue that showed lower levels of cognition towards that showing high levels of cognition. A great many studies have indicated the important function of elaborate talk (Howe et al., 2019; O'Connor et al., 2015), and the empirical evidence from our study also supports this. The process of elaboration impels students to make their thoughts explicit, use evidence to justify their opinions, and think critically and reflectively, promoting deep understanding and productive learning achievement (Muhonen et al., 2018; van der Veen & van Oers, 2017).

Research suggests that extended dialogue exchanges are more indicative of effective language use as a collaborative and cognitive tool than brief exchanges (Mercer, 2008). In terms of dialogic length, science classroom discussions were found to be the most extensive, with mathematics following, while literacy lessons typically involved shorter sequences. In science classes, the dialogue progression was particularly prolonged, originating from 'Ipk' and concluding at 'Sp'. This path began with engaging dialogue about prior-known knowledge (Ipk), proceeded to responses based on this knowledge (Pk), encompassed seeking personal information (Ipi), sharing personal information (Pi), moved to requesting elaboration (Ie), providing elaboration (El), extended to seeking integration (Ic), offering integration (Co), and concluded with inviting speculative thinking (Is) and providing speculative ideas (Sp). This extensive sequence was less likely to include speculative talk in mathematics classes and was less pronounced in literacy sessions. This discrepancy is likely attributable to the inherent nature of the disciplines and the diverse aims of their pedagogical development. Science education, for instance, highlights hypothesis formation and cultivating innovative problem-solving skills (OECD, 2020). Science educators can encourage dialogic interactions by first inviting detailed explanations, then facilitating the weaving and synthesizing of ideas following elaborate discourse, and finally inviting students to speculate beyond existing knowledge. Conversations in both science and literacy settings tend to adopt a prolonged sequential structure that includes the expression of personal information, elaborate discourse, and responses. This sequential pattern exemplifies exploratory dialogue, characterized by a collective and constructive process that involves organized interactions essential for reasoning and knowledge advancement. Exploratory dialogue is instrumental in the co-construction of ideas and shared reasoning, and it is acknowledged as enhancing educational benefits (Muhonen et al., 2016).

In conclusion, our research revealed that although there were some common features, the sequential patterns of dialogue in mathematics, science, and literacy teaching had their unique characteristics. For mathematics classes, a typical sequence involved guiding students, inviting them to share their personal information, engaging in elaborate discussions, and finally reaching a consensus. In science classes, a notable pattern unfolded with a focus on problem analysis and elaboration, leading to a comparison and summarization of the content and ending with a discussion on applying the knowledge to new problem-solving scenarios. The dialogue patterns in literacy lessons often began with sharing personal opinions, progressed to detailed explanations, and might prompt questions about difficulties or the coordination of ideas or result in summarizing the discussion. The sequences identified in mathematics and science classes were generally more extensive than those in literacy classes. A distinctive five-step sequence in science classes was observed, which was represented by the sequence Ipk→ Pk→ Ipi→ Pi→ Ie→ El→ Ic→ Co→ Is→ Sp, where each pair of dialogues constituted a step. This sequence was partly present in mathematics and literacy classes but less frequently extended into coordination and speculation. Discussions about prior-known knowledge and personal information often occurred in conjunction and served as a launchpad for extended dialogue sequences. Elaborate discussions tended to emerge in the middle of the exchange. At the same time, those focusing on coordination, speculation, and uptakes/construction were typically seen as a collective and occurred later in the dialogic process. We found that the transition from expressing personal information to requesting elaboration and from providing elaboration to inviting coordination were key moments that advanced the dialogue from lower cognitive levels to higher ones.

Revealing patterns of classroom dialogue in diverse quality levels

In this section, we will demonstrate how dialogic patterns differ in lessons conducted by different levels of teachers. Table 4.5 shows the per cent of occurrence of each type of interaction in the classroom teaching of the three quality levels. Among them, the implementation of dialogue by preliminary and intermediate teachers had similarities, which were different from those conducted by expert teachers. Compared to preliminary and intermediate teachers, dialogue by expert teachers was more capable of carrying out interactive teaching that reflects higher-order thinking and complex cognitive abilities. In the classroom teaching of primary and intermediate teachers, questions and answers around prior-known knowledge and textbook content accounted for nearly half of all dialogues, followed by a larger proportion of personal information expression and guidance dialogues. These three types of dialogues are lower-order cognitive levels of interaction, which only need to be based on the content of the textbook, relying on the memory of the recitation. In contrast, the elaborate interaction, which reflects higher-order thinking, accounted for about 8%, the coordinated interaction and constructed dialogue accounted for about 5%, and the speculated interaction, which is closely related to the ability to innovate, accounted for less than 1%.

In the classroom teaching of expert teachers, the proportion of dialogic types involving prior-known knowledge was much smaller than that of the last two types of teachers (only 33%). The second largest proportion was elaborate interaction (19.7%), which was two to three times the proportion of the same kind of dialogue in the classrooms of preliminary and intermediate levels. The proportions of other types of interactions reflecting higher-order thinking were also higher than that of preliminary middle school level teachers, such as coordinated interaction accounting for 8.6%, 5.7% for uptakes/construction interactions, and 2.5% for speculation interactions. Compared with preliminary and intermediate teachers, expert teachers paid more attention to provoking students' expression and encouraging active participation. The proportion of questions asked by expert teachers was either similar to or lower than the proportion of students' expressions. In contrast, the proportion

Table 4.5 Frequency table of classroom conversations for junior, intermediate, and expert teachers (in per cent)

	Ipk	*Pk*	*Ipi*	*Pi*	*Ie*	*El*	*Ic*	*Co*	*Is*	*Sp*	*Iu*	*Up*	*Ag*	*Qu*	*Gu*
Preliminary	23.7	23.4	8.3	6.5	5	4	2.7	1.3	0.5	0.4	2.3	0.5	7.1	1	13
Intermediate	24.6	21.3	9	5.6	4.3	3.1	2.9	1.6	0.5	0.3	2.3	0.5	6.7	1.4	16
Expert	11.8	21.4	9.4	9.3	7.2	12.5	3.3	5.3	1.2	1.3	3	2.7	5.8	0.9	5.1

of teachers' talk was significantly higher than that of students in the classrooms of preliminary and intermediate teachers. The type of interaction in which the difference in student-teacher ratios was more pronounced was 'elaborated interaction', in which the expert teacher's questions were answered 7:13 by the students, while the question-answer ratio in the primary teacher's classroom was 5:4. In the intermediate teacher's classroom it was 4:3.

Table 4.6 shows the transformation of dialogue for primary, intermediate, and expert teachers. The transformation patterns of classroom interactions for beginner and intermediate teachers were similar, and the percentage of classroom interactions is lower overall than that of classrooms taught by expert teachers. The transformation with the highest per cent in all types of teachers' classrooms was Ipk-Pk, in which the teacher's questioning around prior-known knowledge (Ipk) was followed by the student's response on prior-known knowledge (Pk). A certain type of questioning tends to elicit the same type of response, and instructional dialogues usually accompany the expressions involving prior-known knowledge. It is noticeable that, in the preliminary and intermediate level lessons, when the preceding interactions were of the type that exemplified higher-order cognition, subsequent interactions tended to shift back to types of interactions involving lower-order cognition. For example, when teachers asked elaborated questions (Ie), a large portion of students' responses, in addition to the corresponding explanations and elaborations (El), would be converted into responses to prior-known (Pk) or students' re-questions about prior-known (Ipk), thus shifting the interaction back to the basics category. Beginning and intermediate teachers rarely initiated innovative talk (Is) in the classroom, so it was rare for students to give innovative answers (Sp). In expert teachers' classrooms, dialogue showing higher-order thinking and complex cognition continued to elicit responses and feedback at higher cognitive levels, with more prominent interaction sequences being analytical interactions. The expert teacher posed an elaborated question (Ie), and then most of the responses were explanations and elaborations of the problem (El), and a proportion of these were converted into further explorations of the causal mechanisms (Ie), thus allowing the problem to be elaborated in layers (El). This is in contrast to preliminary and intermediate teachers' classrooms, where a large proportion of responses were converted to triggering a review of the prior-known (Ipk, Pk). In addition, expert teachers' classrooms also had more inductive, transferable, and response-constructive interactions than those of the first two types of teachers,

Table 4.6 Per cent of classroom discourse transformation for junior, intermediate, and expert teachers

		Ipk	*Pk*	*Ipi*	*Pi*	*Ie*	*El*	*Ic*	*Co*	*Is*	*Sp*	*Iu*	*Up*	*Ag*	*Qu*	*Gu*
Ipk	**Preliminary**	6.48	11.15	1.93	0.27	0.85	0.17	0.68	0.05	0.11	0	0.52	0.02	0.58	0.11	2.83
	Intermediate	5.29	11.3	1.59	0.33	1.15	0.27	0.64	0.07	0.1	0.01	0.43	0.02	0.6	0.14	1.86
	Expert	1.48	7.78	0.46	0.22	0.48	0.34	0.2	0.12	0.02	0.02	0.06	0.1	0.09	0.04	0.41
Pk	**Preliminary**	8.09	3.49	1.5	0.46	0.94	0.81	0.57	0.48	0.05	0.02	0.56	0.08	0.25	0.33	2.41
	Intermediate	7.96	5.63	1.49	0.6	0.79	0.75	0.61	0.41	0.15	0.02	0.54	0.15	2.18	0.27	2.03
	Expert	4.39	5.62	1.87	0.62	1.23	1.59	0.59	0.86	0.19	0.09	0.62	0.4	2.06	0.11	1.26
Ipi	**Preliminary**	1.07	1.47	1.48	3.01	0.31	0.13	0.17	0.08	0.04	0.03	0.02	0.01	0.6	0.07	0.9
	Intermediate	0.95	0.99	1.08	3.16	0.28	0.09	0.09	0.02	0.02	0.02	0.12	0.01	0.75	0.08	0.67
	Expert	0.68	0.49	1.38	4.71	0.39	0.47	0.17	0.14	0.05	0.09	0.09	0.11	0.21	0.05	0.36
Pi	**Preliminary**	0.9	0.53	0.8	0.64	0.33	0.27	0.12	0.1	0.02	0.03	0.33	0.02	0.7	0.2	0.79
	Intermediate	0.67	0.54	0.8	0.96	0.42	0.35	0.19	0.06	0.02	0.02	0.22	0.03	0.76	0.04	0.92
	Expert	0.36	1.23	1.69	1.09	0.88	0.97	0.25	0.35	0.11	0.09	0.45	0.31	0.74	0.12	0.41
Ie	**Preliminary**	0.98	0.53	0.42	0.03	0.58	1.09	0.16	0.02	0.02	0	0.03	0.01	0.18	0.06	0.42
	Intermediate	0.96	0.65	0.26	0.16	0.78	1.47	0.07	0.02	0	0	0.07	0	0.15	0.02	0.36
	Expert	0.26	0.62	0.24	0.36	1.12	3.68	0.17	0.18	0.05	0.07	0.11	0.04	0.15	0.05	0.12
El	**Preliminary**	0.46	0.62	0.24	0.13	0.26	0.27	0.08	0.03	0.01	0.02	0.13	0.05	0.49	0.06	0.37
	Intermediate	0.72	0.59	0.29	0.14	0.63	0.51	0.12	0.1	0.01	0	0.16	0.01	0.41	0.07	0.25
	Expert	1.21	1.22	1.03	0.52	1.28	3.01	0.55	0.84	0.14	0.08	0.57	0.28	1.11	0.17	0.39
Ic	**Preliminary**	0.82	0.28	0.27	0.06	0.08	0.01	0.42	0.48	0.02	0	0.05	0.02	0.11	0.01	0.46
	Intermediate	0.66	0.42	0.19	0.1	0.11	0.02	0.44	0.37	0.02	0	0.03	0.01	0.11	0.03	0.38
	Expert	0.22	0.19	0.18	0.25	0.2	0.27	0.46	1.17	0.08	0.02	0.06	0.01	0.07	0.03	0.08
Co	**Preliminary**	0.27	0.26	0.11	0.04	0.1	0.05	0.11	0.11	0	0	0.12	0.05	0.25	0.02	0.23
	Intermediate	0.28	0.2	0.14	0.03	0.06	0.08	0.13	0.11	0.02	0	0.02	0.01	0.12	0.01	0.1
	Expert	0.55	0.65	0.52	0.24	0.39	0.63	0.31	0.75	0.14	0.05	0.24	0.14	0.34	0.03	0.29
Is	**Preliminary**	0.03	0.05	0.05	0.02	0	0.01	0	0	0.09	0.17	0	0	0	0	0.06
	Intermediate	0.06	0.06	0.03	0.02	0.02	0.01	0	0	0.07	0.2	0.01	0	0	0	0.05
	Expert	0.03	0.02	0.06	0.04	0.08	0.08	0.03	0.03	0.12	0.61	0.01	0	0.02	0.01	0.05

(Continued)

Table 4.6 (Continued)

		Ipk	*Pk*	*Ipi*	*Pi*	*Ie*	*El*	*Ic*	*Co*	*Is*	*Sp*	*Iu*	*Up*	*Ag*	*Qu*	*Gu*
Sp	**Preliminary**	0.05	0.04	0.02	0.04	0.05	0	0.01	0	0.02	0.01	0.04	0	0.02	0	0.02
	Intermediate	0.12	0.01	0.02	0.01	0.02	0.01	0	0.01	0.02	0.02	0.05	0	0	0.02	0.08
	Expert	0.08	0.14	0.11	0.06	0.12	0.12	0.1	0.09	0.17	0.11	0.03	0.03	0.11	0.02	0.05
Iu	**Preliminary**	0.39	0.52	0.16	0.2	0.08	0.06	0.11	0.08	0	0.02	0.16	0.22	0.07	0.07	0.31
	Intermediate	0.36	0.53	0.18	0.23	0.05	0.12	0.02	0.02	0.01	0.03	0.2	0.26	0.05	0.02	0.19
	Expert	0.22	0.33	0.21	0.3	0.14	0.38	0.05	0.11	0.01	0.01	0.18	1.03	0.04	0.02	0.03
Up	**Preliminary**	0.05	0.04	0.04	0.03	0.05	0.03	0.02	0.02	0	0	0.11	0.02	0.06	0.01	0.05
	Intermediate	0.11	0.09	0.06	0.01	0.02	0.01	0.03	0.02	0	0	0.07	0.02	0.06	0.01	0.05
	Expert	0.31	0.47	0.27	0.2	0.2	0.19	0.07	0.16	0.03	0.01	0.27	0.17	0.24	0.05	0.11
Ag	**Preliminary**	2.08	0.41	0.77	0.25	0.33	0.07	0.2	0.08	0.03	0	0.14	0.02	0.53	0.09	2
	Intermediate	1.95	0.36	0.74	0.28	0.32	0.1	0.26	0.07	0.02	0	0.22	0.01	0.98	0.08	1.72
	Expert	0.98	1.01	0.55	0.36	0.37	0.46	0.17	0.36	0.04	0.07	0.31	0.1	0.42	0.06	0.52
Qu	**Preliminary**	0.15	0.38	0.1	0.17	0.02	0.02	0.01	0	0	0	0.02	0.01	0.11	0.23	0.23
	Intermediate	0.17	0.24	0.05	0.07	0.02	0.02	0	0	0	0.01	0.02	0	0.18	0.14	0.12
	Expert	0.06	0.08	0.08	0.11	0.08	0.13	0.05	0.02	0.01	0.01	0.05	0.03	0.04	0.11	0.02
Gu	**Preliminary**	3.85	2.56	1.51	0.49	0.55	0.24	0.42	0.18	0.05	0.02	0.22	0.02	0.77	0.19	5.61
	Intermediate	2.98	1.98	1.41	0.47	0.32	0.2	0.26	0.02	0.09	0.04	0.1	0.02	0.76	0.11	4.46
	Expert	0.68	1.47	0.77	0.24	0.26	0.24	0.13	0.09	0.05	0.02	0.01	0.01	0.14	0.01	0.97

Table 4.7 Means and deviations for different categories of classroom dialogue

Code	*Total*		*Primary school*		*Secondary school*		*High school*	
	M (%)	*SD (%)*	*M (%)*	*SD (%)*	*M (%)*	*SD (%)*	*M (%)*	*SD (%)*
Invite prior-known knowledge	16.99	7.87	19.20	3.89	18.31	9.00	15.10	7.08
Prior-known knowledge	20.57	7.51	24.91	6.61	19.46	6.85	20.55	8.06
Invite personal information	11.12	6.18	5.43	1.98	10.89	6.43	12.82	5.79
Personal information	9.67	5.55	12.71	3.98	7.62	5.28	10.94	5.49
Initiate elaboration	5.82	3.59	2.84	1.08	5.59	4.02	6.82	3.10
Elaboration	7.70	4.76	5.46	2.18	7.14	5.97	8.85	3.46
Invite coordination	3.25	2.49	2.71	1.59	3.31	2.48	3.33	2.71
Coordination	2.35	1.90	2.46	2.53	1.71	1.86	2.95	1.56
Invite speculation	0.52	0.82	0.08	0.30	0.45	0.89	0.69	0.79
Speculation	0.44	0.72	0.02	0.06	0.39	0.72	0.61	0.76
Invite uptakes/ construction	2.64	2.51	6.01	3.23	2.02	2.33	2.38	1.71
Uptakes/ Construction	1.73	2.20	4.65	3.40	0.78	1.66	1.92	1.50
Agreement	6.69	3.30	4.66	2.58	7.87	2.78	6.03	3.55
Querying	0.99	1.27	1.27	1.54	1.05	1.41	0.86	1.04
Guide	6.71	3.39	7.59	3.43	6.42	3.45	6.15	3.31

those addressing personal viewpoints. The averages for elaboration discussions, indicating higher cognitive engagement, were also significant. However, discussions focused on speculation had the lowest averages. The categories of agreement and direction were relatively consistent across math classes, although there was a lower percentage of questioning. In primary school math lessons, the highest averages were seen for reinforcing prior-known knowledge, sharing personal views, and providing guidance. For secondary and high school math lessons, the highest averages were for reinforcing prior-known knowledge, sharing personal views, and engaging in elaboration. Speculation and asking questions were consistently low-scoring across all educational stages, and uptakes/construction talk were infrequent in secondary and high school classes.

The data in Table 4.8 reveal that the one-way ANOVA analysis detected significant differences in dialogic interactions across math lessons at different educational stages. These differences pertained to aspects such as personal information, elaboration, coordination, speculation, uptakes/construction, and agreement. No significant differences were found in dialogic contributions concerning familiar content, coordination invitations, queries, and guidance. The differences were primarily observed between primary and secondary/high school math lessons, with secondary and high school students' contributions being more similar. Primary school students made significantly fewer invitations for subjective opinions compared to

Table 4.8 Differences in dialogic patterns between the three stages of education

Category				
(I)	*(J)*	*F*	*P*	*Mean Difference(I-J) (%)*
Invite prior-known knowledge		2.740	0.069	
Primary school	Secondary school			0.89
Primary school	High school			4.10*
Secondary school	High school			3.20
Prior-known knowledge		2.807	0.065	
Primary school	Secondary school			5.45*
Primary school	High school			4.36
Secondary school	High school			−1.09
Invite personal information		8.391	0.000	
Primary school	Secondary school			−5.46*
Primary school	High school			−7.38*
Secondary school	High school			−1.92
Personal information		7.470	0.001	
Primary school	Secondary school			5.09*
Primary school	High school			−7.38*
Secondary school	High school			−3.33*
Initiate elaboration		7.259	0.001	
Primary school	Secondary school			−2.75*
Primary school	High school			−3.98*
Secondary school	High school			−1.23
Elaboration		3.385	0.037	
Primary school	Secondary school			−1.67
Primary school	High school			−3.39*
Secondary school	High school			−1.71
Invite coordination		.341	0.712	
Primary school	Secondary school			−0.60
Primary school	High school			−0.62
Secondary school	High school			−0.02
Coordination		5.900	0.004	
Primary school	Secondary school			0.76
Primary school	High school			−0.49
Secondary school	High school			−1.25*
Invite speculation		3.214	0.044	
Primary school	Secondary school			−0.37
Primary school	High school			−0.61*
Secondary school	High school			−0.24
Speculation		3.951	0.022	
Primary school	Secondary school			−0.37*
Primary school	High school			−0.59*
Secondary school	High school			−0.21

(Continued)

Table 4.8 (Continued)

Category				
(I)	*(J)*	*F*	*P*	*Mean Difference(I-J) (%)*
Invite uptakes/construction		17.430	0.000	
Primary school	Secondary school			3.98*
Primary school	High school			3.63*
Secondary school	High school			−0.35
Uptakes/Construction		22.583	0.000	
Primary school	Secondary school			3.87*
Primary school	High school			2.73*
Secondary school	High school			−1.14*
Agreement		7.412	0.001	
Primary school	Secondary school			−3.21*
Primary school	High school			−1.37
Secondary school	High school			1.84*
Querying		.614	0.543	
Primary school	Secondary school			0.23
Primary school	High school			0.41
Secondary school	High school			0.18
Guide		2.214	0.721	
Primary school	Secondary school			1.67
Primary school	High school			1.43
Secondary school	High school			0.34

secondary and high school students, yet they were more prone to sharing personal opinions. Similarly, invitations for elaboration were less frequent in primary school math lessons than in secondary and high school lessons, and responses to elaboration were also less common in primary lessons compared to high school ones. In secondary and high school math lessons, coordination contributions varied. Invitations for speculation were significantly less common in primary school lessons than in high school ones, and primary school students typically provided fewer speculative responses than their secondary and high school counterparts. On the other hand, primary math lessons had more invitations for uptakes/construction than secondary and high school lessons, with secondary school students being the least likely to contribute to uptakes/construction and to reach agreements.

The focus on incorporating prior-known knowledge into classroom discussions across all three educational stages indicates a prioritization of foundational understanding over mathematical instruction. Teachers facilitate the connection between new and old knowledge by discussing students' prior learning during lessons. This approach is notably prevalent in primary education, where the connection between pre-existing knowledge and new guidance is consistently emphasized. This emphasizes the importance of securing a solid grasp of basic concepts early on in mathematical education, which forms the basis for advanced reasoning and critical thinking skills (Song et al., 2023). Prior research has highlighted the dynamic and interconnected nature of mathematical knowledge (Evitts, 2005), emphasizing the role of teachers in recognizing and fostering connections among key mathematical concepts to support students in constructing and applying their understanding (Eli et al., 2011).

Personal information plays a vital role in mediating the link between students' personal experiences and their engagement with mathematical learning throughout all stages of education studied. The substantial presence of subjective expression suggests its significance in this process, with secondary students exhibiting more expressions of this kind compared to primary and high school students. This discrepancy could imply that as students age, they face fewer opportunities to discuss social aspects within mathematics classrooms or might be disinclined to share subjective viewpoints. Discourse research in mathematics education often focuses on secondary students, revealing social dynamics. For example, Kieran (2001) found that students may struggle to comunicate their ideas effectively during problem-solving interactions. Similarly, Chan and Sfard (2020) identified barriers to idea exchange in pair collaborations, potentially leading to misunderstandings. These studies underscore the necessity to investigate how students engage with social elements in mathematics learning environments and to provide instruction on effective communication within these settings, especially as students progress to higher levels of mathematics.

The types of dialogue that reflect high levels of cognitive engagement, such as elaboration, coordinated, and speculative discussions, are indicative of profound thinking and often involve intricate processing methods (Hennessy et al., 2016). This research suggests that within the context of mathematics instruction, these higher-order conversations were more apparent in secondary and high school settings. Numerous investigations, as noted by Howe et al. (2019) and O'Connor et al. (2015), have underscored the significance of analytical dialogue, a pattern also confirmed by our empirical data. The analytical process involves students in articulating their reasoning, substantiating their viewpoints with evidence, and engaging in critical and introspective thinking, which in turn fosters deep comprehension and academic success (Muhonen et al., 2018; van der Veen et al., 2017). However, this study found that instances of coordination and speculation were relatively rare. Coordinated talk generally entails students constructing links between ideas, contrasting and integrating various knowledge concepts, and collaboratively establishing rules and principles. Speculative dialogue, on the other hand, encourages innovative problem-solving and nurtures creativity. Both types of dialogue are crucial for mathematical learning, as emphasized by the OECD (2020), and should be nurtured and given greater prominence in educational practice.

- **Notable patterns of classroom dialogue across different educational stages**

Figures 4.10–4.12 show the results of the sequential pattern mining, reflecting the collective process of dialogue contributions. The nodes refer to different types of classroom dialogue, and the edge/path direction represents the evolution

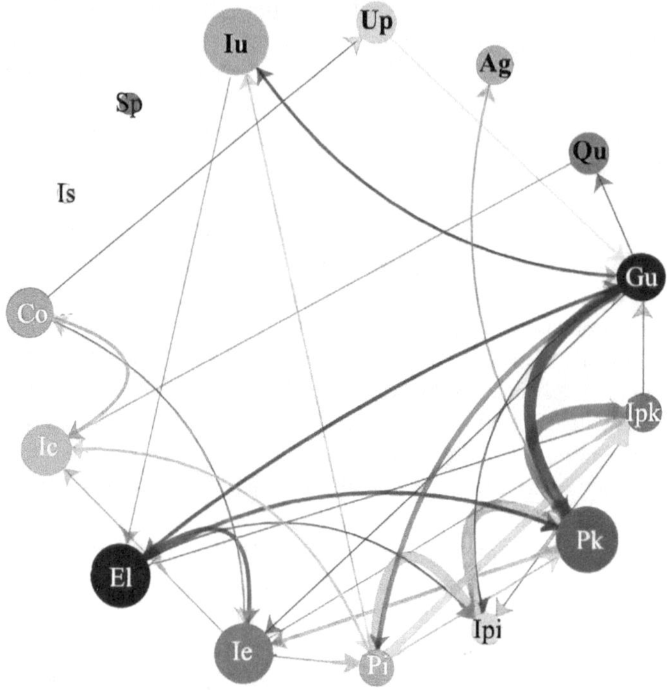

Figure 4.10 Sequential patterns of dialogue in primary school

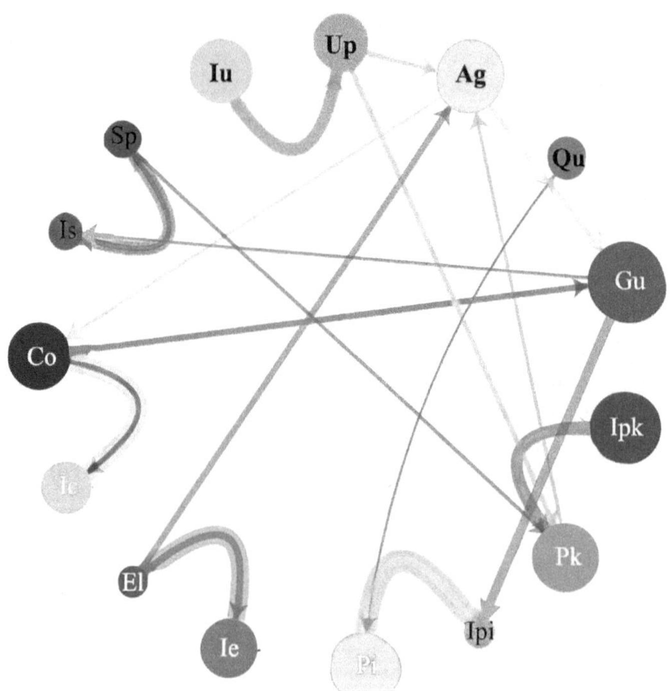

Figure 4.11 Sequential patterns of dialogue in secondary school

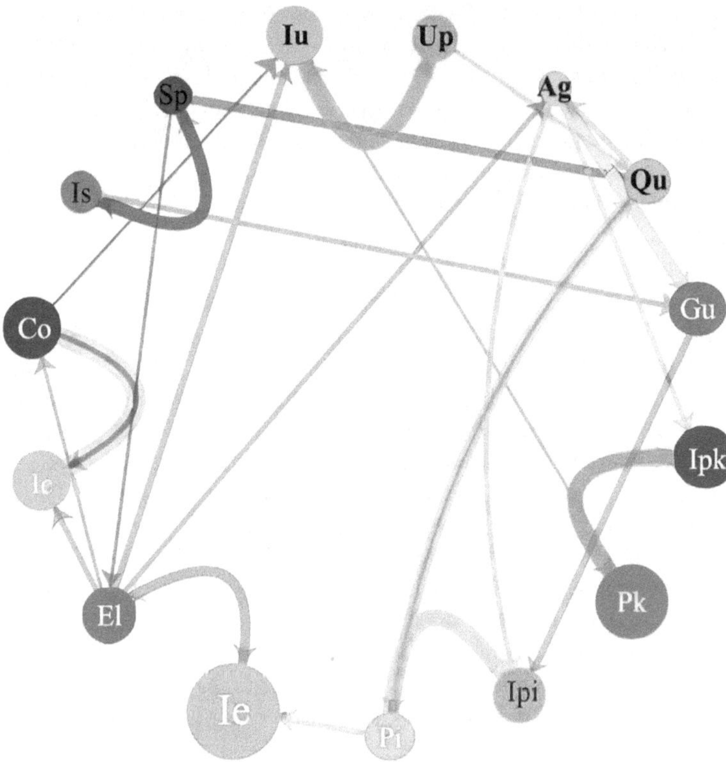

Figure 4.12 Sequential patterns of dialogue in high school

of dialogic categories. The paths shown in the figures are significant in the dialogic contributions of mathematics lessons. The arrows for paths indicate the evolution of dialogic contributions and how dialogic categories make transformations. The size of the edges/paths varies to reflect the varying strength of the relationships between the categories: a thick path is viewed as more important in the graph network.

Pairs of classroom dialogue of the same kind were frequently observed in mathematics lessons, and those dialogic categories included inviting prior-known knowledge-giving a response based on prior-known knowledge, inviting personal information-giving personal information, inviting elaboration-giving elaboration, and inviting coordination-giving coordination, and so on. Coordination was also likely to transform into inviting elaboration talk or into uptakes/construction. Guide was closely linked to dialogue concerning previously learnt knowledge and personal information, and there were a great number of paths connecting the five categories, particularly in primary schools and secondary schools. There were similarities between the sequential patterns of mathematics lessons in secondary and high schools. Paths connecting pairs of dialogue categories of the same kind were frequently identified, and sequences inviting speculation-giving speculation, and inviting uptakes/construction-giving uptakes/construction were also prominent.

A few paths were identified in secondary school lessons that made sense, which involved giving elaboration→ guide→ prior-known knowledge, inviting elaboration→ giving personal information→ querying/guide→ giving prior-known knowledge, and querying→ giving personal information→ inviting personal information→ reaching agreement. In high school lessons, there was a long prominent sequence starting from inviting personal information→ giving personal information→ inviting elaboration→ giving elaboration→ inviting coordination→ giving coordination.

There were more paths connecting dialogic categories relating to speculation in mathematics lessons at high school compared to those of primary or secondary schools, for example, speculation extending to querying, guide, or coordination. More paths progressed through querying, and for example, there were many instances of sequences connecting querying with speculation, or personal information. In comparison, the dialogic paths of mathematics lessons in primary school were less likely to involve speculation, uptakes/construction, and querying.

The sequential patterns of classroom dialogue in the three stages of education have their own characteristics, although dialogic patterns in secondary and high schools share more similarities. Variation between the three stages of education is particularly obvious in terms of high-cognitive dialogue, namely, elaboration, coordination, speculation, and uptakes/construction. There was more free talk in primary school mathematics lessons, and students there were more likely to express their personal information and discuss it with the teacher and their peers. They tended to build on previous talk and make extensions. In comparison, the dialogue in secondary and high school lessons embodied more in-depth thought and demonstrated critical thinking. Teachers were more likely to induce students to elaborate reasoning processes and encourage them to apply what they have learnt to solve novel problems. The switch from primary to secondary education shows a more pronounced transformation than the transition from secondary to high school. Research has illuminated the challenges students face during these educational transitions, particularly in the context of mathematics. These studies either compare common content across various educational levels or focus on the requirements for advanced mathematical studies. However, many of these investigations centre on the secondary to high school transition, assuming that shifts in mathematical culture, including the use of symbols, mathematical terminology, and pedagogical approaches, can lead to academic hurdles for students (Gueudet, 2008).

In primary school, dialogic interactions frequently centre on familiar knowledge, personal information, and guidance, remaining at a fundamental cognitive level and not often extending to speculative or probing dialogues. Prominent sequences in secondary and high school classes engage both lower and higher cognitive levels, with discussions often involving the application of previously learnt knowledge, personal information, and the enhancement of cognitive processes, followed by mutual questioning and problem-solving strategies. High school mathematics lessons, in particular, often exhibit distinctive lengthy sequential patterns that commence with personal information, proceed to elaboration discussions, and culminate in coordinated problem-solving. This suggests that extended dialogue sequences significantly contribute to collaborative thinking and comprehensive understanding, as opposed to isolated statements. This kind of interaction is instrumental in engaging students in mathematical reasoning and thinking. Speculative and probing contributions are more common in high school mathematics lessons. This is likely due to the complexity of tasks that necessitate advanced problem-solving and cognitive skills (McCulloch et al., 2018). These types of dialogues not only facilitate the practical application of learnt concepts but also promote critical thinking and reflective practice. Studies like Hew and Lo (2020) have corroborated the manner in which high school students engage in constructing and validating hypotheses in math classes, aligning with our observations.

Implications

The empirical evidence presented earlier has practical implications for educational practices and the effective implementation of dialogic pedagogy. It can be utilized in the professional development of teachers, enhancing their management skills to foster collective, cumulative, exploratory, and productive classroom dialogue. It is important to highlight that these findings are based on the analysis of lessons from three subjects, mathematics, science, and literacy, taught in China. It is possible that different dialogic patterns may arise in other subjects and social contexts. Future research should expand on these findings to deepen our understanding of sequential patterns across a broader spectrum of settings and contexts. The results are better interpreted as exploratory rather than confirmatory. Despite this, the identified collective patterns were derived from a nationally representative dataset. The lessons examined in this study were significantly influenced by OECD guidelines (2019), which are widely regarded as a global standard. Consequently, the findings should be generalizable and serve as a strong foundation for future research.

This study contributes novel insights into the domain of classroom dialogue and technology. Firstly, it integrates data mining methodologies, ordinarily associated with computer science, into the realm of classroom dialogue. This chapter introduces a set of sequential pattern mining techniques to discern how dialogic exchange shapes and captures the sequential patterns inherent in classroom dialogue. These techniques have proven effective in extracting insights into the behavioural and cognitive processes unfolding during classroom interaction. Data mining analytics has the potential to transcend the constraints of traditional qualitative analysis of transcripts or descriptive statistics related to category occurrences. The judicious application of data mining analytics will enhance our methodological approaches and set a new direction for the examination of classroom dialogue. This approach is burgeoning and holds promise, and it is our hope that the methods we employ will inspire additional scholars to undertake similar pioneering efforts. Secondly, this study captures sequential patterns within extensive datasets of classroom dialogue, shedding light on the progression of both productive and exploratory communication. The findings illuminate the communicative process and offer significant insights into the conduct of dialogic pedagogy. Drawing on sophisticated theories and compelling arguments, there is a consensus that productive classroom dialogue should be characterized by collective and cumulative progression. However, few studies have provided a clear demonstration of the interconnected chains of collaborative reasoning. Our research fills this gap by presenting compelling empirical evidence that supports the sociocultural theory and unveils the shared patterns amid seemingly disordered expressions. Thirdly, we differentiate the dialogic structures that manifest in various subjects, quality levels, and educational stages.

The research presented here offers a valuable understanding of the effective planning and handling of classroom dialogue. First and foremost, I proposed a Double Helix Upward Pattern to describe the productive collective feature of classroom dialogue (see Figure 4.13). This is taken from a typical structure of DNA, and it adapts extremely well to the context of verbal exchange in whole-class settings. One helix is about the talk made by a teacher, while the other signals students' contributions. Normally, teachers and students should understand each other well, and a type of initiation will lead to the same type of response. Ideally, dialogue should be built upward from an understanding of basic knowledge to the expression of personal opinions, followed by an elaboration of thoughts. After that, the verbal exchanges keep moving upward to seek integrated lines of knowledge and summarize key patterns, which can then be applied to new scenarios to solve novel problems. This double-helix interactive model should be adopted where both teachers and students collectively contribute to enhancing the interactive function. Attain excellence in classroom instruction. Teachers should improve questioning

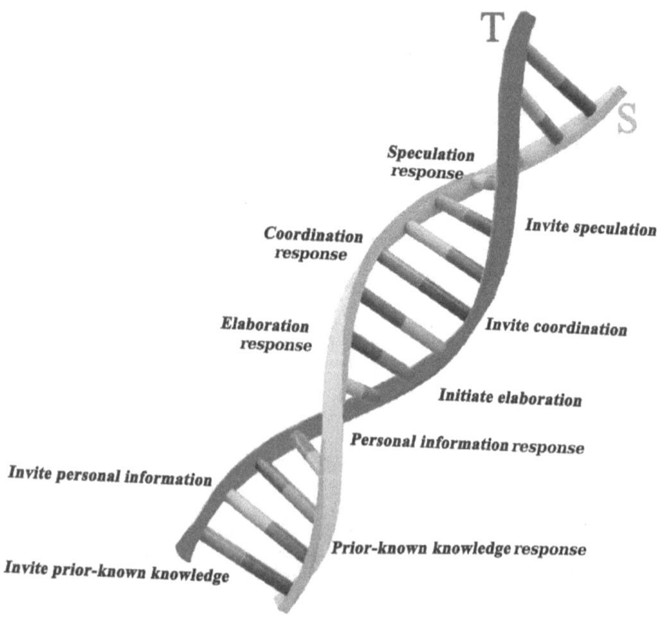

Figure 4.13 A Double Helix Upward Pattern

strategies and the effectiveness of guidance to facilitate students' collaborative knowledge construction through problem-solving scaffolds. It is essential to transition from surface interactions to profound ones, with an emphasis on developing interactive teaching approaches aimed at cultivating higher-order thinking and complex cognitive skills.

The following excerpt provides an illustration of such the Double Helix Upward Pattern in one primary school math lesson and its topic is Possibility (Table 4.9).

Table 4.9 An example of math lesson: Possibility

Role	*Content*	*Coding*
T:	Let's engage in an interesting activity. Can you tell me how many points are there in total? Let's count together.	Invite prior-known knowledge-Guide
S:	The dots on the dice represent the numbers 1, 2, 3, 4, 5, and 6. So, the sum of the numbers has a total of 11 variations.	Prior-known knowledge
T:	Great, let's conduct an experiment. The teacher has a set of cards with a sum of five points, while you have a set with a sum of six points. I will ask a volunteer to come up and roll the dice, announcing your sum out loud. Considering this rule, who do you think is more likely to win, given the scenario described?	Invite personal information-Guide
S:	Teacher, I believe our chances of winning are relatively high because we have a total sum of 6 points, which increases the likelihood of rolling the desired outcome.	Personal information-Elaboration
T:	(During the experiment) We noticed that although the teacher has cards with a total of five points, and you have cards with a total of six points, I seemed to win more often. Can anyone explain why that might be?	Initiate elaboration
S:	The points selected by the teacher are relatively small, which have a higher probability of being rolled. Although the points we selected are more, we must roll two specific numbers to meet the requirements when throwing the dice. Therefore, the teacher won.	Elaboration
T:	Well, that's a good analysis. Let's count and see how many combinations the teacher has. And how about the students? What have you noticed?	Invite coordination-Invite prior-known knowledge-Agreement-Guide
S:	I've observed a consistent trend: due to the teacher's question combinations being twice as numerous as the student's, the teacher enjoys a higher probability of victory. Moreover, the chance of winning is maximized when the numbers are closer to the middle, marking the peak point of winning probability.	Coordination-Elaboration

(Continued)

Table 4.9 (Continued)

Role	*Content*	*Coding*
T:	You are very good at identifying and summarizing patterns, and your observations are very accurate. Based on the pattern we have just summarized, please review the following game rule designed by a mall for redeeming consumption vouchers according to the sum of points rolled on two dice. By comparing these two schemes, if you were the shopkeeper, which one would you choose?	Invite speculation-Agreement-Guide
S:	I would opt for option B. This is because option A follows a pattern where the numbers closer to the middle are larger, whereas option B necessitates that the numbers towards the edges are greater. Option B features larger numbers, which inherently implies a higher sum of money, making it less likely to be selected.	Speculation-Elaboration
T:	This shopkeeper is quite intelligent. He chose plan B in his pursuit of higher profits. How about you? Do you have a similar choice? If there are other views or methods that could bring different returns or outcomes, how would you evaluate them? What better alternatives do those who disagree with this choice possess?	Invite uptakes/construction-Agreement
S:	I have a different answer from the student before me; I choose option a. Although it may result in a loss, it can attract a large number of customers. Moreover, this shop owner might be the kind of person who is very generous and willing to help others without asking for anything in return. After all, in our lives, there really are some people who are like that. Additionally, we could design another plan.	Uptakes/Construction-Personal information-Elaboration-Speculation

The following excerpt provides an illustration of such a Double Helix Upward Pattern in one primary school science lesson, and its topic is Sand, Rock, and Clay (Table 4.10).

It emphasizes the significance of not underestimating discussions related to subject matter or fundamental knowledge, as they are fundamental for reasoning skills. The study highlights the importance of analytical talk, which is crucial for both academic achievement and profound understanding, as well as for the advancement of quality interaction. Through the processes of justification, elaboration, and critical thinking, dialogue can advance beyond mere comprehension of subject matter to include higher-level intellectual and cognitive contributions. Engagement in conversation that involves coordination, speculation, and inquiry should be fostered, particularly with teachers encouraging students to generate hypotheses and apply previously acquired knowledge to resolve new challenges. In mathematics

Table 4.10 An example of science lesson: Sand, Rock, and Clay

Role	*Content*	*Coding*
TT:	Do you remember what we learnt in the last class?	Invite prior-known knowledge
SS:	We learnt how to make rock and mineral specimens.	Prior-known knowledge
TT:	Great. Through this activity, we gained a deeper understanding of rocks. In our everyday lives, rocks are a constant presence. Reflecting back on your childhood, what games do you recall playing that revolved around rocks?	Invite personal information
SS:	I remember as a child playing a game with my friends where we would collect various stones and see who could find the most unique and beautiful one. After learning in the last class, I now know that those stones were composed of different minerals, some hard, some soft, and others with stunning colours.	Personal information-Prior-known knowledge
TT:	Very good. Let's delve into the world of geology, examining the intricate relationship between rocks, sand, and clay. Please turn to page 52 of your textbook. We are all familiar with natural occurrences such as the sun, wind, water, and earthquakes, which shape rocks by either breaking them down into smaller fragments or eroding them. Now, take a look at these huge rocks under the sun, why are there some tiny rocks underneath?	Initiate elaboration-Guide-Prior-known knowledge
SS:	Teacher, I think it is because the heat from the sun causes the rocks to expand with heat and then cool and contract at night, and this repeated thermal expansion and contraction causes the rocks to crack. Meanwhile, rocks are gradually broken into small particles by many natural forces such as water and living things.	Elaboration
TT:	Well, that's a very sensible analysis. Indeed, just as you said, this physical weathering over time and biological action will gradually break up the rocks. So, do sand and clay follow the same principles? Rock, sand, and clay – how are they related? Please turn to page 53 of your books to look for the traces of rocks, sand, and clay. Think deeply and share your findings.	Invite coordination-Agreement-Guide-Prior-known knowledge
SS:	The rock is relatively large, and both sand and rock feel rough to the touch. In comparison, the particles of clay are smaller, and it also has a deeper color.	Coordination

(Continued)

Table 4.10 (Continued)

Role	*Content*	*Coding*
TT:	Excellent, you've observed with great detail. We just explored the characteristics of the biological strata through our observations and touch. Inspired by this principle, have any of you formed new hypotheses while observing the relationship between rocks, sand, and clay? Consider the alterations that rocks experience under external pressures. Might these changes provide insights into the relationships between rocks and soil?	Invite speculation-Agreement
SS:	Based on my observation and analysis, I infer that old rocks undergo a series of natural processes, gradually weathering and eventually shedding to form sand and clay. These materials, in turn, may transform into new rocks, representing a cyclical process of rock formation and reformation.	Speculation
TT:	Well, that's a very splendid conjecture. He mentioned the transformation between rocks, sand, and clay is a cyclical process where they can mutate into one another. Who can assist him in fleshing out the details and describing the precise manner in which they convert or transform into one another?	Invite uptakes/ construction-Agreement
SS:	On the basis of his answer, I add that rocks are broken down into smaller particles through the process of weathering. Over time, these smaller particles accumulate and transform into sand. When sand is mixed with clay and subjected to compaction and the action of water, it can give rise to new types of rock.	Uptakes/Construction

and literacy classes, dialogue can be led by teachers who initiate student input, guide them to provide further explanations, and then prompt them to expand on previous discussions, thus promoting exploratory dialogue. In science classes, a productive dialogue can be achieved through a sequential approach: problem justification and analysis; comparing, connecting, and summarizing key knowledge; and applying this knowledge to address new situations, which could enhance critical thinking and the development of advanced cognition. The advancement of dialogic pedagogy signifies a critical indicator of teachers' professional growth in the contemporary era and is essential for high-quality educational practices. We observed that the dialogue in classrooms led by novice and intermediate teachers is similar and differs from that of expert teachers. These differences are primarily reflected in the effectiveness of questioning, the initiation of interactions requiring higher-order thinking and complex cognitive skills, and the extendibility of the interactive role. Experienced teachers' instructional models are characterized by interactivity, inquiry, and stimulation, setting a commendable standard for beginning and intermediate teachers to improve their professional abilities.

The marked disparities observed in dialogue structures indicate that students undergo significant transformations in their mathematical learning as they progress from primary to middle schools. These shifts encompass not only the manner in which mathematics educators interact with them concerning mathematical concepts but also the nature of the discourse itself. The passage from primary to higher levels of math education proves to be a pivotal moment, as classroom conversation styles exhibit substantial diversity. It is anticipated that educators and students at the secondary and high school levels will engage in more cognitively demanding discussions, which include elucidating, comparing, and integrating ideas, as well as forming hypotheses about them. Certain prototypical lengthy dialogue patterns have been identified within secondary and high school math classes. One notable pattern commences with a call for previously acquired knowledge, transitions into personal viewpoints, proceeds to analytical discussion, and concludes with coordinated communication. Educators are encouraged to adopt and strategically utilize these patterns within their math instruction. The research suggests that challenges students face during these transitions might necessitate attention even at the primary education level. Furthermore, academic transitions should be examined with a particular focus on dialogues that promote higher-order thinking. By recognizing these aspects, classroom conversations can be conducted more efficiently and constructively, leading to the effective utilization of language in supporting learning outcomes. Moreover, these insights are beneficial for enhancing teachers' abilities in managing dialogue and developing tailored strategies for fostering productive communication at various educational stages. Such understanding should ease the transition between different educational levels.

5 Enhancing dialogue productiveness using generative artificial intelligence

This chapter discusses the importance of bringing in large language models (LLM) to enhance dialogue productiveness in classroom settings. As a subfield of generative artificial intelligence, LLM shows powerful abilities in dealing with complex tasks concerning natural language processing and generating. To leverage its potential, the author's team develops an LLM-based teaching assistant tool, the Productive Dialogue Explorer, to improve the productiveness of classroom dialogue. The novel tool was designed with four AI refinement functions, namely, AI elaboration, AI coordination, AI speculation, and AI construction. These were proposed after considering the productive features of dialogic pedagogy. The tool can automatically generate personalized refinements for selected turns of dialogue. A quasi-experiment was conducted to test its effectiveness in promoting dialogue productiveness. Results indicated that the teachers who used the Productive Dialogue Explorer significantly outperformed their control group counterparts in managing dialogue involving complex ways of thinking. Dialogic contributions concerning making elaborations, seeking coordination, and building up constructions significantly increased. Findings indicated that this large language model assistant only plays a limited role in polishing speculated talk. Regarding how the teachers perceived the Productive Dialogue Explorer, they generally viewed it as helping enrich verbal exchanges and found it most useful in polishing coordinated talk. Feedback provided by this tool was recognized as specific and adaptive to context. The results suggest that the prominent language model technique can support teacher professional development in a scalable and efficient way. A wide range of teachers will be empowered to develop a better understanding and strategically use talk to boost educational achievement.

The necessity of bringing in large language models in enhancing dialogue productiveness

Classroom dialogue has been applied extensively worldwide and has become familiar to policy-makers, academics, and practitioners (Kim & Wilkinson, 2019). Typical forms spotlighted as especially productive towards educational achievement include elaboration, coordination, speculation, and construction (Howe et al., 2019).

DOI: 10.4324/9781003543039-5

A number of research studies have shown that dialogic pedagogy, when used strategically, will boost teaching and learning achievements (Vrikki & Evagorou, 2023). For example, it will deepen students' understanding of course content (van der Veen et al., 2017), help with critical thinking (Koichu et al., 2022), improve reasoning (Resnick et al., 2015), and facilitate learning outcomes (Howe et al., 2019). Practically, the use of dialogic pedagogy is often less effective, and teachers tend to lack sufficient skills to support its productive implementation (Jacobs et al., 2022). Teachers often struggle with low levels of student engagement, resulting in frequent but superficial dialogue that does little to inspire deeper thought (Zhao et al., 2022). The typical initiation-response-feedback pattern is often followed rigidly, but its role in promoting critical thinking and understanding is frequently overlooked. For example, teachers seem less confident in their questions when it comes to provoking elaboration of ideas and seeking novel implications (Howe et al., 2019). Fragmented chains of talk are common and it is challenging to develop collective and constructive exchanges (Song et al., 2022). Professional training for teachers is recommended, yet training relies heavily on human expertise, which is not scalable and requires extensive practice (Heck et al., 2019). It seems unlikely that most teachers will be able to receive personalized and prompt feedback from human experts on how to enrich their verbal contributions (Shin et al., 2023). When they do, the feedback is often less personalized and specific to support reflection and instructional change, as experts might not be sufficiently familiar with the dialogue scenarios and course content (Jacobs et al., 2022). It is highly demanding, with experts needing to be familiar with course content, as well as being a professional in the field of classroom dialogue and experienced in dialogic teaching practices. Additionally, it is time-consuming to refine verbal exchanges sentence by sentence for teachers' lessons (Song et al., 2020), which makes it challenging to achieve scalable professional development. It is therefore essential to provide support for implementing dialogic pedagogy more efficiently and effectively.

The large language model (LLM) technique might be a feasible solution for addressing the issues mentioned earlier. This is because such a solution has the potential to provide targeted and prompt feedback for teachers to help improve their skills in managing dialogic pedagogy. The recent advancement of LLMs, such as the GPT series, LLaMA, and ChatGLM, has dramatically enhanced the performance of natural language processing tasks and shown impressive capabilities in generating contextually rich dialogue (Farrokhnia et al., 2023). LLM-based teaching assistant tools are capable of generating content automatically and intelligently. The content generated can be context-based and logical, which might sometimes surpass human experts (Guo et al., 2023). This section introduces how we explored the possibility of using the LLM technique to facilitate the enhancement of dialogue productiveness in classroom settings. We take account of the productive features of dialogic pedagogy and generate personalized feedback automatically to help polish verbal exchanges towards collective reasoning. To examine its effectiveness and understand how it affects classroom dialogue, this study conducted a quasi-experiment for three months and compared teachers' performance in dialogic classroom practices. We also collected teachers' perceptions and evaluations of the refinement content provided by the LLM technique. This research is expected to support teachers' professional development and provide personalized insights to improve their instructional strategies. Productive classroom dialogue promises to provide access to a more comprehensive range of teachers and students and boost educational achievement.

Generative artificial intelligence, large language models and their use in education

Generative AI (Gen AI) is a type of artificial intelligence technology that can produce various types of content, including text, imagery, audio, and synthetic data. Gen AI is a subset of deep learning, which means it uses artificial neural networks and can process both labelled and unlabelled data using supervised, unsupervised, and semi-supervised methods (Park & Doo, 2024). It creates new content based on what it has learnt from existing content. The process of learning from existing content is called training and results in the creation of a statistical model when given a prompt. Gen AI uses the model to predict what an expected response might be, and this generates new content. Essentially, it learns the underlying structure of the data and can then generate new samples that are similar to the data it was trained on (Hao et al., 2024). The power of Gen AI comes from the use of transformers, which was introduced in a seminal paper by Vaswani et al. in 2017 (Bengesi et al., 2024). The Transformer model is a neural network architecture that has gained immense popularity due to its superior performance on various natural language processing tasks.

A large language model (LLM) is a specific type of generative artificial intelligence system that focuses on generating and understanding human language. Recent developments in LLM technology demonstrate remarkable capabilities (Raiaan et al., 2024). The GPT series launched by OpenAI is one of the most distinguished large models and has attracted wide attention around the world. Furthermore, several open-source models have also been released, such as LLaMA, BLOOM, and ChatGLM. These models contain hundreds of billions (or more) of parameters. They are trained on massive text datasets, such as books, articles, and web pages, to learn the structure and patterns of language (Minaee et al., 2024). LLMs exhibit strong capacities to understand natural language and solve complex tasks. They can be used to generate coherent, fluent text in response to input, such as completing sentences, generating articles, or translating between languages. As part of the broader field of generative AI, large language models contribute to developing and understanding machine learning algorithms that can generate new content in the form of text. Here, we briefly introduce three typical emergent abilities for LLMs.

- *In-context learning.* GPT-3 formally introduced the in-context learning (ICL) ability. Assuming that the language model has been provided with natural language instruction and/or several task demonstrations, it can generate the expected output for the test instances by completing the word sequence of input text without requiring additional training (Balkus & Yan, 2022).

- *Instruction following.* By fine-tuning with a mixture of multi-task datasets formatted via natural language descriptions, LLMs are enabled to follow the task instructions for new tasks without using explicit examples, thus having an improved generalization ability (Jovanovic & Voss, 2024).
- *Step-by-step reasoning.* With the chain-of-thought (CoT) prompting strategy, LLMs can solve such tasks by utilizing the prompting mechanism that involves intermediate reasoning steps for deriving the final answer. Prompting is the major approach to using LLMs for solving various tasks (Gu et al., 2024). A well-designed prompt is very helpful to elicit the abilities of LLMs for accomplishing specific tasks.

Education is also an important domain of application where LLMs potentially exert significant influence. Existing work has found that LLMs can achieve student-level performance on standardized tests in a variety of subjects of mathematics (e.g. physics, computer science) on both multiple-choice and free-response problems (Wang et al., 2024). In addition, empirical studies have shown that LLMs can serve as writing or reading assistants for education (Randall, 2019). A recent study reveals that ChatGPT is capable of generating logically consistent answers across disciplines, balancing both depth and breadth (Herbold et al., 2023). Another quantitative analysis shows that students utilizing ChatGPT (either keeping or refining the results from LLMs as their answers) perform better than average students in some courses from the computer security field (Richards et al., 2024). Several prospective papers have recently explored various application scenarios of LLMs in classroom teaching, such as teacher-student collaboration, personalized learning, and assessment automation. It can generate personalized feedback and recommendations for improvement of teaching and learning and facilitate classroom communication between students and teachers (Jeon et al., 2023; Tan et al., 2023).

To be more specific, LLM techniques such as ChatGPT can become a human teacher's assistant in information retrieval, knowledge question and answer, and decision analysis. It can help teachers deal with fundamental and repetitive work such as information retrieval, knowledge explanation, classroom question and answer, test paper generation, etc. It can provide teachers with creative ideas and methodological suggestions for complex work such as curriculum design, classroom production, assessment guidance, and so on (Yacobson et al., 2024). Moreover, LLM can automatically generate a large amount of content based on text prompts without human intervention, freeing content production from over-reliance on professionals and enabling every teacher to become a creator of teaching content (Bonner et al., 2023). The AIGC model significantly improves content productiveness. It is able to understand the information needs described by the teacher's natural language, find relevant information from massive data resources, and unlike the simple sorting of information by a search engine. It is able to generate textual results with a better structural framework and semantic logic according to certain algorithms (Huang et al., 2024). In terms of instructional design, it is able to analyse and reorganize course materials according to dialogue prompts and generate design contents with certain logic and creativity, such as teaching cases, teaching prompts, teaching questions, and answers. In material creation, it can generate customized teaching materials, such as scenario stories, based on sample materials and creation requirements. In terms of dialogue and communication, LLMs are able to conduct multiple rounds of natural language interaction with users. They can deeply understand the language environment and user's intention and generate responses that are more in line with the user's linguistic style and more logically consistent so as to support interaction between teachers and students (Bonner et al., 2023). Teaching feedback can help teachers quickly analyse the quality of students' work and give targeted feedback and teaching suggestions. Finally, LLMs will personalize the learning process to a large extent. Khan Academy Showcase Khanmigo, an experimental AI tool powered by the GPT-4 model, plans to build this smart tool into an intelligent teaching assistant and virtual tutor for online learning environments, providing one-on-one tutoring in the form of dialogues, asking personalized questions and answers to guide students to deeper learning, and helping teachers develop lesson plans and mark assignments, customize learning programmes for each student, and explore how the GPT-4 model can be effectively applied to learning and teaching (Wang et al., 2023).

Development of an LLM-based teaching assistant tool – Productive Dialogue Explorer

Dialogic pedagogy, though frequently used, could be more challenging in terms of being implemented effectively in practice. It seems insufficient to rely merely on manual methods to provide personalized and efficient feedback on how verbal exchanges should be processed. Previously, very few studies have used the LLM technique tailored to the needs of dialogic pedagogy. When they do this, the tools typically give descriptive information about classroom dialogue and show the status of teachers' performance, such as by undertaking automatic coding and indicating the percentage of occurrence of dialogic categories. However, the tools are less likely to help polish dialogic contributions or to generate a feasible alternative solution in order to improve their productiveness.

We developed an LLM-based teaching assistant tool, the Productive Dialogue Explorer, to support teachers' reflections about their dialogic pedagogy. This is a web-based tool that has both English and Chinese versions. Each participating teacher was assigned a personal account. Teachers logged into the account to view the transcribed results of classroom dialogue and utilized its AI refinement functions to enrich dialogic contributions. It offered personalized support and helped the teachers to reflect on their course instruction. The above literature review has indicated that the productiveness of dialogic pedagogy is limited for three main reasons. Firstly, teachers lack clear criteria for assessing the quality of dialogic teaching. Secondly, teachers more often cannot obtain personalized and prompt feedback on their class performance as this requires a lot of human expertise and time. Thirdly, classroom talk is often processed at a low cognitive level, which hides the effectiveness of pedagogy. Accordingly, the architecture of the Productive Dialogue Explorer consists of the following four main modules that work in coordination to provide personalized and efficient teaching assistance for teachers (see Figure 5.1). This would result in a more personalized and

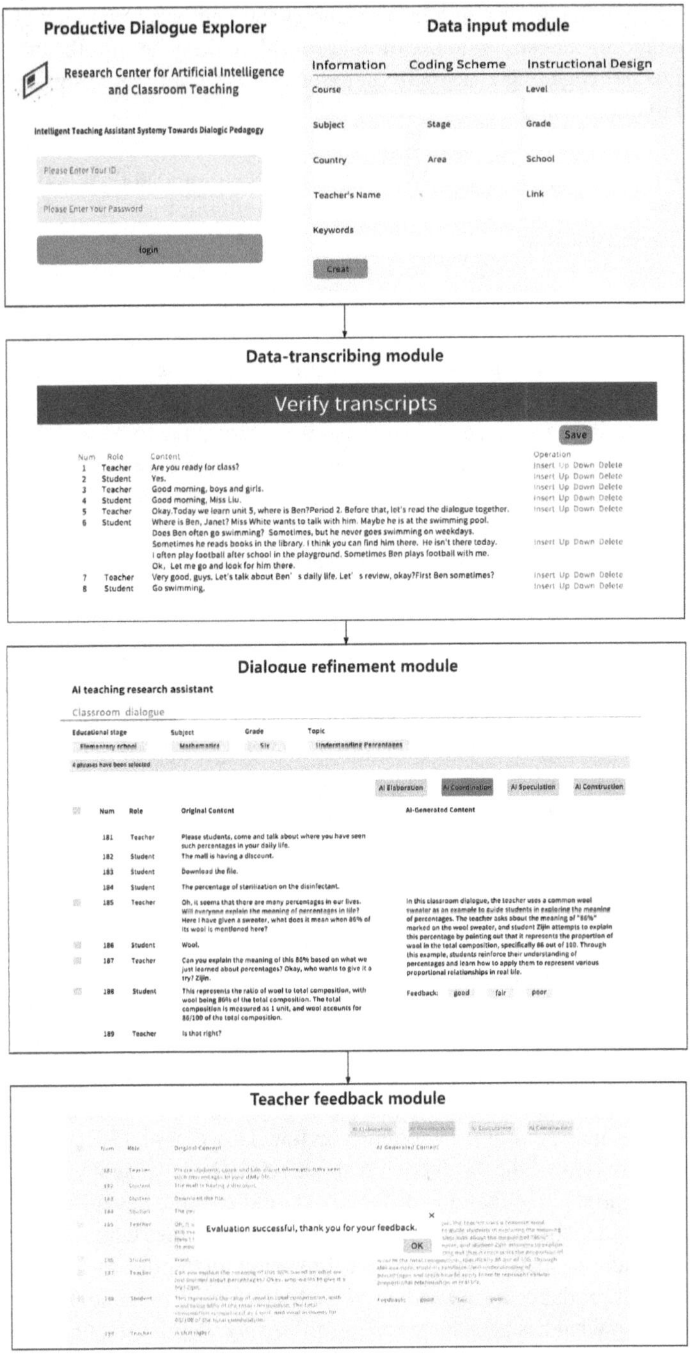

Figure 5.1 Flowchart of the four main functional modules

productive approach to teaching, where teachers are empowered to develop a better understanding and strategic use of talk. It is also likely helpful for the building of effective and engaging classroom dialogue, encouraging higher-order thinking and deep understanding.

1. *Data input module.* This module allows teachers to upload their audio or video recordings of classroom dialogue. Course-relevant information, such as subject, grades, and educational context, are also accessible.
2. *Data-transcription module.* This module can automatically transcribe the uploaded recordings into text form using embedded software, IFLYTEK Voice Transcription Software. The software is probably the most frequently used voice transcription software globally. It employs natural language processing techniques and provides real-time transcription of talk into text. Its classroom dialogue transcription accuracy was quite high, approximately 90%. Subsequently, human researchers corrected the rest of the incorrect dialogic transcripts. The combination of machine and human transcription increased the efficiency of the process. The transcripts will demonstrate the turn level detected by the speaker switch in the tool, which allows teachers to track the progress of verbal exchanges.
3. *Dialogue refinement module.* This component incorporates the large model technique to automatically generate personalized refinements to automatically polish dialogic contributions. A large model, ChatGLM was selected to be embedded in the teaching assistant tool. This is because ChatGLM has performed well in terms of text processing and generation in both Chinese and English. It uses technologies similar to ChatGPT and is optimized for Chinese dialogue. Besides, it is open-source and allows users to deploy the model locally, which has enabled us to incorporate it into our teaching assistant tool. More importantly, ChatGLM has passed security clearance and obtained official authorization from the Chinese government to be used with school teachers and students.

   During our study, teachers chose a turn or turns of dialogue that first needed to be refined. Then, four types of functions could be selected to generate feasible and personalized solutions based on the situational context, which are *AI elaboration*, *AI coordination*, *AI speculation*, and *AI construction/uptakes*. These four functions are derived from the productive features of dialogic pedagogy in CI-PCD. As indicated in the literature review, Howe et al. (2019) undertook a systematic review of the productive features of dialogic pedagogy. According to the review, productive dialogic pedagogy should encourage students to provide reasoning and justification for their answers, which comes with *AI elaboration*; teachers ought to lead students to seek links and attempt to coordinate knowledge, which produces *AI coordination*; rich discussion to make novel explorations beyond what has been learnt relates to *AI speculation*; and finally, dialogue should be collective and cumulative so that participants build on each other constructively, which leads to *AI construction/uptakes*.

There were four main steps involved when generating refinements for the selected turns of classroom dialogue. The first step was data preprocessing. To prepare the data for the large model, the transcripts of classroom dialogue were preprocessed by the LangChain model, which works by providing modular abstractions/prompts necessary to work with language models. The model represented dialogic transcripts as continuous vectors and created dialogue prompts, which were suitable for the input format of large models. The second step was specifying the turn or turns of dialogue that teachers wanted to refine as the input for the dialogue chain. Third, the criteria of refinement were specified, and we proposed templates for the four AI refinement functions. An example of one of the criteria of AI construction was: *Please refine the dialogue by making it more constructive and show collective ways of contributing by teachers and students*. Fourth, a suitable prompt for ChatGLM was generated based on the dialogue chain input and the criteria. ChatGLM then used its generative pre-trained transformer model to generate refinement texts based on the prompt. Examples of refinements generated by the Productive Dialogue Explorer are provided in Table 5.1.

4. *Teacher feedback module*. This module allows teachers to provide feedback about the refinement content generated by the intelligent assistant tool. Three-point ratings were provided, namely, good, fair, and poor, which were shown after each of the refinement results. We selected three ratings, instead of five or seven ratings, because their distinctions were easier for the teachers to identify.

Exploring the possibility of LLM-based tool in improving classroom dialogue

This section aimed to investigate the possibility of using the LLM-based teaching assistant tool, Productive Dialogue Explorer, to promote the productiveness of dialogic pedagogy. Previously, there is little empirical evidence to demonstrate how LLMs function in authentic educational settings, nor how they perform in relation to promoting teaching achievement. In the author's team, the LLM-based tool has been developed to automatically generate personalized refinements in verbal exchanges along with the productive features of dialogic pedagogy, namely, elaboration, coordination, speculation, and construction. Specifically, two research questions were addressed here. *(1) How effective is the LLM-based tool in promoting the productiveness of dialogic pedagogy? (2) What feedback do teachers provide regarding this LLM-based teaching assistant tool?* It is expected that this research will support teachers' professional development and increase their management skills in dialogic classroom practices.

Table 5.1 Examples of AI refinement results provided by the Productive Dialogue Explorer

Function	*Original content*	*AI Generated content*
AI Elaboration	We can calculate it using the multiplication table.	Classmates, let's look at this problem. This student suggests using the multiplication table, which is a good idea. The multiplication table is the foundation of our learning in multiplication. By mastering it proficiently, we can quickly perform multiplication calculations. Please practice more after class and become skilled in the multiplication table, as it will significantly help you in your future studies.
AI coordination	Student: $6\times2=12$. Student: $6\times8=48$. Student: $6\times40=240$. Teacher: Hmm, okay. What observations do you have about this set of equations, Classmate B? Student: We can calculate it using the multiplication table. Teacher: Oh, any other findings? Classmate C. Student: The multiples of 12 and 48 are 4, then the multiples of 48 and 240 are, the multiple relationship is 5, and then it increases by 1 in sequence. Their multiple relationship is 6. Teacher: Classmate D. Student: I found that the results of these calculations, the last digit is always the same as the second factor in front of it, $6\times2=12$.	This classroom dialogue is about multiplication operations. The students demonstrated their ability to calculate multiplication using multiplication tables, such as $6\times2=12$, $6\times8=48$, and $6\times40=240$. Then, the teacher guided the students to observe these equations in order to discover patterns. Classmate C pointed out that both 12 and 48 are multiples of 4, while 48 and 240 are multiples of 5, with a consecutive increase of one for each multiple relationship. This is their multiple relationship. Classmate D noticed that the last digit of the results in these equations is always the same as the second factor of the preceding factor, for example, in $6\times2=12$. Overall, through observation and discussion, the students discovered and understood patterns in multiplication operations.
AI speculation	Teacher: Let's do an experiment to verify. Children, look here, I have brought a prop called a triangle. When we strike the triangle, it will produce sound. So, if I want to make the sound of this triangle louder, what should we do? Oh, I see this group over here. Sweetie, you tell me.	We can migrate this experiment to other fields, such as music. We can let children try different instruments, observe the intensity and timbre of the sounds they produce, and then teach them how to change the volume and pitch of the sound by striking or playing the instrument. We can also migrate this experiment to the field of physics. We can let children explore the generation and propagation of sound, as well as the influence of different materials and shapes on sound. Through these experiments, children can learn about the basic principles of sound and its characteristics, thereby cultivating their scientific thinking and experimental abilities.

(Continued)

Table 5.1 (Continued)

Function	*Original content*	*AI Generated content*
		We can also migrate this experiment to the field of art. Let children try creating music with a triangle bell, exploring variations and combinations in sound and rhythm, thereby cultivating their musical sense and creativity. Through innovative migration, we can expand this simple experiment into broader fields, allowing children to learn more knowledge and skills from it while also stimulating their curiosity and creativity.
AI construction	Teacher: Well we know that this sun, wind and water, earthquakes and all these activities can cause some fragmentation of this rock or make it form small particles take a look at these huge rocks under the sun, why are there some tiny rocks underneath? Student: Erm because maybe here was originally with those maybe, there was no bag here originally, it formed here after the earthquake and it cracked all of these things. Teacher: Good.	Teacher: Well we know that this sun, wind and water, earthquakes and all these activities can cause some fragmentation of this rock or make it form small particles take a look at these huge rocks under the sun, why are there some tiny rocks underneath? STUDENT: Teacher, I think it is because the heat from the sun causes the rocks to expand with heat and then cool and contract at night, and this repeated thermal expansion and contraction causes the rocks to crack. After a long time, these cracks will get bigger and bigger and the rocks will become smaller and smaller pieces. TEACHER: Well, that's a very sensible analysis. Indeed, just as you said, this physical weathering over time will gradually break up the rocks. So are there any other factors? Besides the sun, who else wants to share their opinion? ANOTHER STUDENT: Teacher, I also know that water also breaks up rocks. When water penetrates into the cracks of rocks and then freezes and expands in winter, it will hold up the cracks even more, so the rocks will break more easily too. TEACHER: Great, you mentioned the freezing and thawing of water, which is a very important weathering effect. Besides that, what other natural forces affect the shape of rocks? Third student: Teacher, there are also biological effects, I guess. For example, the roots of plants grow in the cracks of the rocks, and they will keep expanding and hold the rocks apart. Teacher: Yes, you are very right. Biological action is also an amazing way of weathering. So now we know that rocks are gradually broken into small particles by many natural forces such as the sun, water, and living things.

Participants

This study involved 40 teachers from three primary schools in China. The involvement of teacher participants was based on taking into consideration certain ethical issues. The participant teachers were informed of the study's purpose and process, and their participation was voluntary. The participants consisted of 28 female and 12 male teachers, ranging in age from 27 to 41, with an average age of 34 (SD= 3.61). The teachers' length of teaching ranged from 3 years to 17 years. Among them, 18 taught mathematics, 16 literacy, and 6 science. These subjects were selected due to their global popularity in the field of classroom dialogue and because they are often viewed as being of high importance in terms of students' development (Howe & Abedin, 2013). The participants had not accessed LLM-based teaching assistant tools prior to the study and did not use other similar tools during the study period.

Procedures and measures

A quasi-experiment design was adopted whereby the participants were divided into two groups (20 teachers in each group). These two groups were generally matched in terms of gender, age, length of teaching, and subject. The experimental group used the LLM-based teaching assistant tool to refine dialogic pedagogy, while the control group was not subject to any intervention. The experiment lasted for three months. Furthermore, we used interviews to understand the teachers' perceptions of the effectiveness of this LLM-based teaching assistant tool. The procedure for our study is listed in the following list. There were five steps, the first and last of which were applicable to all teacher participants, while the second, third, and fourth steps applied to the experimental group only (see Figure 5.2).

(1) **Pretest of dialogic pedagogy performance.** Teacher participants' dialogue pedagogy performance was assessed. We collected a recording of a daily lesson (40 minutes) for each participant. The lessons were audio recorded in order to protect the confidentiality of the students whose informed consent was obtained. The classroom dialogue was transcribed into text form. Systematic coding, where talk transcripts were allocated to a set of predefined categories (Mercer, 2008), was used to assess the productiveness of dialogic pedagogy. Coding instruments used in this study were selected to make links to the productive dimensions of dialogic pedagogy. The instrument called Coding Instrument for Productive Classroom Dialogue (CI-PCD) (Song et al., 2020, 2021, 2022) was used (see Chapter 3). This instrument was selected for three main reasons. Firstly, its coding categories are closely related to the main productive features of dialogic pedagogy, as summarized by the Cambridge team (see Howe et al., 2019; Hennessy et al., 2021). Secondly, the categories have been proposed based on a systematic review of publications on dialogic pedagogy over two decades (see Song et al., 2021). Features/dimensions that enjoy wide recognition and applications in various studies were kept. This improved the applicability of the coding instrument and the research findings based on

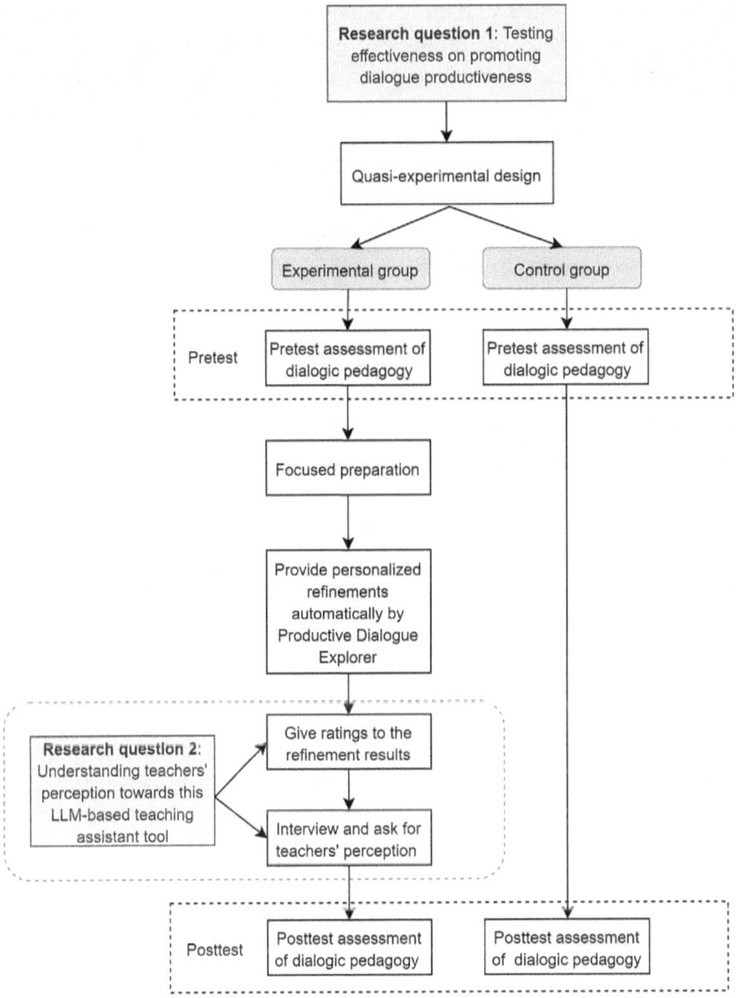

Figure 5.2 Research procedure of this study

it. Thirdly, CI-PCD has been tested on primary and secondary lessons several times, showing good reliability and validity (e.g. Song et al., 2021, 2022).

There were nine main coding dimensions in the CI-PCD to assess the quality of dialogic pedagogy. These were elaboration, coordination, speculation, construction, prior-known knowledge, personal information, agreement, querying, and guidance. In these dimensions, elaboration, coordination, speculation, and construction show higher-order thinking, as making these contributions involves complicated information processing methods (Pehmer et al., 2015). The remaining dimensions were considered because they are constantly evident in classroom dialogue and their appearances are very likely to be initiations or follow-ups relating to the productive forms of dialogue (Song et al., 2022). These dialogues usually reflect lower-order thinking, as they are associated with rote memorization, simple recall of information, and following procedural instructions. They involve minimal reflection and analysis, and they rely on pre-existing knowledge and basic cognitive skills (Sychev et al., 2021). On the above dimensional basis, dialogic forms, namely, initiation and response, were incorporated, and the six former dimensions were further divided to show reciprocal exchanges between the teacher and students. Notably, the dialogic form 'feedback' is likely to appear together with new initiation turns, and its addition makes coding less reliable (Hennessy et al., 2020). Thus, feedback form was excluded (see Hennessy et al., 2020; Howe et al., 2019).

Teachers' classroom performance in relation to dialogic pedagogy was examined according to the CI-PCD instrument. The dialogic transcripts were coded at a turn level identified through the speaker switch. For each turn, multiple coding categories could be attached. For example, a turn '*The diagram in the textbook is of a sphere, just like the football in gyms. It's shaped like this because it can roll, and it doesn't have any sharp edges*' demonstrated knowledge learnt in textbooks, and links to daily life and shows an analytical process. The categories of prior-known knowledge, personal information, and elaboration were therefore coded simultaneously. This way of coding is recommended as coders can fairly reliably distinguish and detect it (Hennessy et al., 2021).

(2) **Focused preparation**. Each teacher was given a personal account for the experimental group to access the web-based teaching assistant tool. The researchers organized two training periods for the experiment group, each lasting three hours. The first training session was conducted in relation to dialogic pedagogy, when the significance of this pedagogy and its productive features were explained to the teachers. The second session was designed to instruct the teachers in the use of the Productive Dialogue Explorer. They were informed how the tool worked and shown how to upload lesson recordings, generate refinements for their dialogic contributions, and make evaluations for the AI-generated results. Technicians were assigned to instruct the participants in the experiment group to ensure they were familiar with the tool's operation method.

(3) **Providing intelligent teaching assistance through using the Productive Dialogue Explorer**. Each participant teacher in the experimental group was assigned a personal account to access the Productive Dialogue Explorer, through which they could upload their recordings of classroom dialogue, generate refinement results of their dialogic contributions, and give their evaluations of the AIGC results. During the experiment, teachers were asked to upload audio recordings of their lessons six times. These were then transcribed automatically by the embedded IFLYTEK Voice Transcription Software and subsequently corrected by research assistants. IELYTEK can convert voice into text in real-time with an accuracy of 90%. Participants could view their

dialogic transcripts approximately one hour after they had uploaded their recordings, which was prompt and time-efficient. Then, the teachers were asked to use a series of AI refinements (i.e. AI elaboration, AI coordination, AI speculation, AI construction) to polish their dialogic contributions. Personalized refinement results were generated automatically in real-time for the selected turn or turns of verbal exchanges. After this, teachers were asked to give evaluations for the results generated by the teaching assistant tool and to choose one of the evaluation levels, that is, good, fair, or poor. By viewing the AI-generated results, teachers were encouraged to reflect on strategies that contribute to the productiveness of dialogic pedagogy and adopt these strategies in their daily lessons.

(4) **Collecting feedback.** To understand the teachers' feedback about the LLM-based teaching assistant tool, we conducted an interview to probe their perceptions of the refinement results generated by the Productive Dialogue Explorer. Nine teachers were selected randomly from the experimental group, three of whom taught mathematics, literacy, and science. The interview questions were adapted from Jacobs et al. (2022), who designed an intelligent teaching assistant application, TalkMoves, to promote rich classroom discussions. Jacobs et al.'s interviews obtained satisfactory results, indicating that they are generalizable for other studies concerning classroom dialogue. On this basis, our interview questions considered the usefulness of the teaching assistant tool in terms of promoting the productiveness of dialogue pedagogy, teachers' tendencies towards teaching behavior change, and their trust in the tool. The interview questions were as follows:

- *How useful do you find the refinement content generated by the Productive Dialogue Explorer?*
- *How likely are you to change your dialogic pedagogy based on the refinement content received from the Productive Dialogue Explorer?*
- *Do you trust the refinement results generated by the Productive Dialogue Explorer?*

(5) **Posttest of dialogic pedagogy performance.** At the end of the experiment, all teacher participants were asked to audio record one lesson to assess their latest performance in relation to dialogic pedagogy. The researchers collected these recordings and then transcribed to enable systematic coding. The coding process was the same as the first step.

Data analysis

To address the first research question, we compared the coding results of the participants' first and last lessons to investigate whether and how the use of the LLM-based teaching assistant tool, the Productive Dialogue Explorer, promoted the productiveness of dialogic pedagogy. The number of times contributed under each coding category was counted for each lesson. Given that the participants' lessons varied with respect to subject and course content, percentages of dialogic categories, rather than frequency and their standard deviations, were calculated. Independent samples t-tests were conducted to examine the comparability of baseline scores between the experimental group and the control group, with no significance found (see Table 5.2). This suggests that the two groups were comparable at the baseline. To examine the effectiveness of the LLM-based teaching assistant tool, we conducted independent samples t-tests to compare the differences in the percentages of dialogic categories between the two groups on the last assessment.

To address the second research question, teacher participants in the experimental group were asked to give a rating (i.e. poor, fair, or good) following each refinement result. Rating percentages for each refinement function (i.e. AI elaboration, AI coordination, AI speculation, and AI construction) were calculated to reflect the teachers' evaluations of the content generated by the LLM-based teaching assistant tool. Effects of subject, gender, age and length of teaching on the teachers' ratings were tested. Regarding the interview data, we used an open-coding approach to understand the teachers' perceptions of the tool's usefulness for increasing dialogue productiveness. The open-coding approach is a method for identifying and reporting themes within data based on research interests or aims. It does not need to follow particular analytical steps (Given, 2008). This method is often used when interviews play a subordinate role in understanding statistical results. Data from the interviews offered insights into how the intelligent teaching assistant tool supported the teachers' reflection and instructional change.

Table 5.2 Group difference of dialogic contributions in the posttest assessment

Coding categories	*Experimental group*	*Control group*	*Group difference*	
	M(SD)	*M(SD)*	*t*	*p value*
Invite elaboration	2.53 (1.45)	1.52 (1.40)	2.66	.01*
Elaboration	4.10 (1.40)	2.50 (2.37)	2.53	.01*
Invite coordination	1.27 (2.36)	1.10 (1.11)	.46	.65
Coordination	2.59 (1.46)	1.05 (1.84)	3.66	.00**
Invite speculation	0.52 (1.22)	0.42 (0.83)	0.46	.65
Speculation	0.63 (0.77)	0.56 (1.03)	0.26	.79
Invite construction	7.37 (1.13)	3.66 (2.96)	4.33	.00**
Construction	8.93 (3.42)	2.82 (3.16)	7.86	.00**
Invite prior-known knowledge	15.63 (4.88)	18.20 (8.21)	−1.42	.16
Prior-known knowledge	25.78 (8.10)	28.87 (10.49)	−1.24	.22
Invite personal information	5.30 (2.91)	8.24 (5.49)	−2.50	.02*
Personal information	6.96 (4.98)	9.80 (5.18)	−2.09	.04*
Agreement	7.85 (2.64)	8.16 (3.19)	−.29	.77
Querying	0.76 (4.54)	0.92 (0.69)	−.55	.58
Guidance	9.79 (1.28)	12.17 (3.17)	−1.55	.13

*Note:** $p < .05$, ** $p < .01$.

Results

Given that the two groups of teachers' performance matched in the pretest assessment, the effectiveness of the LLM-based teaching assistant tool can be inferred from the group difference in dialogic contributions revealed in the posttest assessment. As shown in Table 5.2, there were significant differences in dialogic contributions between the experimental and control groups. Teachers in the experimental group scored significantly higher than those in the control group on dialogic categories inviting elaboration $(\text{mean} = 2.53 > 1.52, p < 0.01)$, elaboration $(\text{mean} = 4.10 > 2.50, p < 0.01)$, coordination $(\text{mean} = 2.59 > 1.05, p < 0.001)$, inviting construction $(\text{mean} = 7.37 > 3.66, p < 0.001)$, and construction $(\text{mean} = 8.93 > 2.82, p < 0.001)$. These categories represent productive features of dialogic pedagogy and show higher-order thinking. The percentage scores on inviting personal information $(\text{mean} = 5.30 < 8.24, p < 0.001)$ and personal information $(\text{mean} = 6.96 < 9.80, p < 0.001)$ contributed by the experimental group, a coding category which represents lower-order thinking, were significantly lower than those contributed by the control group.

In terms of answering the first research question, using the LLM-based teaching assistant tool and referring to the content it generated had positive effects on the teachers' dialogic pedagogy. Our findings indicate that the teachers who utilized the tool outperformed their control group counterparts in managing classroom dialogue, with significantly more verbal exchanges relating to elaboration, coordination, and construction. Contributing these kinds of dialogue necessitated a complex cognitive process closely related to higher-order thinking (Pehmer et al., 2015). Specifically, these forms of contribution required the ability to integrate information, to question assumptions, and to evaluate evidence, which matter greatly to the productiveness of dialogic pedagogy (Kim et al., 2019).

Beyond the benefits highlighted earlier, several other points should be noted. Firstly, no significant increase was found in terms of dialogic contributions related to speculation. This suggests that the refinements generated by the large model are less helpful in supporting speculated dialogue. Speculation refers to talk that leads to extended and novel explorations based on logical reasoning. It is a type of strategic communication that can be used to explore ideas and relates closely to innovation and creativity (Song et al., 2021). This, to a certain extent, certifies the claim that large model techniques remain limited in the role that they can play in tackling innovative tasks (Jeon et al., 2023). Secondly, dialogue improvements were similar amongst teachers in the three investigated subject areas, namely, mathematics, literacy, and science. This indicates that the LLM-based teaching assistant tool is likely to have the same benefits for dialogic pedagogy across different subjects. This is likely to be because the large model technique is advantageous in generating targeted and personalized feedback tailored to specific course contexts. The technique is powerful in natural language processing and generation and is trained with huge amounts of data from different areas. Therefore, the refinement dialogue generated is very likely to be sensible and provide teachers with insights that can be used to make dialogic improvements.

Regarding the second research question, the teachers' feedback about the AI-generated results is shown in Table 5.3. For the four refinement functions, the percentages of good ratings were the highest, followed by those of fair, while the percentages of poor ratings were the lowest. This indicates that the teachers were generally satisfied with the refinement results generated by the Productive Dialogue Explorer and that they found it helpful in promoting teaching productiveness. In general, AI coordination was found to be most useful, as its good rating was the highest (81.82%), followed by AI construction with a good rating of 72.06%. Comparatively, AI speculation was perceived relatively poorly, with the highest poor rating being 16.67% . This result is compatible with the findings reported above and confirms the effectiveness of the teaching assistant tool in promoting the productiveness of dialogic pedagogy. The participant teachers reported that they were generally satisfied with the results generated by the large model. This is probably because, firstly, the AI-generated results were specific and connected to the individual's needs and context, ensuring they were meaningful and applicable. Secondly, the teachers perceived that the feedback was provided in a timely manner, so that they could use it to make adjustments or improvements. The teachers suggested that they make changes to their classroom teaching practices, and they reported that their dialogic pedagogy is more productive. The AI-generated refinements were considered to be supportive of the teachers' professional development and their reflections concerning dialogic pedagogy.

The teachers' perceptions of the effectiveness of the LLM-based teaching tool in promoting dialogue productiveness were assessed through refinement evaluation data and the results of the interviews. Encouragingly, most of the interviewees found the Productive Dialogue Explorer helpful in helping them refine dialogic contributions, polish questions, and provide feedback on students' answers. Eight of the nine interviewees reported that the Productive Dialogue Explorer helped them reflect on the dialogic process and that its use supports their professional development. Their questions became more *effective*, and their feedback was more *specific* and *adaptive* to the context. Three teachers found themselves more *skillful* in terms of leading students to build ideas into chains of knowledge construction and thinking. A literacy teacher suggested that to obtain a feasible solution,

Table 5.3 Rating percentages of AI refinement functions

AI refinement function	*Ratings*		
	Poor	*Fair*	*Good*
AI elaboration	8.62%	32.62%	58.77%
AI coordination	1.51%	16.67%	81.82%
AI speculation	16.67%	29.29%	54.04%
AI construction	2.94%	25%	72.06%

teachers need to wisely select AI refinement functions and choose sufficient turns of dialogue so that the AI tool can understand the contextual background.

Teacher A (Mathematics): *It is indeed helpful. While my posed questions may sometimes not be thoughtful or inspiring, the machine seems to always come up with a smart and prompt solution.*

Teacher B (Science): *You know, to manage a classroom discussion is challenging as children can come up with different answers and sometimes I don't know how to give them appropriate feedback. This tool can figure out proper and personalised feedback to students very quickly, in only a few seconds. It gives me a lot of inspiration.*

Teacher C (Literacy): *At first, I randomly selected a small piece of the transcript and then clicked on an AI refinement function. The results were not ideal. Then, it turns out that episodes of dialogue I chose were incomplete. Also, I did not clearly recognize my improvement needs, to elaborate them or to construct them. Then I carefully reviewed my dialogue transcripts and figured out the specific refinement requirements. Following this, I used the tool again and the results were much better.*

All the teachers reported that they were *willing to change* their dialogic pedagogy based on the refinement content received from the Productive Dialogue Explorer. Seven of the nine teachers stated that they believed their dialogic pedagogy performance had *improved*. The changes were identified as more students were willing to *participate* in classroom discussions, verbal exchanges tended to be more *diversified*, and contributions became more *collective* and involved more *reasoning*. A science teacher reported, 'I sorted the AI refinement results and added up the useful strategies. I then used the strategies in future lessons'. Six of the nine teachers indicated that they trusted the refinement results generated by the LLM-based teaching assistant tool. Regarding reasons for their trust in the tool, *sensibility* of the AI-generated content was mentioned by most of the teachers. Also, a few of the teachers indicated they trusted the large model as it had obtained *official authorization*. A literacy teacher expressed, 'I trust the AI results in the same way people dine in a restaurant. You don't know the chef, but you feel safe to order a meal, as the chef is supposed to be qualified'. The other three teachers were cautious about the results generated by the AI tool, especially when they were concerned with theorems and formulae.

The teachers generally showed high trust in the Productive Dialogue Explorer, given its sensible results and official approval. However, it is essential to note that while the large model-based teaching assistant tool can be a valuable tool for improving dialogue productiveness and encouraging critical thinking, it should be used with caution when the results matter standard answers. Therefore, it is essential to evaluate the sources and evidence provided by large models critically. Furthermore, it is suggested that teachers should preferably be clear about their pedagogy goals and have a well-developed understanding of the ways in which productive dialogue most effectively functions. Making a wise selection of the turns of dialogue and AI refinement functions, which are also referred to as prompts, will improve the results generated by the teaching assistant tool. This has been confirmed by other studies, which show that the use of prompts is essential for harnessing the power of large language models in a controlled and effective manner (Demszky et al., 2023). A prompt is a short piece of text that serves as a starting point for a model to generate a response or output. Dialogue prompts help large models understand the context and desired outcome of a conversation, allowing for more coherent and relevant responses.

Implications

The purpose of this chapter was to explore the effectiveness of a large model-based teaching assistant tool in improving the productiveness of classroom dialogue. A tool, the Productive Dialogue Explorer, was developed. It was designed to meet the needs and characteristics of dialogic pedagogy. Utilizing the ChatGLM large model, the tool showed its capability to generate refinement results for selected turns of dialogue across four aspects, namely, AI elaboration, AI coordination, AI speculation, and AI construction. Results from the quasi-experiment proved that the use of this LLM-based teaching tool was effective in improving the productiveness of dialogic pedagogy. The teaching assistant tool functioned well in terms of managing dialogue involving complex ways of thinking and reasoning. The benefits were particularly obvious regarding elaboration, contributing coordination, and building up dialogic construction. However, the tool only displayed a limited effect in polishing speculated talk. The refinements generated were perceived as being helpful and trustworthy in empowering teacher participants to make use of the dialogic approach in teaching and learning. It was largely conducive to providing prompt and personalized feedback that is adaptive to course contexts.

It is important to note several limitations that may open avenues for future research. Firstly, this study only explored the AI tool in the context of three subjects (i.e. mathematics, literacy, and science). Therefore, in the future, the tool could be investigated in the context of other subjects. Furthermore, in this study, the ChatGLM large model was selected to be adapted for the teaching assistant tool based on its being open-source and exhibiting good performance in both English and Chinese. In the future, more large models could be tested with dialogue transcripts to examine their effectiveness. Different large models could also be applied collaboratively to increase their performance in dialogue generation.

However, despite these limitations, this study makes innovative contributions to the field of classroom dialogue and educational technology. The LLM technique has attracted enormous attention around the world, given its powerful ability in language processing and generation. There is sustained debate about how this technique could be used to support teaching and learning. This study confirms that LLM techniques can be used effectively to improve teaching when they are adapted to the productive features of dialogic pedagogy. Secondly, increasing teachers' management skills concerning dialogic pedagogy has become a pressing issue as this type of teaching links closely to the development of students' critical thinking and deep understanding. Given its high human expertise demands, support for teachers is far from sufficient and efficient. This study represents an innovative approach to supporting and improving teaching and learning processes. Personalized and prompt assistance is likely to be available for a wide range of teachers. Refinements generated by this study's LLM-based teaching assistant tool provide valuable insights regarding how to enrich dialogic pedagogy. The tool has the potential to improve dialogue productiveness in the aspects of elaboration, seeking coordination and building up constructions. This effectiveness may lead to productive learning achievements and higher-order thinking among students. Thirdly, this study offers a promising solution for problems relating to teacher professional development. The evidence generated by the study implies that LLM-based teaching assistant tools can be applied to support teachers' self-reflection, particularly in domains related to dialogic pedagogy. Scalable professional support for teachers could, therefore, be possible. More teachers, especially those in less-developed contexts where experts are not widely available, could have opportunities to increase their classroom dialogue practices.

6 Applying AI technique to improve teachers' professional capabilities in dialogic pedagogy

From the previous chapters, we have known that the productiveness of classroom dialogue is directly related to the high-quality development of schools and the cultivation of innovative talents. At the same time, implementing dialogic pedagogy is challenging for many educational practitioners, and professional support for teachers in this aspect is greatly needed. In order to make good use of the AI technique and leverage its powerful abilities to orchestrate dialogue productiveness, the author's team has built up an intelligent teaching assistant tool named Productive Dialogue Explorer. It integrates various intelligent techniques, many of which have been introduced in previous chapters. Pie charts and bar charts illustrate the percentage of occurrence for each dialogic category, identifying productive forms of dialogic pedagogy. Additionally, tracking dialogue sequences reveals the interaction process and uncovers the evolutionary patterns of dialogic contributions. This method allowed teachers to detect underlying structures and dynamics in the interactions, as well as identify factors that contribute to effective communication and learning. After obtaining a better understanding of pedagogical performance, Productive Dialogue Explorer provides another function to assist in refinements of dialogic contributions by retrieving multiple large language models. Teachers select one or more turns of dialogue, which is one of the functions that AI is expected to accomplish. With these prompts, the platform can produce a personalized refinement plan for these selected talk turns. With the help of this platform, the author conducted a three-year project 'AI-assisted Teacher Professional Development on Dialogic Pedagogy' in a school (covering primary and secondary education) in China. Twenty-eight teachers participated in the project on a voluntary base throughout the three years. The significant positive changes in classroom dialogue and more contributions linked to productive features of talk have strengthened my confidence about the suitability of the AI techniques proposed and how they should be incorporated into classroom dialogue areas. In the following sections, I will provide a detailed introduction to the teacher professional development project, including its implementation, changes in dialogic contributions, and teachers' reflections on how the AI-assisted project impacted their management skills in dialogic pedagogy.

DOI: 10.4324/9781003543039-6

Implementation of AI-assisted teacher professional development on dialogic pedagogy

This project aimed to increase teachers' management skills in dialogic pedagogy and increase productiveness to boost educational achievement. The latest artificial intelligence technology was utilized to innovate means for teaching evaluation and explore patterns and features shared across high-level classroom talk. It was also expected to assist in teachers' self-reflection and efficacy in pedagogical development. Ideally, the project aimed to promote the teaching method from a 'knowledge-based' indoctrination approach to a 'literacy-based' inquiry, interactive, and inspirational approach. An innovative paradigm of dialogic pedagogy empowered by artificial intelligence can be leveraged. The project generally consisted of three main components.

1. **Thematic training and pedagogical workshops**. During the experiment, a total of nine thematic training sessions were conducted, as shown in Table 6.1. The training was intended to give participants' teachers a better understanding of dialogic pedagogy and what productive classroom dialogue expects from them.
2. **Assessment of performance on dialogic pedagogy.** Management accounts were set up for school administrators better to understand the overall situation of teachers' pedagogical performance. Individual accounts were set up for each participating teacher to help teachers gain an in-depth understanding of their

Table 6.1 Training sessions

Training topics	*Element*
Overview of the project	Clarifying the content and value of the project
Understanding productive dialogic pedagogy	Understanding dialogic pedagogy's definitions, productive forms, coding instrument, and benefits
Understanding the potentials of artificial intelligence	Understanding the usages of latest AI techniques and how they can be applied to teaching and learning
Enhancing the productiveness of questioning	Improving the effectiveness of classroom questioning
Improving the productiveness of feedback	Improving the effectiveness of teacher feedback
Organizing dialogue for constructive discussion	Introducing trends in classroom structure
Improving abilities in initiating elaboration	Enhancing teacher's skills to guide students in analysing, reasoning, and justifying ideas
Improving abilities in initiating coordination	Carrying out dialogue linking knowledge points, connecting and comparing knowledge, and summarizing and generalizing patterns
Improving abilities in initiating speculation	Enhancing teachers' skills in leading students to transfer and apply what have learnt to solve new problems

own changes in dialogic pedagogy. My team worked collaboratively with the school, organizing participant teachers to record their lessons and then uploading these recordings to the platform six times a year. Through the personal account, teachers viewed their performance reports and understood the limitations and strengths of their dialogic teaching. The quality of the effectiveness of classroom questioning and feedback was assessed.

3. **Intelligent dialogue improvement and optimization.** With the platform's auto-suggestion function, dialogic contributions were optimized automatically. Multiple strategies were provided to teachers, which were tailored to the specific needs of the talk and the context of the curriculum. Workshops were organized three times each year, and teacher participants, dialogic experts, and school principals were involved. These relevant people joined together to have a good discussion of how to strategically use the results produced by the intelligent Productive Dialogue Explorer platform.

In order to gain an understanding of the project's effect, the project team carried out a questionnaire survey on the participating teachers, in which 75.8% of the teachers indicated that they were very satisfied, 24.2% indicated that they were generally satisfied, and there were no teachers who indicated that they were dissatisfied. As shown in Figure 6.1, we can observe the trend of the indicators of various types of dialogues, in which the indicators of lower-order thinking, that is, talk about basic knowledge and expression of subjective opinions, show a decreasing trend. In contrast, the indicators of higher-order thinking, namely, elaboration, coordination, speculation, and uptakes, increase significantly. This suggests that, after participating in the AI-assisted project, the teachers have paid more attention to the cultivation of students' higher-order thinking by using

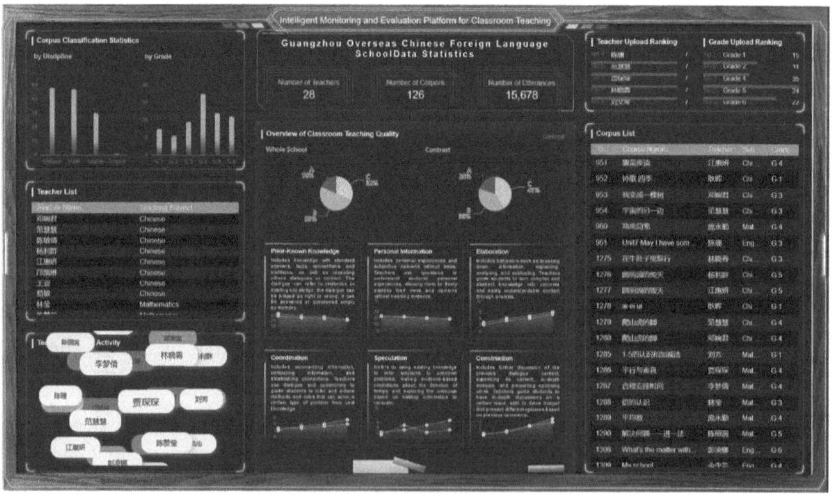

Figure 6.1 Visualized map of teachers' performance on dialogic pedagogy

thought-provoking questions and feedback. They are more capable of scaffolding students to elaborate their thinking process and dig into the problems to enhance their in-depth understanding of the problems. Their abilities in summarizing and sublimating principles or typical patterns that are helpful in addressing types of problems have been significantly improved. Furthermore, teachers strengthen their abilities to cultivate speculated talk and encourage students to explore novel exploration.

Application and practical examples

The following is a collection of feedback from participating teachers on the AI-Assisted Teacher Professional Development Project. Teachers have shared their insights from different perspectives on the use of AI technology in dialogic teaching. They demonstrated the effects of the improvements through examples of specific dialogic transcripts. It is hoped that the following examples will increase frontline educational practitioners' understanding of AI usage in dialogic education.

Reflection of a grade-8 literacy teacher on classroom dialogue

I find that every word and every action of the teacher in the classroom deeply affect the students. In the real-time transcribed text of the classroom dialogue, the teachers' talk is sometimes *not concise enough*. They are *redundant and repetitive*. Some teachers often unconsciously repeat what they have already said or use lengthy sentences to express simple meanings. It is also manifested in the improper use of words and ambiguity of expression. In the past, it happened a lot that my questions lacked focus. Pupils often have difficulty concentrating, and this is particularly evident in the lower educational grades. *Lack of focused questioning* often manifests itself in overly broad or vague questions. For example, a teacher may ask in class, 'What do you think about this text?' Such a question, although open-ended, leaves students at a loss because they don't know which angle or level they should answer. Such a question lacks a clear point of reference and makes it difficult for students to think deeply. In the teaching process, the use of concise language can convey the core information more quickly, thus enabling students to absorb knowledge more effectively within a limited time. Through the AI system Productive Dialogue Explorer, I can intuitively find out the problems of dialogic pedagogy and *timely adjust* our way of expression to ensure that the teacher can deliver knowledge more effectively and improve the learning efficiency of the students.

For example, one of the dialogic transcripts is about an ancient poem, 'The Lakeside Temple at Down'. This course is to let the students imagine the picture while reading and read aloud with emotion. When teaching, a set of pictures of West Lake was shown, with the intention of letting students feel the picture in the poem visually and then read out the beauty of West Lake. The following is the comparison of the original classroom dialogue and the modified ones suggested by Dr. Song's intelligent platform.

Original dialogue transcripts:

Teacher: *Let's enjoy the beauty of West Lake in June through a set of pictures. See what West Lake looks like in June?*
Student: *(looking at the picture)*
Teacher: *Do you like it?*
Student: *Yes.*
Teacher: *Please imagine the picture at that time and read out the author's love for West Lake.*

AI refinements:

Teacher: *Let's enjoy the beauty of West Lake in June through a set of pictures. After looking at the West Lake in June, what impression does it leave on you?*
Student: *(look at the picture) West Lake is very big and green, the water is clear and transparent, the scenery is picturesque, and I feel very comfortable standing by the lake.*
Teacher: *Do you like it and why?*
Student: *Yes. I like it because there are many famous people in Chinese histories had been to the place and left with outstanding poems or stories.*
Teacher: *Please imagine that you are standing by the West Lake right now, seeing such a view and could you try to bring up your own poem?*

Another example is a set of dialogue transcripts which is about making phone calls. The teaching objectives are as follows: (1) Understand the steps of the phone call and the initial learning to call and answer the phone independently. (2) When you make a phone call, you can be polite, make a simple self-introduction, express yourself clearly, and ask the other party to repeat when you can't hear. The author, in teaching, sets up three scenarios, respectively – call about classmates playing football, call with the teacher to ask for leave, others call when the father is not at home – and let the students according to the order of the three scenarios in turn role-playing, so that the students will learn to make a phone call in the three times to play. The intelligent platform offers refinements for more constructive dialogue. *(1) Group work. Let students discuss a certain phone call scenario and design a dialogue plan together. Cultivate students' sense of cooperation and teamwork, and at the same time, improve their conversational thinking skills. (2) Guide students to think about different points of view, for example, discussing different people's attitudes and word choices in telephone communication and how these factors affect the effectiveness of communication.*

Reflection of a grade-6 literacy teacher on dialogic pedagogy

In most of the classes I observed, the dialogue was rather casual and trivial, and the students' thinking *lacked breadth and depth*, which had something to do with the teacher's guidance and feedback in response to students' answers. Using the Productive Dialogue Explorer platform and looking back at the dialogue transcripts, I found that the classroom dialogues were not firmly focused, which led to poor teaching results. I reflect on classroom language use and analyse which questions can effectively stimulate students' thinking and which questions may hinder students' understanding. Primary school teachers should not only pay attention to the consolidation of students' basic knowledge in daily teaching but also consciously guide the *upgrading of students' thinking mode* through strategic use of language and lay the foundation for the formation of students' thinking.

The number and frequency of questions asked in class seem less critical. Since the implementation of the new curriculum, some teachers do not understand the concept of dialogic pedagogy. This makes us teach from the previous 'full irrigation' into today's 'full of questions'. Dozens of questions can be asked in one lesson. The intensive questioning will *leave little time for students to think*. Through participating in the training and workshops, I find that while it is encouraging to increase the number of questions asked and the motivation to respond, I think the *quality of the dialogue* is its core value in enhancing the effectiveness of the classroom. Questioning, especially with selective questions such as 'is it right', 'like it or not', 'is not', and so on, reduces the efficiency of the classroom and fails to promote students' interest in learning. Teachers' language in the classroom should be rich in expression.

Original dialogue transcripts:

Teacher: *You are in 100 per cent spirits today, all sitting up straight and loud. In the last lesson, we followed the master of observation, Fabre, into this world of observing insects. What are the characteristics of cricket dwellings observed along with Fabre? Who will say it?*

AI refinements:

Teacher: *Class, you have done a fantastic job today. Everyone is sitting upright and refreshed. Thinking back to the last lesson, we followed the master of observation, Fabre, on a marvellous journey to explore the world of insects. Together, we observed the cricket's dwelling in detail and discovered some of its unique features. Now, I would like to ask you to share what characteristics you have observed in the cricket's residence. Please be brave and raise your hand to speak! By the way, this way let's make the whole process more logical; students should practice at the end of the lesson, plus connecting words to say the process; the cricket follows these processes to build this residence, and in the process, you experienced how the jaws move the earth?*

It can be seen that the classroom educational language expression after AI paraphrasing is *richer* and more likely to *stimulate students' interest in learning.*

Combined with the *design of interesting situations*, games, etc., the use of lively and interesting teaching language enhances students' classroom experience, which is more attractive to students. The following is another example of my dialogue transcripts and how they are improved by the AI construction function.

Original dialogue transcripts:

Teacher: *So what does Faber have to say about the cricket's residence?*

AI refinements:

Student A: *Teacher, I've read* The Book of Insects, *and Faber thought the cricket's dwelling was very ingenious.*

Teacher: *Very good, Student A. Can you be specific about what aspects of the cricket dwelling Faber found so ingenious?*

Student B: *Faber mentions that the entrance to the cricket's residence was designed to be hidden so that enemies could avoid it while still allowing the cricket to enter and exit safely.*

Teacher: *Very detailed, Mr B. Moreover, how did the cricket build such an elaborate dwelling?*

Student C: *Faber observed that crickets pick soft soil and then dig bit by bit to build burrows that fit their bodies.*

Teacher: *Excellent, Class C. Have you noticed that Faber uses a lot of vivid language and metaphors when describing the cricket's residence? What is the purpose of such a writing technique?*

Student D: *I think this writing style makes it easier for the reader to empathize as if he or she has witnessed the whole process of building a cricket's home.*

Teacher: *Ding said it very well. Through such descriptions, Faber not only helps us understand the structure of the cricket's dwelling but also gives us the pleasure of observing natural creatures. This is exactly what makes the book* The Book of Insects *attractive.*

Teachers need to *clarify the objectives* of classroom teaching and carry out classroom questioning in a *targeted and hierarchical manner*. In the original teaching clip, the teacher just put forward a general question for students to extract information directly from the text to answer, which failed to stimulate students' thinking development. After the AI paraphrase, the question was subdivided into 'Can you tell me specifically what about the cricket's dwelling that Faber thought was ingenious?' 'And how did the cricket build such an ingenious dwelling?' This guides students to think step by step and then really feel the greatness of Fabre's writing about insects.

A reflection from a grade-1 mathematics teacher on dialogic pedagogy

After joining Prof. Song's training project and using the intelligent tool, I gained a deeper understanding of dialogic pedagogy and the design of dialogue for higher-order thinking. The process of reflecting on dialogic transcripts is actually a process of recognition of how I taught. Students cannot *maintain a long period of concentration*. Thus, we teachers need to guide students through *effective questioning and evaluation* of the learning process and results to help students maintain a better state of mind and avoid stagnant thinking, daze, desertion, and other phenomena. In the stage of reflection and evaluation, teachers can ask, *'Have we completed the task?' 'Are there any new discoveries?' 'Can you find any other ideas for solving the problem?' 'How do you evaluate your solution and other students' solutions?' 'What problems, in reality, do you think can be solved by what we learnt in today's lesson?' 'Do you have any other thoughts about today's content?'* Questions such as these prompt students to reflect on the basic knowledge, sort out the thinking process, analyse the solution method, fully mobilize students' enthusiasm for thinking, and broaden their minds.

Students are *not passive recipients of knowledge*; they are the main body of learning. Students should internalize the new knowledge into the old knowledge. The key lies in *knowledge collision*, condensing into their own knowledge of the vein. Students can raise questions about the knowledge and methods taught by the teacher. The teacher should affirm and guide students in thinking, use cognitive conflict, and inspire students to find ways to solve problems so that students can experience the process of mathematical 're-discovery' and develop students to question *critical thinking*. Teachers should be *precise in their questioning* and ask questions at crucial points. The questions should be thorough and should not be superficial and passing. No coherent random questioning is easy to cause fragmentation of students' thinking. It is common for us to see that a teacher threw out a question, not waiting for students to think about it thoroughly, and then rushed to answer. Teachers should make a good selection of questions, leaving students enough time to think and have group discussions.

For example, the 'Knowledge of the Hundred Numbers Table' is an important part of mathematics teaching and learning, helping students to understand and master the arrangement and composition of numbers from 1 to 100. The intelligent platform provides me with *actionable ideas for improvement*. The platform gives suggestions for improvement in relation to making speculated talk.

1. Stimulation of innovative thinking. Encourage students to create their own number series and explain the rules of their arrangement, which can cultivate students' innovative thinking ability. Let students try to represent the hundreds table in different ways, for example, using graphs, symbols, or stories to represent the patterns among numbers.

2. Facilitation of classroom dialogue. Teachers should encourage discussion and sharing among students and allow students to discuss in small groups what they have learnt about the hundreds table and the patterns they have discovered. Teachers can guide students' thinking and dialogue through open-ended questions, such as 'How do you know that this number should go here?' or 'How did you discover the pattern in this number sequence?'

Teaching about the Hundred Numbers Table is not just about memorization and repetition but also about *deepening students' understanding* and *making explorations*. Classroom dialogue is useful for developing students' *mathematical thinking* and problem-solving skills. Reproducible operational suggestions can help teachers gain a deeper understanding of the classroom and the higher-order thinking goals and practical implementation strategies for student development.

Reflection of a grade-4 teacher on mathematics dialogue

Through participating in Prof. Song Yu's programme, I learnt that context creation plays an important role in the process of problem exploration. 'Contextual teaching' refers to the teaching method in which the teacher purposefully introduces or *creates vivid and concrete image-based scenarios* to help students understand the teaching materials and develop their mental functions. According to the old saying, doubt is the opportunity for enlightenment. Teachers are good at provoking doubt in order to cause students to think positively. Indeed, the question is the spark that ignites students' independent learning and is the source of blooming students' innovative thinking. Teachers should cleverly set up the problem situation and stimulate students to actively participate in the desire to explore so that they want to learn mathematics.

When teaching the lesson 'Least Common Multiples', in order to make students enjoy this boring conceptual lesson, the teacher *brought a fun game* to the students at the beginning of the lesson. He drew a kitten with a broken tail inside a square hexagon and a kitten with a broken tail inside a square quadrilateral. Please guess: rotate the quadrilateral where the tail is located, and guess how many times the tail and the body can be rejoined. After everyone has guessed correctly, replay the game: draw a kitten with a broken tail in a square octagon and a kitten with a broken tail in a square pentagon. Guess how many times the tail and the body will be put back together by rotating the pentagon in which the tail is located. By comparing and contrasting the data obtained from the two games, the concept of 'least common multiple' is introduced, and students are guided to find the least common multiple of several numbers. Throughout the lesson, students' interest was high, and the teacher was able to make a boring conceptual lesson a memorable one.

In mathematics classroom teaching, special attention should be paid to the cultivation of students' ability to *express themselves in mathematical language*, which should be complete and concise. Let students speak boldly, especially those who are not good at speaking, and encourage them to speak more and train them to speak more in the teaching process. For the lower grades, let them learn to speak and try to say in the classroom; let them first use their whisper, then talk to each other in small groups, and finally speak out in whole-class dialogue. Table 6.2, shows how the intelligent platform assist me in polishing my dialogic teaching.

Reflection of an English foreign language teacher on dialogic pedagogy

Take English as an example; in classroom dialogue, many teachers will ask, 'Did you understand?' 'Is that right?' 'Is that right?' In fact, this is a rather obvious, repetitive, and useless case of dialogic questioning. The platform constructed by

Dr. Song's team can detect this repetitive and useless discourse in class so that the teacher can recognize the impact of his/her conscious or unconscious invalid discourse on the timeliness of the classroom and optimize classroom dialogue. An example of the course design of dialogic pedagogy can be seen in Table 6.3.

Table 6.2 Transcribed dialogue of Multiples of Recognition

Teacher:	Class begins. Hello, everyone.
Students:	Hello teacher.
Teacher:	Sit down. For this question let's play a musical game; the teacher taps one part and you tap a few parts, then each part and each part should be spaced out, and when you tap think about how many times you actually tap, got it? Children. Ready, the teacher claps 2, students clap 3 2, listen, start. Watch the pause between the two taps and the two taps. The teacher claps 3, the children clap 4 3s. Here we go. Children clap 6, teachers clap 2 6, children first. Pay attention. Get the children to say it. [AI rephrasing] Class, let's do a fun music game to help us understand rhythm better. I'll start by tapping twice, and you follow with three taps, remembering that each set of taps has to be properly spaced out. Now, I'm going to start clapping, so count how many times you clap. Are you ready? Here we go. Listen to my beat. I'll clap three times, and you'll clap three times for each of the four groups, with a pause between each group. Now, I'm going to start tapping, and you're going to follow. Again, this time I'll clap six times, and you'll clap six times for two groups. Remember, there should be a pause between each group as well. Okay, now you start clapping and I'll count to see how well you're doing. Okay, now can any of you say how you counted?
Students:	Two sixes are 12.
Teacher:	Who is the total, who is the multiplier, and who is the number of copies each?
Students:	12 is the total number, 6 is the number of copies each, and 2 is the multiplier.
Teacher:	Very good, this is what we have learnt before, so in our cheerful clapping game, rabbits come to our classroom, what is the favourite food of rabbits?
Students:	Radishes.
Teacher:	What specific information do you know from the diagram? Anyone. Let's see how we can distinguish between the radish in the first row and the radish in the second row. [AI evaluation] The previous classroom dialogue embodies the concept of game-based teaching. The teacher guides students to understand and consolidate mathematical knowledge by means of a musical game, which can stimulate students' interest in learning, enhance the fun of the classroom, and help to increase students' participation and motivation. During the game, the teacher guides students to pay attention to the grouping and spacing of numbers, which helps students understand the concepts of the composition of numbers and multiples.

(Continued)

Table 6.2 (Continued)

	Summary and Evaluation: 1. Innovative teaching methods: The teacher uses gamification to teach mathematics, which is in line with the characteristics of students' attention being easily distracted at the basic education stage and helps to improve students' learning efficiency. 2. Consolidation of knowledge: Reviewing previously learnt knowledge, such as the composition of numbers and totals, in the form of questions and answers helps to consolidate students' basic knowledge. 3. Guided thinking: Teachers guide students to think and express themselves in the games, such as asking students about the information they get from the diagrams, which helps to develop students' observation and expression skills. **Problems and Suggestions for Improvement:** 1. Student participation: Although the teacher interacted, the students' participation might not have been balanced. To encourage more students to participate, it is suggested that teachers go off the podium more often and walk among students during the game. 2. Knowledge development: During the game, teachers could guide students more in thinking about the mathematical principles of the game, such as how to understand concepts like division through the game. 3. Teaching evaluation: Teachers can provide immediate evaluation of students' answers to help students build up correct concepts and provide clarifications and additions when necessary. 4. Classroom management: Teachers need to maintain good order in the classroom during the game to ensure that all students can keep up with the pace of the game and understand the mathematical concepts behind the game. 5. Safety precautions: In games that involve movements such as clapping, teachers should remind students to pay attention to the strength of the movements to avoid injuries caused by excessive movements. Overall, this classroom dialogue demonstrated the teacher's innovation and enthusiasm for the teaching and learning process. However, further optimization is needed in the areas of student participation, knowledge expansion, teaching evaluation, and classroom management.

Table 6.3 Dialogic pedagogy design for Unit 11 I like the Spring Festival

Course Basic Information					
academic discipline	English (language)	grade	sixth grade	school term	in autumn
problem	***Unit 11 I like the Spring Festival best Let's talk***				
textbooks	Book Name: Compulsory Education Textbook English (Starting from Grade 3) Grade 6 Upper Publisher: Educational Science Publishing House Publication date: July 2014				

(Continued)

Table 6.3 (Continued)

Course Basic Information

Parts of speech study

- What: This lesson is a daily dialogue for primary school students about their favourite festivals. During the classroom activity, Ben asked Xiaoling about his favourite festival. During the conversation between Ben, Xiaoling, and Janet, Ben and Janet learnt about the name, time, typical activities, and meaning of the traditional Chinese festival 'Spring Festival' through Xiaoling's introduction.
- Why: Through the dialogue between Xiaoling and her classmates, the author helps the students learn to describe the traditional festival 'Spring Festival' in English, understand its cultural connotation of 'Spring Festival', gradually form an identity with the excellent traditional Chinese culture, and be firm in their cultural self-confidence.
- How: The dialogue is a typical daily dialogue for students, involving vocabulary related to introducing festivals, such as favourite, festival, gift, wish, clean their houses, buy new clothes, make everything new and fresh, lucky money, visit our family, have a big dinner with; communicating, introducing their favourites using core language, such as: 'What's your favourite festival?' Visit our family, have a big dinner with them; communicate, introduce their favourite language, for example, 'What's your favourite festival? Best', 'When is . . .? It is . . .', 'What do people usually do before/during . . .? They usually. . .'. The general present tense is used when asking others and introducing their favourite festivals, which students have been exposed to and learnt in previous lessons. The dialogue is simple, easy to understand, realistic, and educational.

Teaching Goal

- By the end of this lesson, students will be able to:

1. In the activities of watching, listening, and speaking, acquire and sort out the knowledge of the three primary school students in the dialogue about the traditional Chinese festival 'Spring Festival', including the name of the time, the time, typical activities, and their meanings.
2. With the help of the teacher and the teaching video, act out the dialogue in roles and try to introduce the traditional Chinese festival 'Spring Festival'.
3. With the help of the 'Learning Task Sheet', share in small groups their plans and ways of introducing the traditional Chinese festival 'Spring Festival'.

- The core language needed to complete the objectives of this lesson is listed below.

[Core words and phrases]

favourite, festival, gift, wish, lucky money, each other, clean their houses, buy new clothes, make everything new and fresh, visit our family, wish them a happy . . ., have a big dinner with

[Core sentence pattern]

What's your favourite festival? Best.

When is . . .? It is . . . (usually in January or February)

What do people usually do before/during . . .? They usually . . .

Teaching Process

Organizing teaching to introduce the unit theme

1. Based on the pictures, students predict the theme of the unit and learn the new word festival inspired by the teacher.
2. Introduce what you will learn in this lesson.
3. Reminder of supplies for this lesson.
4. Briefly describe the learning objectives of this lesson.

(Continued)

Table 6.3 (Continued)

Course Basic Information

[Design intent] At the beginning of the class, guide students in understanding the main learning content and learning objectives of this lesson. The student-oriented classroom plays an important role in the effectiveness of teaching.

Activity-driven, learning new knowledge

1. Inspired by the teacher, students, based on the pictures and existing experiences, predict the festivals that the three partners will talk about and perceive the language related to the Chinese New Year, such as 'clean the houses, buy new clothes'.
2. Students watch the video dialogue, understand the main idea of the dialogue, choose the pictures to answer the questions, and get the information that 'Xiaoling's favourite festival is the Spring Festival'. Moreover, help students sort out the information on the name and time of the 'Spring Festival' through the Thinking Maps, such as what and when. 'The Spring Festival is the Chinese New Year. Usually, it is in January or February'. Furthermore, through the question, 'What do people do with the Spring Festival? The Spring Festival is the Chinese New Year. Usually, it is in January or February'. The question 'What do people usually do at the Spring Festival?' elicits students' thinking.
3. Students look at the pictures, listen to the dialogues, and tick the right pictures about people's activities in Chinese New Year, and learn the phrases of typical activities in Chinese New Year, such as 'clean their houses', 'buy new clothes', etc. They can understand and learn the word lucky by using explanations and example sentences.
4. With the teacher's help, students divide the phrases of typical activities of the Spring Festival into two parts – 'activities before the Spring Festival' and 'during the Spring Festival' – and read the dialogues carefully to understand the details of the dialogues, and understand and learn the vocabulary with the help of new questions and examples. At the same time, through the mind map, we help students to sort out the knowledge points from what, when, and how, and pave the way for 'application practice' and 'transfer and innovation'.

before

clean their houses buy new clothes ⇨ Why do people do so many thing before the Spring Festival?

during

giving their some lucky money ⇨ Do Children give each other gift?

visit their family ⇨ What will people do when they go to visit their family?

have a big dinner ⇨ What do people usually eat for the big dinner?

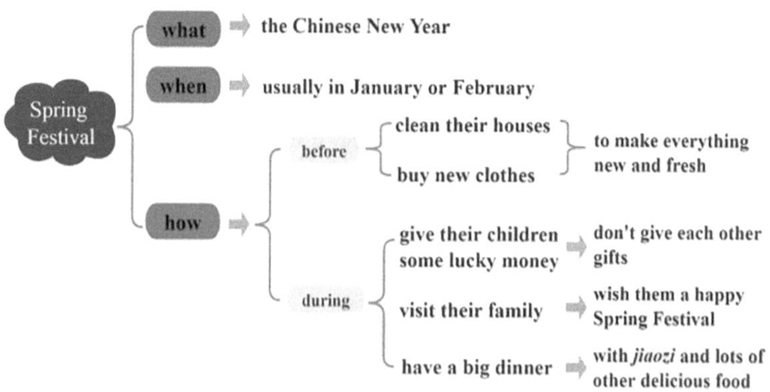

(Continued)

Table 6.3 (Continued)

Course Basic Information
The learning activities in this stage aim to help students understand the dialogues in context and learn the vocabulary and core language in the dialogues. Under the guidance of the teacher, students will gradually understand the dialogue from the general idea to the details through three levels of activities: 'Watching the video of the dialogue', 'Listening to the audio of the dialogue', and 'Reading the dialogue silently'. In vocabulary learning, we can understand the content of the dialogue, from the main idea to the details, through the three levels of activities. In vocabulary learning, students are helped to accumulate and expand their vocabulary through word decoding, English explanations, and example sentences.
Situational drills to consolidate new knowledge 1. Students listen to the recording and follow the dialogue, paying attention to the voice, intonation, rhythm, etc. Teachers read aloud the three long and difficult sentences in the dialogue, and students learn to read the long and difficult sentences with the meaning group by listening and imitating reading aloud. 2. Video of students role-playing and selecting characters to read the dialogue aloud. [Design Intentions] The learning activities in this stage aim to help students learn the skills of reading long and difficult sentences aloud and further understand the contents of the dialogues by following the dialogues. Through role-playing, students can use language to understand the meaning and promote the internalization of language, transitioning from learning to understanding to applying practice and preparing for authentic expression in later lessons. IV. Summarizing core language and strengthening cultural confidence 1. Students reflect on what they have learnt in the lesson, sorting out and summarizing the core language of the dialogue under the teacher's guidance. 2. Cultivation of cultural awareness and enhancement of civilization and social responsibility. 3. Classroom summaries and assignments to consolidate language knowledge in a timely manner. The summary part, through the three parts of 'words', 'phrases', and 'sentences', guides students to recall, organize, and summarize the core language of this lesson. The core language of this lesson is to cultivate students' habit of actively reviewing and summarizing what they have learnt. The design of homework adopts two parts – 'compulsory' and 'optional' – and the 'optional' homework can be downloaded from the 'Homework Practice' sheet. The 'optional' homework can be downloaded from the 'Homework Exercise' sheet and completed according to one's learning progress and needs.

Through the use of the Productive Dialogue Explorer platform, I uploaded the classroom recordings of the lesson, which were transcribed into teaching transcripts through the platform. That is, 32.79% of the questions were on basic knowledge, 39.96% of the responses were on basic knowledge, and the total percentage of teacher-student questions and answers on basic knowledge accounted for 72.74%. The proportion of teacher-student dialogue on analysis, coordination, and speculation, which are conducive to cultivating students' higher-order thinking, is low. I can clearly see the distinctive differences when comparing dialogue led by expert teachers. This makes me motivated to improve my classroom dialogue and enhance their productiveness.

Original dialogue transcripts:

Teacher: *(shows the picture) What animal is it? What does it wear?*
It is wearing a pair of . . . (PJs)
Teacher: *Pyjama, a suit of pyjama. What colour is the pyjama?*
It is red.
Teacher: *Children, you know red is the typical colour of China. Chinese people love red. Today, we are going to learn something about a traditional Chinese festival.*

AI evaluation:

This dialogue appears to be taking place in a classroom session where the teacher tries to guide the students to understand and explore the symbolism of red in Chinese culture. The students have already mentioned that red is the colour of China and the teacher is further reinforcing this point and leading the students to think about the reasons why red is a symbol of China. Teachers can inspire students to think about the deeper meaning of the colour red in Chinese culture here and encourage them to express their impressions and opinions about the colour. This activity is designed to explore cultural symbols and colours in order to increase students' awareness of Chinese culture. Engaging in such a dialogue is invaluable for the study and teaching of basic education as it encourages students to think about and explore the cultural signs and symbols of the country while also stimulating their interest in reading and learning. Through posing questions, teachers can stimulate students to think critically and creatively, which is a crucial aspect of basic education.

Through the analysis of AI technology, I found that although it is a conventional design to organize the class from the story that students are discussing and introduce new knowledge, for this lesson, the topic of red as the representative colour of China should be put into the 'transfer and innovation' part of the classroom or the overall design of the unit, and the teacher should guide students to carry out reasoning and argumentation activities for the value orientation behind the parts of dialogue. Teachers should guide students to reason and argue about the values behind them. In the 'Master Teacher's Formula' analysed by AI technology, the coaching teacher found the 'theme' and screened the programme in the corpus, and after thinking and adjusting, the introduction link of the original lesson was changed to observing the pictures related to the Spring Festival to introduce the new lesson. 'Red is the representative colour of China' is placed in the third lesson of the unit, and the three aspects of the Spring Festival, namely, the typical colour of the Spring Festival, the typical food of the Spring Festival, and the typical colour activity of the Spring Festival, are discussed. In the third lesson of this unit, we will summarize and share the three aspects of the Spring Festival: the typical colour of the Spring Festival, the typical food of the Spring Festival, and the typical colour of the Spring Festival.

Original dialogue transcripts:

Teacher: *Yeah, I like the Spring Festival. Look at the children here; it is the Spring Festival. Now I have a video for you. Please watch the video and answer these three questions. Question One: What do I refer to? I like the Spring Festival. What do I refer to? And when is the Spring Festival? So we have pictures for you to choose from. What is the Spring Festival? Also, we have some Chinese there for you to choose. Now, children watch the video. OK. Now, let's check. So, what do I refer to? Refer to Jimmy, Xiao Lin or Jiaming? Is that Jimmy or Jiaming? What do I refer to? You, please.*

AI refinements:

Teacher: *Yes, I enjoy the Spring Festival. Listen, everyone. I have a video for you to watch. While you're viewing it, please answer these three questions. First question: Who does 'I' refer to in the statement 'I like the Spring Festival'? Secondly, when is the Spring Festival? To help you answer, I've provided some images for you to choose from, along with some Chinese words related to the Spring Festival. Now, let's watch the video together. Okay, it's over. Now, let's go over the answers. So, who does 'I' refer to? Is it Jimmy, Xiao Lin, or Jiaming? Is it Jimmy or Jiaming? Can you please tell me?*

From the above comparison of the two parts of the dialogue, it can be seen that the AI-modified discourse is rigorous. Considering the difficulty of second language learning, teachers' classroom language is mostly short sentences or sentences with incomplete structure for the sake of students' better understanding, especially in the teaching of the lower grades. Through the aid of teachers' language, expression, and body language, students can also understand the teacher's questions and intentions, which can promote the classroom process.

Reflection of a grade-9 school teacher on mathematics dialogue

Mathematical language is the carrier of mathematical thinking and an important tool for mathematical learning and communication. Cultivating secondary school students' mathematical language ability is conducive to improving their mathematical comprehension, creativity, and application, as well as cultivating their logical thinking ability. However, there are some common problems in their verbal expression in mathematics, such as unclear and inaccurate expression, inappropriate use of vocabulary, and difficulties in understanding the meaning of problems. Attending Prof. Song's project made me realize that students' mathematical language expression ability can be enhanced with the support of artificial intelligence. An example of my dialogic transcripts can be viewed in Table 6.4.

Table 6.4 Example transcripts: Division of decimals to solve problems rounding up and rounding down

Teacher:	Recently, we have been learning division. Division is a very important operation in math; it can help us solve many life problems. Please see: These two problems also need to use division calculations. Can you see these two division equations directly and say their results? The first problem is Zihan.
Students:	They are renting three boats in total.
Teacher:	Ugh, there are students, um, please speak.
Students:	It should be that they are renting 4 boats in total, as this $14 \div 4 = 3$, and there are still two people left over.
Teacher:	Yu. So? What are the remaining 2 going to do?
Students:	To add another boat.
Teacher:	So we have to prepare 4 boats. What about the second question? Jun-ho.
Students:	They're going to want 4. To be to be 4.
Teacher:	Lol, it looks like some students have a different answer for the new branch.
Students:	I think they fill up to three boxes because it says they can be filled, but it doesn't say how many boxes in total.
Teacher:	So the remaining two it can't fill a box, so we can only fill three boxes and have to think about the remaining two?
Students:	No need.
Teacher:	No, okay. Problems like this one are about dividing evenly, but it doesn't have just the right amount of this situation, so how do we go about dealing with the remainder? That's what we're going to continue to learn in today's lesson on the division of decimals: problem-solving. OK, class, look, Xiao Ming's mum is going to prepare a birthday dinner for Xiao Ming and see what problems she encounters in the kitchen. Can you say what information you know? Required problems? Shankai.
Students:	Knowing that the total quantity is 2.5 kg of flavoured oil and the number of servings is 0.4 kg of flavoured oil, find the quantity.
Teacher:	So, what calculation do we use to find the number of shares when the total number and the number of shares per share are known?
Students:	Removal of the law.
Teacher:	Now, please take out your study sheets and make equations and calculations on your study sheets. Yinxia, please go to the board, write these two equations on top, and write in the second. You go to write on the third and write the third set. Just write this one equation. Just write on the third write on yours. Where do you write it? Why can't you do this step? You write it up. Okay. In groups of two, please discuss which of the answers on the board you agree with. Which one do you disagree with? Say something.
	[AI evaluation]
	In the above classroom dialogue, the teacher is teaching the application of the division of decimals in real life. The teacher begins with two real-world problems that involve the concept of equal division. The first problem is about a group of people renting a boat, and the students calculate through division that they need to rent four boats. The second problem was about filling a box with sweets, and students considered the possibility of not filling the box. The teacher guided the students to think about what to do with the remainder.

(Continued)

Table 6.4 (Continued)

	The teacher then introduced a new element of decimal division, using the problem of distributing the spiced oil for
	Xiao Ming's mother's preparation for her birthday dinner is an example for students to apply decimal division to solve real-world problems. Students were guided by the teacher to understand the use of division to calculate the amount of perfumed oil in each portion. The teacher encourages students to practise on their own and discuss the possibility of different answers within the group. Through this interactive teaching method, students are able to understand and master the concept of decimal division better and its application in real life.
Students:	(student discussion)
Teacher:	You just write this. And then it's done. Okay, have a seat. The three students above have written their equations above, all using division equations, as if the answers seem to be a bit different. Then please ask your classmates to say what you think. Jinteng.
Students:	The second one.
Teacher:	What about the others? Tell us the reasons. Okay, please add more from your classmates. Shihan.
Students:	Well, I agree with the second one, because in the first one, it's 2.5 ÷ 0.4 equals 6.25, but not only does it not have a unit, but where does it get the 6 from?
Teacher:	Good. Think about this for a moment: Are there any more students who want to say something? Which one can we rule out first? Zihang.
Students:	Firstly, we can rule out the third one because then it has decimals, and there's no way the bottle can be used for the kind of 0.25 bottle.
Teacher:	That is to say, now that the quotient appears to be a decimal, we are solving the problem of how many bottles are needed, depending on the situation. The bottles are bound to be taken as whole numbers, so in this question, we are going to take an approximation of the quotient as a whole number. Firstly, eliminate the third one based on the actual situation, and then come back to it. What is the answer? Why? Tell us the reason. Qu Yicheng.
Students:	I don't think the second one is very good, but because it divides by 0.4 and then equals 6 remainder 0.1, it is very good.
Teacher:	Right. Will the students please explain again why it is 7? Some students just now agreed that it was seven.
Students:	Because if it's 6, it can't fill all of the scented oil into the 6 glass bottles; there's still some leftover scented oil, so it would take 7 bottles to fill all of the bottles.
Teacher:	Okay, so how do you know there's a surplus? How much is left over? Kingwood.
Students:	Taking the total and dividing it by its 0.4 gives a number of 6.25, which is 6.25 bottles, but it is approximately 6 bottles if it takes the approximation to a whole number. And then take then um, but take um, but if it's 6 bottles, the remainder is still 0.25 kg left.
Teacher:	Hey, is that 0.25 kg left? Come on, let's have a look. Just now, we all said 6 bottles can't hold all. Then 6 bottles, please see how many kilograms of sesame oil they can hold. Do the maths, Purple Rain.
Students:	6 bottles will hold 2.4 kg of flavoured oil.

(Continued)

Table 6.4 (Continued)

Teacher:	What about the rest?
Students:	0.1 kg of sesame oil is left.
Teacher:	So what about the remaining 0.1 kg? Lu Yi.
Students:	To get another bottle for it.
Teacher:	So we need to add one more bottle to our final answer, which is 7. Right? Students compare. Since we take a whole number, we can just approximate it to 7. Which one do you think you like better, the second one this student just wrote or the teacher's kind? Zihang.
Students:	I think the teacher's one is better because it's easier and you can directly see the number of points. [AI evaluation] Summary and Evaluation of Excerpts from Classroom Dialogues: In the previous classroom dialogues, the teacher guided students to discuss different solutions and values of division application problems. Students participated in the discussion by presenting their views and calculations, while the teacher promoted students' thinking and deepened their understanding by asking questions and asking them to explain their reasons. **Advantages:** 1. The teacher encourages students to take the initiative to think and express their views, which helps to increase students' participation and motivation. 2. The teacher guides students by asking questions and develops students' logical thinking and problem-solving skills. 3. The teacher pays attention to the application of units and emphasizes the combination of practical situations and mathematical calculations, which helps students to establish correct mathematical concepts. **Deficiencies and Suggestions for Improvement:** 1. The teacher did not give timely feedback on whether the points made by students were correct or not, which students might misunderstand. Suggestions for improvement are that the teacher should briefly confirm the correctness of the answers after students' responses or allow students to evaluate each other. 2. Although the teacher encourages students to express different views, there is less interaction between students throughout the dialogue. Suggestions for improvement are that the teacher can guide students to have group discussions to promote communication and co-operation among students. 3. When answering the questions, the teacher focuses more on the quickness of the results and does not show enough of the steps and ideas for solving the problems. Suggestions for improvement are that the teacher should pay more attention to the problem-solving process and guide students in explaining in detail the derivation and choice of each step. Overall, this classroom dialogue shows a good atmosphere of interaction and inquiry, but there is room for improvement in some details. By optimizing these aspects, students' learning outcomes and mathematical literacy can be further enhanced. . . .
Teacher:	Okay, please take your seats.
Students:	I'll sit down.
Teacher:	Okay, I'll ask one of my students to tell me how to make an equation. Robin.
Students:	Take $25 \div 1.5$.

(Continued)

Table 6.4 (Continued)

Teacher:	OK, now let's ask the students to make their own vertical formulas and calculate the answers on the study sheet. I'll ask a student to come up and write a vertical calculation. Please sit down. Class, look at the blackboard and see what Zejun and this student wrote; which one do you agree with? Shun Xin.
Students:	I agree more with the one that Deng Zejun wrote on the board because it directly applies the approximate equivalent here, which is equal to 16. But what about this one on the board? It writes 16.66 loops, which is not enough to make one of the 0.66 loops that are left here, so it could have been simpler to just use the approximate equivalent.
Teacher:	Hey, that means this question is first. Its quotient is a decimal; how do we go about it? Yiju.
Students:	We need to press the quotient if it is a decimal. We can add one because we need to remove one.
Teacher:	That means we have to?
Students:	Because of the remaining 6.6, the 0.6 cycle is now not enough for Auntie Zhang not enough to fill a gift box.
Teacher:	Okay, so students, actually, from what the students said, I know that we know that the quotient is a decimal, and you can actually tell that it's the part that has a remainder. Then, if there is a remainder, we should first consider the approximation of the quotient as an integer because, according to the actual situation, the number of our gift boxes should be an integer, so we have to rule out this one first. Then, since we are taking integers, just now is this one exactly? Was it 16 on the blackboard or 17? Zengkai. [AI rephrasing] Class, we can see from your answers that when we know that the quotient is a decimal, we can be sure that there is a remainder. Then, if we want to find an approximate quotient of an integer, we need to consider the actual situation. For example, if we count the number of gift boxes, that number should be a whole number. So, when we say we want to take an integer quotient, we need to determine whether there are 16 gift boxes or 17 gift boxes. Sun Kay, can you help us with this?
Students:	It should be 16 on the board because the 0.6 cycles it has left over are not enough to pack, so it can only become 16.
Teacher:	Right. Students know that there are leftovers, and there are leftovers if you fill up 16, but how much is left over? Is it 0.66? Please verify this by doing the maths in your study sheet. How much red ribbon was used to fill 16 and pack 16? Um okay, Zi Yun, please.
Students:	A total of 24 metres of ribbon was used to wrap the 16 boxes.
Teacher:	And then what?
Students:	However, it left a metre of ribbon that was still smaller than 1.5 metres, so not enough to wrap an extra gift box.
Teacher:	That is not enough to pack a gift box; we directly rounded off, so we can only pack 16 gift boxes that root according to the rounding method or into one method; why not 17 ah? Think about how much is needed to pack 17. Ze Jing.
Students:	Because it packed 16 metres after consuming 24 metres of red ribbon, there was still 1 metre of red ribbon left. Packing a gift box needs 1.5 metres of red ribbon, so 1.5 metres minus 1 metre still needs 0.5 metres of ribbon. It is not enough to pack a gift box, so it can only use 25 metres of ribbon, which is only enough to pack 16 gift boxes.

(Continued)

Table 6.4 (Continued)

Teacher:	Oh, that's 17; packing 17 of that red ribbon is not enough. Come on, let's see if we need 2 for 17. Do we need 25.5 metres? Then we don't have enough red ribbon, so we can't pack 17. Then, students like this, no matter what the fractional part, the remainder is because we don't have to think about it round; we just round it off. We call the method of taking approximations like this the method of going to the end. Okay, please change the equation like this. Well, if the red ribbon keeps changing, then students think about how many gift boxes they can pack with these red ribbons to the far end.
Students:	All of these red ribbons are only good for packing 16.
Teacher:	Say why.
Students:	Since the first one equals 16.3, well, that 3 can just be omitted. If it was equal to 17, it wouldn't be enough. In the second question, 16.5, the next 0.5 can be omitted and rounded off. However, it's not enough to make it equal to 17.16.66 is a loop, so it doesn't work either.
Teacher:	OK. That means that the quotient is a decimal, and we know that it must have a remainder, but it doesn't matter how much it has left over. We don't have enough to pack a gift box, so we'll just round it off. So we're going to round up to the nearest whole number for this one. Students, it seems that the rounding method and the method of rounding to one cannot be applied in this problem; we can only use the tail method; no matter how much the decimal part is, we have to round off the tail to get the whole number. What are the similarities and differences when you compare these two problems? OK, please say.
	[AI coordination]
	The previous classroom dialogue mainly revolved around how to take an approximation of the quotient, especially how to choose the appropriate method of taking the quotient when it comes to practical situations. The teacher guided the students to understand that in order to ensure that the number of gift boxes is a whole number when the quotient is determined to be a decimal and there is a remainder, it is necessary to use the trailing method to take the approximate number. Specifically, students worked out that even if the remaining ribbon was not long enough to wrap another gift box, the remainder needed to be rounded off because the total length was insufficient to support more gift boxes.
	In this process, the teacher asked students to verify and think for themselves how to determine an approximation for taking the quotient based on the actual situation. Through practical calculations, students find that whether there are 16 or 17 gift boxes, only 16 gift boxes can be taken because the remaining length of the ribbon is not enough to pack another gift box, which is a practical application of the tailing method.
	The teacher also asked the students to compare the applicability of different methods of taking numbers (tailing, rounding, rounding up, and rounding down) in real situations, and guided the students to understand why they could only use the tailing method in this problem. Overall, this dialogue is designed to help students understand and master the application of the trailing method in real-world problems.

(Continued)

Table 6.4 (Continued)

Students:	Uh, they're all the same in that they're both approximately equal to, behind, they're both behind, um no, behind, um, the difference is that that scented oil is going to be, it's going to be required to be sought, sought to be approximately equal to is going to be larger, that scented oil is going to be valued larger, the gift box this is going to be valued smaller.
Teacher:	I'm sorry, I'm sorry. Some students would like to add that he just made a very important point: both are written approximately equal to the same point, so why should both be written approximately equal to, ah? Shihan.
Students:	Because this one sums out to decimals.
Teacher:	So, what's it going to be?
Students:	So it can only be counted approximately.
Teacher:	Approximate is the same as asking for its approximation as an integer. That's the same point. And what about the differences? Who's going to say more? Ding Han.
Students:	Well, fragrance oil is all; it has to be all part of the end. Ah, red ribbon, then. That is a red ribbon, and then it is packaged in gift boxes. There may be leftovers, but they are not used.
Teacher:	Okay, that means that the two questions use different methods; the first one is the method of progressing to one because it has to take into account the remainder and prepare another bottle, whereas the second one considers the test also has to take into account the remainder. No need. Directly rounded off, using the tail method will result in different results. Think about when we use the method of rounding off or rounding up in real life. Look at this question. Can you ask a maths question based on known information? Pan Nan.
Students:	How many vehicles are required to transport 40 tonnes of goods?
Teacher:	Is there any more? Shun Xin.
Students:	40 tonnes of cargo can fill several vehicles.
Teacher:	Fill up a few cars and will both problems be solved the same way?
Students:	Not the same.
Teacher:	Hey, everyone will react differently, so students, now please take out your study sheets, make equations, and calculate according to these two problems. Make a direct equation and calculate. Write the answer. Please be seated. Please look at the steps he took to solve these two problems. Can you say you agree with the way he wrote them? Why? Wanting.
Students:	Ah, I agree that he wrote it this way because the first question, um, he counted it to 15.38, and then it asked how many cars would be needed to carry it all, and then it was 10 um to estimate 15.38 as 16.
	[AI evaluation results]
	This classroom dialogue shows the teacher and students discussing the application of the method of rounding up and rounding down in real life. The teacher guides students to understand and differentiate between the two mathematical calculation methods, that is the method of rounding up to one and the method of rounding off, through two different questions. The rounding-up method is to round up and add one unit when the total is not enough to fill a unit, while the trailing-off method is to round off the remainder directly, regardless of the fact that there is less than one unit. Students, inspired by the teacher, were able to come up with mathematical problems related to real-life situations, which reflected the teaching concept of combining mathematical knowledge with real-life situations. Students were more engaged and motivated and were able to think and solve problems on their initiative.

(Continued)

Table 6.4 (Continued)

	However, there are some shortcomings and suggestions for improvement in the classroom dialogue: 1. Problem guidance could be more in-depth: The problems raised by the teacher could be more specific and in-depth to help students better understand the specific contexts and conditions applicable to the two calculation methods. For example, examples can be given to illustrate under what circumstances the method of rounding up to one must be used and under what circumstances the method of tailing off is used. 2. The time for students to think and discuss can be appropriately extended: After asking questions, the teacher can give students more time to think and discuss and encourage them to express their own views, which can improve their depth of understanding and problem-solving ability. 3. Teacher's feedback can be more specific: After students have answered the questions, the teacher's feedback can be more specific, not only affirming the correctness of the students but also pointing out deficiencies in thinking or expression and guiding the students to think more deeply. 4. Enhancing the accuracy of mathematical language: Students may lack accuracy in their expressions. For example, in the question 'How many cars are filled?' students should understand that this is an uncertain question because it may not be possible to fill up a whole number of cars exactly. The teacher can guide students to pay attention to the accuracy of the mathematical language and the completeness of the question. Overall, this classroom dialogue is a good start towards improving students' mathematical thinking and problem-solving skills through further guidance and inspiration.
	. . .
Students:	There's not enough money if it uses the Progressive One method.
Teacher:	Oh, is there any more? You say.
Students:	This should go to the end method because if it is approximately equal to 14 pens, then there is definitely not enough money, and you can't buy 14 pens.
Teacher:	That means after buying 13, it still has some money left over. Is there enough left over to buy another one?
Students:	Not enough.
Teacher:	So we're going to take the whole number to 13 branches using the detailed method. Class, what have you learnt from this lesson today? Xin Zhi.
Students:	I learnt that to find approximations, you can round up to one and go to the end.
Teacher:	The method of progressing to the first and the method of going to the end. What else?
Students:	I learnt the use of the method of going in one and going out the end.
Teacher:	How does it work? How exactly does it work?
Students:	The first method will usually be loaded with stuff to use, and then going to the end method over here is how much it can be filled or how much it can do.
Teacher:	Um well, Zihao, you have something to add, please.
Students:	I know where I can use the rounding up to one method and where I can use the rounding down to the end of my life.

(Continued)

Table 6.4 (Continued)

Teacher:	Well, can you talk about it?
Students:	For example, in life, there are some things like transporting goods. If it is to fill how many cars, then it is to go to the end of the method. However, if it's to finish loading the goods, then it's the rounding method. [AI elaboration] As a teacher-researcher, I need to acknowledge that this student was able to integrate the rounding method (tailing and rounding) in mathematics with real-life situations, which is very important. The fact that the student was able to apply the mathematical concepts to daily life after understanding them shows that they not only grasped the knowledge but also internalized it into problem-solving skills. Tail removal refers to the practice of truncating the result directly to the tails and retaining only the integer part when calculating. For example, if we want to calculate how many cars are needed to fill 50 boxes of goods, and each car can hold 5 boxes, we will use the trailing method to calculate $50 \div 5 = 10$, so 10 cars are needed. The rounding-up method means rounding the result upwards to the nearest whole number when calculating. For example, if we want to calculate how many cars are needed to load 100 boxes of goods, each of which can hold 9 boxes, we would use rounding up to the nearest integer: $100 \div 9 = 11 \ldots.1$. Since there is still 1 box of goods to be loaded, we need to add another car, for a total of 12 cars. This student's explanation clearly expresses the application scenarios of the method of going to the end and the method of going into one in life, which helps other students understand these two concepts better. In basic education, we encourage students to think about problems in this way because it is an important way to develop their practical application and logical thinking skills. At the same time, it is also in line with the principle of practical teaching advocated in our national education policy, which allows students to learn by doing and practice by learning.

Lack of clarity and accuracy

When pupils try to describe mathematical problems or solutions in words, they often encounter difficulties in expression. One of the most obvious is a *lack of comprehension of mathematics concepts*; that is, they know what they want to say but cannot find the right words to describe it accurately. At the same time, the sentence structure is often complex or confusing, making it difficult for the listener to understand the true meaning. This may be due to several reasons. Firstly, children may not have been exposed to enough maths-specific concepts or may not have a deep enough understanding of such concepts. Secondly, their thinking is not mature enough to *integrate fragmented ideas into a complete and organized description*. Finally, *dialogue organization* is also an important factor. Even if they have clear ideas, they may have difficulty expressing them fluently because they lack effective dialogue organization skills. Terminology in mathematics has specific meanings and uses. Lack of familiarity with their meanings and usages often leads to *inappropriate use of concepts when describing or answering mathematical problems.* For example, they may confuse conceptual terms such as 'divisor' and 'divisor'. Such confusing use makes their mathematical expressions appear imprecise and unprofessional. In addition, students may sometimes use everyday language instead of *technical terms* to simplify their descriptions. Although this may sometimes help them understand mathematical concepts better, it is not *accurate and standardized* enough for formal mathematical communication and expression.

Difficulty in understanding the complicated meaning of questions

When faced with *complex or abstract mathematical problems* involving generalizations, some students may have difficulty understanding them. This may be due to the fact that the concepts or information in the questions are beyond their current level of knowledge, or that the questions themselves are presented in a way that is obscure and difficult to understand. In such cases, students often find it difficult to understand the meaning of the questions. Naturally, they have difficulty *translating the textual descriptions of the questions into mathematical models and mathematical language.* This difficulty not only is at the initial stage of solving the problem but may continue throughout the whole problem-solving process. This is because once there is a deviation in the initial understanding, the subsequent mathematical modelling and solving will be problematic. Therefore, understanding the meaning of the problem and accurately translating textual information into mathematical language is a challenge that teachers need to overcome in teaching mathematics.

Group discussions to develop students' expressive skills in a collegial atmosphere

In the context of core literacy, teachers should learn to organize group discussion activities so as to promote students' development in a *collective atmosphere* and to enhance students' dialogue skills in mathematics. In addition, teachers should create opportunities for students to *express themselves through group activities.* For example, I organized group activities in the Measurement of Angles section. *Observe and discuss in small groups to recognize a protractor. What shape is a protractor? What is its function? What parts does it consist of?* These are the questions that students need to solve in the group discussion. Teachers set aside time to arrange for students to have group discussions and encourage students to actively express themselves in the group to get to know the protractor comprehensively. Another example is a course introducing the use of the protractor. I encouraged each group to analyse and discuss the content of the textbook within the group and summarize the steps of using the protractor. In this process, students expressed their views and focused on the two 'coincidences' proposed in the textbook. How to operate? How to read? In the end, they successfully understood the factors affecting the size of an angle and mastered the use of the protractor.

Refining teachers' language and modelling expression

In order to develop pupils' mathematical language skills effectively, teachers need to *refine our language* in the teaching process to model the correct use of mathematical language. Teachers should ensure that they use *correct mathematical terms, symbols, and definitions*, and *avoid vague expressions*. For example, when introducing parallel lines, the phrase '*two lines in the same plane that never intersect is called a parallel line*' can be used rather than an expression such as '*two lines that do not intersect*'. Such precise expressions not only help students understand mathematical concepts better but also develop their habit of using mathematical language correctly. We teachers should *present ideas logically and clearly*, and avoid incoherent or confusing expressions. *Appropriate connectives and transitions* can be used to link ideas and proof steps to ensure that students can understand and follow the teacher's thinking smoothly. For example, when solving a mathematical problem, words such as 'firstly', 'secondly' and 'finally' can be used to guide students through the steps and logical reasoning of the problem. In the classroom, teachers can try to avoid lengthy and complex narratives and instead express their ideas and *key points in a clear and concise manner*. Sentences and phrases can be used to explain mathematical concepts and theorems in a concise manner, avoiding the use of excessive vocabulary and cumbersome expressions.

Creating an atmosphere of expression and inspiring students to express themselves

In order to develop pupils' ability to express themselves in mathematics, teachers need not only standardize their language but also create a positive atmosphere to stimulate pupils' desire and ability to express themselves. In the class, teachers can set up some mathematical problems for students to actively participate in the discussion. Teachers can give students ample opportunities to speak and encourage them to express their ideas, opinions and solutions. At the same time, teachers should listen to students, respect their different views, and give them timely recognition and constructive guidance. Through this kind of interactive communication, students will have the opportunity to practise and improve their ability to express themselves in mathematical language. We can guide students' thinking by asking open-ended questions and encouraging them to express their ideas and thoughts in mathematical language. Teachers can *use guided questioning* to help students organize their thinking and language, and give them sufficient time and space to express themselves. Teachers can also lead group discussions, encourage students to share and learn from each other, and give them timely guidance and feedback. Through this kind of stimulating questioning, students will be able to think actively and express their ideas and opinions freely. Teachers can also promote expression through classroom presentations and demonstrations. Teachers can guide students through classroom presentations in which they independently organize their own words to express a mathematical concept, theorem, or solution to a problem. Teachers can give students sufficient time to prepare, and provide relevant information and guidance to help them improve their language skills. At the same time, teachers can organize mathematical presentations to encourage students to use graphs, charts, objects, or demonstrations to show their mathematical knowledge and problem-solving processes. Through such presentations and demonstrations, students will have the opportunity to demonstrate their learning outcomes and further develop their language skills in mathematics.

References

Affeldt, S., Labiod, L., & Nadif, M. (2020). Spectral clustering via ensemble deep autoencoder learning (SC-EDAE). *Pattern Recognition*, *108*, 107522.

Aguiar, O. G., Mortimer, E. F., & Scott, P. (2010). Learning from and responding to students' questions: The authoritative and dialogic tension. *Journal of Research in Science Teaching: The Official Journal of the National Association for Research in Science Teaching*, *47*(2), 174–193.

Alexander, R. (2018). Developing dialogic teaching: Genesis, process, trial. *Research Papers in Education*, *33*(5), 561–598.

Alexander, R. (2019). Whose discourse? Dialogic pedagogy for a post-truth world. *Dialogic Pedagogy: A Journal for Studies of Dialogic Education*, *7*.

Alexander, R. (2020). *A dialogic teaching companion*. Routledge.

Alexander, R. J. (2001). Border crossings: Towards a comparative pedagogy. *Comparative Education*, *37*(4), 507–523.

Alexander, R. J. (2008). *Towards dialogic teaching. Rethinking classroom talk*. Dialogos.

Alexander, R. J. (2017). Investigating texts about environmental degradation using critical discourse analysis and corpus linguistic techniques. In *The Routledge handbook of ecolinguistics* (pp. 196–210). Routledge.

Amiri, S., Mehvari-Habibabadi, J., Mohammadi-Mobarakeh, N., Hashemi-Fesharaki, S. S., Mirbagheri, M. M., Elisevich, K., & Nazem-Zadeh, M. R. (2020). Graph theory application with functional connectivity to distinguish left from right temporal lobe epilepsy. *Epilepsy Research*, *167*, 106449.

Baghipur, M., Ghorbani, M., Ganie, H. A., & Shang, Y. (2021). On the second-largest reciprocal distance signless Laplacian eigenvalue. *Mathematics*, *9*(5), 512.

Bakeman, R., & Gottman, J. M. (1997). *Observing interaction: An introduction to sequential analysis*. Cambridge University Press.

Balkus, S. V., & Yan, D. (2022). Improving short text classification with augmented data using GPT-3. *Natural Language Engineering*, 1–30.

Bengesi, S., El-Sayed, H., Sarker, M. K., Houkpati, Y., Irungu, J., & Oladunni, T. (2024). Advancements in generative AI: A comprehensive review of GANs, GPT, autoencoders, diffusion model, and transformers. *IEEE Access*, *12*, 69812–69837.

Blanchard, N., Brady, M., Olney, A. M., Glaus, M., Sun, X., Nystrand, M., Samei, B., Kelly, S., & D'Mello, S. (2015). A study of automatic speech recognition in noisy classroom environments for automated dialog analysis. In *Artificial intelligence in education: 17th international conference, AIED 2015, Madrid, Spain, June 22–26, 2015. Proceedings 17* (pp. 23–33). Springer International Publishing.

Bonner, E., Lege, R., & Frazier, E. (2023). Large language model-based artificial intelligence in the language classroom: Practical ideas for teaching. *Teaching English with Technology*, *23*(1), 23–41.

Bonwell, C. C., & Eison, J. A. (1991). *Active learning: Creating excitement in the classroom. 1991 ASHE-ERIC higher education reports*. ERIC Clearinghouse on Higher Education, The George Washington University.

Boyd, M. P., & Markarian, W. C. (2011). Dialogic teaching: Talk in service of a dialogic stance. *Language and Education*, *25*(6), 515–534.

Bradley, E. G., & Kendall, B. (2014). A review of computer simulations in teacher education. *Journal of Educational Technology Systems*, *43*(1), 3–12.

Cazden, C. B. (2001). The language of teaching and learning. *The Language of Teaching and Learning*, *2*.

Chan, M. C. E., & Sfard, A. (2020). On learning that could have happened: The same tale in two cities. *The Journal of Mathematical Behavior*, *60*, 100815.

Chen, M., Chai, C. S., Jong, M. S. Y., & Jiang, M. Y. C. (2021). Teachers' conceptions of teaching Chinese descriptive composition with interactive spherical video-based virtual reality. *Frontiers in Psychology*, *12*, 591708.

Chen, Y. (2015). *Convolutional neural network for sentence classification* [Master's thesis, University of Waterloo].

Chen, Z., Chen, W., Jia, J., & An, H. (2020). The effects of using mobile devices on language learning: A meta-analysis. *Educational Technology Research and Development*, *68*(4), 1769–1789.

Chesnais, A. (2021). Enhancing classroom discourse about measure to foster a conceptual understanding of geometrical practices. *ZDM – Mathematics Education*, *53*(2), 337–357.

Chin, C. A. (2006). Classroom interaction in science: Teacher questioning and feedback to students' responses. *International Journal of Science Education*, *28*(11), 1315–1346.

Chinn, C. A., O'donnell, A. M., & Jinks, T. S. (2000). The structure of discourse in collaborative learning. *The Journal of Experimental Education*, *69*(1), 77–97.

Cobo, M. J., Martínez, M. A., Gutiérrez-Salcedo, M., Fujita, H., & Herrera-Viedma, E. (2015). 25 years at knowledge-based systems: A bibliometric analysis. *Knowledge-based Systems*, *80*, 3–13.

Colace, F., De Santo, M., Lombardi, M., Pascale, F., Pietrosanto, A., & Lemma, S. (2018). Chatbot for e-learning: A case of study. *International Journal of Mechanical Engineering and Robotics Research*, *7*(5), 528–533.

Cooper, R. P., & Shallice, T. (2006). Hierarchical schemas and goals in the control of sequential behavior. *Psychological Review*, *113*(4), 887–916.

Corriveau, C., & Bednarz, N. (2017). The secondary-tertiary transition viewed as a change in mathematical cultures: An exploration concerning symbolism and its use. *Educational Studies in Mathematics*, *95*, 1–19.

da Silva, N. F., Hruschka, E. R., & Hruschka Jr, E. R. (2014). Tweet sentiment analysis with classifier ensembles. *Decision Support Systems*, *66*, 170–179.

Dalal, M. K., & Zaveri, M. A. (2011). Automatic text classification: A technical review. *International Journal of Computer Applications*, *28*(2), 37–40.

Dallimore, E. J., Hertenstein, J. H., & Platt, M. B. (2010). Class participation in accounting courses: Factors that affect student comfort and learning. *Issues in Accounting Education*, *25*(4), 613–629.

D'Ambrosio, B. E. A. T. R. I. Z., Johnson, H., & Hobbs, L. E. S. L. I. E. (1995). Strategies for increasing achievement in mathematics. In *Educating everybody's children: Diverse teaching strategies for diverse learners: What research and practice say about improving achievement*. Association for Supervision and Curriculum Development.

Dascalu, M. I., Bodea, C. N., Mihailescu, M. N., Tanase, E. A., & Ordoñez de Pablos, P. (2016). Educational recommender systems and their application in lifelong learning. *Behaviour & Information Technology*, *35*(4), 290–297.

Datta, D., Phillips, M., Bywater, J. P., Chiu, J., Watson, G. S., Barnes, L. E., & Brown, D. E. (2021). Evaluation of mathematical questioning strategies using data collected through weak supervision. *arxiv preprint*, arxiv:2112.00985.

Dawson, M. R., & Lignugaris/Kraft, B. (2017). Meaningful practice: Generalizing foundation teaching skills from TLE TeachLivE™ to the classroom. *Teacher Education and Special Education*, *40*(1), 26–50.

Delen, E., Liew, J., & Willson, V. (2014). Effects of interactivity and instructional scaffolding on learning: Self-regulation in online video-based environments. *Computers & Education*, *78*, 312–320.

Demszky, D., Yang, D., Yeager, D. S., Bryan, C. J., Clapper, M., Chandhok, S., Eichstaedt, J. C., Hecht, C., Jamieson, J., Johnson, M., Jones, M., Krettek-Cobb, D., Lai, L., JonesMitchell, N., Ong, D. C., Dweck, C. S., Gross, J, J., & Pennebaker, J. W. (2023). Using large language models in psychology. *Nature Reviews Psychology*, *2*(11), 688–701.

Dhahri, M., & Khribi, M. K. (2021). *A review of educational recommender systems for teachers*. International Association for Development of the Information Society.

Diez-Palomar, J., Chan, M. C. E., Clarke, D., & Padros, M. (2021). How does dialogical talk promote student learning during small group work? An exploratory study. *Learning, Culture and Social Interaction*, *30*, 100540.

Ding, Y., Rousseau, R., & Wolfram, D. (2014). *Measuring scholarly impact. Methods and practice*. Springer International Publishing.

Dizon, G. (2020). Evaluating intelligent personal assistants for L2 listening and speaking development. *Language, Learning and Technology*, *24*(1), 16–26.

Dolin, J., Bruun, J., Nielsen, S. S., Jensen, S. B., & Nieminen, P. (2018). The structured assessment dialogue. *Transforming Assessment: Through An Interplay between Practice, Research and Policy*, *4*, 109–140.

Dorofeyuk, A. A. (1971). Algorithms of automatic classification. *Avtomatika i Telemekhanika*, (12), 78–113.

Dwyer, J., Kelcey, B., Berebitsky, D., & Carlisle, J. F. (2016). A study of teachers' discourse moves that support text-based discussions. *The Elementary School Journal*, *117*(2), 285–309.

Eli, J. A., Mohr-Schroeder, M. J., & Lee, C. W. (2011). Exploring mathematical connections of prospective middle-grades teachers through card-sorting tasks. *Mathematics Education Research Journal*, *23*, 297–319.

Ellegaard, M., Damsgaard, L., Bruun, J., & Johannsen, B. F. (2018). Patterns in the form of formative feedback and student response. *Assessment & Evaluation in Higher Education*, *43*(5), 727–744.

English, E., Hargreaves, L., & Hislam, J. (2002). Pedagogical dilemmas in the national literacy strategy: Primary teachers' perceptions, reflections and classroom behaviour. *Cambridge Journal of Education*, *32*(1), 9–26.

Epp, E. M., Green, K. F., Rahman, A. M., & Weaver, G. C. (2010). Analysis of student – instructor interaction patterns in real-time, scientific online discourse. *Journal of Science Education and Technology*, *19*, 49–57.

Erath, K., Prediger, S., Quasthoff, U., & Heller, V. (2018). Discourse competence as important part of academic language proficiency in mathematics classrooms: The case of explaining to learn and learning to explain. *Educational Studies in Mathematics*, *99*, 161–179.

Evitts, T. A. (2005). Investigating the mathematical connections that preservice teachers use and develop while solving problems from reform curricula (Doctoral dissertation, The Pennsylvania State University, 2004). *Dissertation Abstracts International*, *65*(12), 4500.

Ezaldeen, H., Misra, R., Bisoy, S. K., Alatrash, R., & Priyadarshini, R. (2022). A hybrid E-learning recommendation integrating adaptive profiling and sentiment analysis. *Journal of Web Semantics*, *72*, 100700.

Farrokhnia, M., Banihashem, S. K., Noroozi, O., & Wals, A. (2023). A SWOT analysis of ChatGPT: Implications for educational practice and research. *Innovations in Education and Teaching International*, 1–15.

Fisher, R. (2007). Dialogic teaching: Developing thinking and metacognition through philosophical discussion. *Early Child Development and Care*, *177*(6–7), 615–631.

Ford, M., Baer, C. T., Xu, D., Yapanel, U., & Gray, S. (2008). *The LENATM language environment analysis system: Audio specifications of the DLP-0121* (Technical Report LTR-03-2). Lena Foundation.

Fritschner, L. M. (2000). Inside the undergraduate college classroom: Faculty and students differ on the meaning of student participation. *The Journal of Higher Education*, *71*(3), 342–362.

Fryer, L. K., Ainley, M., Thompson, A., Gibson, A., & Sherlock, Z. (2017). Stimulating and sustaining interest in a language course: An experimental comparison of Chatbot and Human task partners. *Computers in Human Behavior*, *75*, 461–468.

Fryer, L. K., Nakao, K., & Thompson, A. (2019). Chatbot learning partners: Connecting learning experiences, interest and competence. *Computers in Human Behavior*, *93*, 279–289.

Fung, D., & Howe, C. (2014). Group work and the learning of critical thinking in the Hong Kong secondary liberal studies curriculum. *Cambridge Journal of Education*, *44*(2), 245–270.

Galton, M., Hargreaves, L., Comber, C., Wall, D., & Pell, T. (1999). Changes in patterns of teacher interaction in primary classrooms: 1976-96. *British Educational Research Journal*, *25*(1), 23–37.

García-Fariña, A., & Jiménez-Jiménez, F. (2018). Observation of communication by physical education teachers: Detecting patterns in verbal behavior. *Frontiers in Psychology*, *9*, 254621.

Geng, Y., Chen, W., Liu, Z., Chiu, A. S., Han, W., Liu, Z., Zhong, Z., Qian, Y., You, W., & Cui, X. (2017). A bibliometric review: Energy consumption and greenhouse gas emissions in the residential sector. *Journal of Cleaner Production*, *159*, 301–316.

Gillies, R. M. (2016). Cooperative learning: Review of research and practice. *Australian Journal of Teacher Education (Online)*, *41*(3), 39–54.

Gillies, R. M., & Baffour, B. (2017). The effects of teacher-introduced multimodal representations and discourse on students' task engagement and scientific language during cooperative, inquiry-based science. *Instructional Science*, *45*, 493–513.

Gillies, R. M., & Nichols, K. (2015). How to support primary teachers' implementation of inquiry: Teachers' reflections on teaching cooperative inquiry-based science. *Research in Science Education*, *45*, 171–191.

Gimenez, E., Salinas, M., & Manzano-Agugliaro, F. (2018). Worldwide research on plant defense against biotic stresses as improvement for sustainable agriculture. *Sustainability*, *10*(2), 391.

Given, L. M. (Ed.). (2008). *The Sage encyclopedia of qualitative research methods*. Sage publications.

Godwin-Jones, R. (2019). In a world of SMART technology, why learn another language? *Journal of Educational Technology & Society*, *22*(2), 4–13.

González-Howard, M., Marco-Bujosa, L. M., McNeill, K. L., Goss, M., & Loper, S. (2018). The argumentation toolkit: A resource for integrating argumentation into your science classroom. *Science Scope*, *42*(3), 74–78.

Graesser, A. C., Wiemer-Hastings, K., Wiemer-Hastings, P., Kreuz, R., & Tutoring Research Group. (1999). AutoTutor: A simulation of a human tutor. *Cognitive Systems Research*, *1*(1), 35–51.

Grimes, D., & Warschauer, M. (2010). Utility in a fallible tool: A multi-site case study of automated writing evaluation. *The Journal of Technology, Learning and Assessment*, *8*(6).

Gu, X., Chen, X., Lu, P., Li, Z., Du, Y., & Li, X. (2024). AGCVT-prompt for sentiment classification: Automatically generating chain of thought and verbalizer in prompt learning. *Engineering Applications of Artificial Intelligence*, *132*, 107907.

Gueudet, G. (2008). Investigating the secondary – tertiary transition. *Educational Studies in Mathematics*, *67*(3), 237–254.

Guo, B., Zhang, X., Wang, Z., Jiang, M., Nie, J., Ding, Y., Yue, J., & Wu, Y. (2023). How close is ChatGPT to human experts? Comparison corpus, evaluation, and detection. *arxiv preprint*, arxiv:2301.07597.

Guo, S., Zheng, Y., & Zhai, X. (2024). Artificial intelligence in education research during 2013–2023: A review based on bibliometric analysis. *Education and Information Technologies*, 1–23.

Gupta, M., & Kumar, P. (2020). Recommendation generation using personalized weight of meta-paths in heterogeneous information networks. *European Journal of Operational Research*, *284*(2), 660–674.

Gupta, V., & Jain, N. (2017). Harnessing information and communication technologies for effective knowledge creation: Shaping the future of education. *Journal of Enterprise Information Management*, *30*(5), 831–855.

Handelsman, M. M., Briggs, W. L., Sullivan, N., & Towler, A. (2005). A measure of college student course engagement. *The Journal of Educational Research*, *98*(3), 184–192.

Hao, J., von Davier, A. A., Yaneva, V., Lottridge, S., von Davier, M., & Harris, D. J. (2024). Transforming assessment: The impacts and implications of large language models and generative AI. *Educational Measurement: Issues and Practice*, *43*(2), 16–29. https://doi.org/10.1111/emip.12602

Harney, O. M., Hogan, M. J., & Quinn, S. (2017). Investigating the effects of peer to peer prompts on collaborative argumentation, consensus and perceived efficacy in collaborative learning. *International Journal of Computer-Supported Collaborative Learning*, *12*, 307–336.

He, Q., Borgonovi, F., & Paccagnella, M. (2021). Leveraging process data to assess adults' problem-solving skills: Using sequence mining to identify behavioral patterns across digital tasks. *Computers & Education*, *166*, 104170.

Heck, D. J., Plumley, C. L., Stylianou, D. A., Smith, A. A., & Moffett, G. (2019). Scaling up innovative learning in mathematics: Exploring the effect of different professional development approaches on teacher knowledge, beliefs, and instructional practice. *Educational Studies in Mathematics*, *102*(3), 319–342.

Heift, T. (2004). Corrective feedback and learner uptake in CALL. *ReCALL*, *16*(2), 416–431.

Henderson, J. B., McNeill, K. L., González-Howard, M., Close, K., & Evans, M. (2018). Key challenges and future directions for educational research on scientific argumentation. *Journal of Research in Science Teaching*, *55*(1), 5–18.

Hennessy, S., Calcagni, E., Leung, A., & Mercer, N. (2021). An analysis of the forms of teacher-student dialogue that are most productive for learning. *Language and Education*, *25*, 1–26.

Hennessy, S., Dragovic, T., & Warwick, P. (2017). A research-informed, school-based professional development workshop programme to promote dialogic teaching with interactive technologies. *Professional Development in Education*, *44*, 1–24.

Hennessy, S., Howe, C., Mercer, N., & Vrikki, M. (2020). Coding classroom dialogue: Methodological considerations for researchers. *Learning, Culture and Social Interaction*, *25*, 100404.

Hennessy, S., Rojas-Drummond, S., Higham, R., Márquez, A. M., Maine, F., Ríos, R. M., García-Carrión, R., Torreblanca, O., & Barrera, M. J. (2016). Developing a coding scheme for analysing classroom dialogue across educational contexts. *Learning, Culture and Social Interaction*, *9*, 16–44.

Herbold, S., Hautli-Janisz, A., Heuer, U., Kikteva, Z., & Trautsch, A. (2023). A large-scale comparison of human-written versus ChatGPT-generated essays. *Scientific Reports*, *13*(1), 18617.

Hew, K. F., & Lo, C. K. (2020). Comparing video styles and study strategies during video-recorded lectures: Effects on secondary school mathematics students' preference and learning. *Interactive Learning Environments*, *28*(7), 847–864.

Hirsch, J. E., & Buela-Casal, G. (2014). The meaning of the h-index. *International Journal of Clinical and Health Psychology*, *14*(2), 161–164.

Howe, C. (2010). Peer dialogue and cognitive development: A two-way relationship? In *Educational dialogues* (pp. 44–59). Routledge.

Howe, C. (2017). Advances in research on classroom dialogue: Commentary on the articles. *Learning and Instruction*, *48*, 61–65.
Howe, C., & Abedin, M. (2013). Classroom dialogue: A systematic review across four decades of research. *Cambridge Journal of Education*, *43*(3), 325–356.
Howe, C., Hennessy, S., Mercer, N., Vrikki, M., & Wheatley, L. (2019). Teacher – student dialogue during classroom teaching: Does it really impact on student outcomes? *Journal of the Learning Sciences*, *28*(4–5), 462–512.
Howe, C., Ilie, S., Guardia, P., Hofmann, R., Mercer, N., & Riga, F. (2015). Principled improvement in science: Forces and proportional relations in early secondary-school teaching. *International Journal of Science Education*, *37*(1), 162–184.
Howe, C., & Mercer, N. (2017). Commentary on the papers. *Language and Education*, *31*(1), 83–92.
Huang, K. L., Liu, Y. C., Dong, M. Q., & Lu, C. C. (2024). Integrating AIGC into product design ideation teaching: An empirical study on self-efficacy and learning outcomes. *Learning and Instruction*, *92*, 101929.
Huang, W., Hew, K. F., & Fryer, L. K. (2022). Chatbots for language learning – Are they really useful? A systematic review of chatbot-supported language learning. *Journal of Computer Assisted Learning*, *38*(1), 237–257.
Hulsman, R. L., & van der Vloodt, J. (2015). Self-evaluation and peer-feedback of medical students' communication skills using a web-based video annotation system. Exploring content and specificity. *Patient Education and Counseling*, *98*(3), 356–363.
Jackson, G. T., Boonthum, C., & McNamara, D. S. (2010). The efficacy of iSTART extended practice: Low ability students catch up. In *Intelligent tutoring systems: 10th international conference, ITS 2010, Pittsburgh, PA, USA, June 14–18, 2010, proceedings, part II 10* (pp. 349–351). Springer Berlin Heidelberg.
Jacobs, J., Scornavacco, K., Harty, C., Suresh, A., Lai, V., & Sumner, T. (2022). Promoting rich discussions in mathematics classrooms: Using personalized, automated feedback to support reflection and instructional change. *Teaching and Teacher Education*, *112*, 103631.
Jadallah, M., Anderson, R. C., Nguyen-Jahiel, K., Miller, B. W., Kim, I. H., Kuo, L. J., Dong, T., & Wu, X. (2011). Influence of a teacher's scaffolding moves during child-led small-group discussions. *American Educational Research Journal*, *48*(1), 194–230.
Jay, T., Willis, B., Thomas, P., Taylor, R., Moore, N., Burnett, C., Merchant, G., & Stevens, A. (2017). *Dialogic teaching: Evaluation report and executive summary*. Education Endowment Foundation.
Jeon, J. (2022). Exploring AI chatbot affordances in the EFL classroom: Young learners' experiences and perspectives. *Computer Assisted Language Learning*, 37(1–2), 1–26.
Jeon, J., Lee, S., & Choe, H. (2023). Beyond ChatGPT: A conceptual framework and systematic review of speech-recognition chatbots for language learning. *Computers & Education*, 104898.
Jie, Z., Shahbaz, M., Chunling, L., & Richard, C.A (2016). What makes a more proficient discussion group in English language learners' classrooms? Influence of teacher talk and student backgrounds. *Research in the Teaching of English*, *51*(2), 183–207.
Jovanovic, M., & Voss, P. (2024). Trends and challenges of real-time learning in large language models: A critical review. *arxiv preprint*, arxiv:2404.18311.
Juzwik, M. M., Borsheim-Black, C., Caughlan, S., & Heintz, A. (2013). *Inspiring dialogue: Talking to learn in the English classroom*. Teachers College Press.
Kasneci, E., Seßler, K., Küchemann, S., Bannert, M., Dementieva, D., Fischer, F., Gasser, U., Groh, G., Günnemann, S., Hüllermeier, E., Krusche, S., Kutyniok, G., Michaeli, T., Nerdel, C., Pfeffer, J., Poquet, O., Sailer, M., Schmidt, A., Seidel, T., Stadler, M., & Kasneci, G. (2023). ChatGPT for good? On opportunities and challenges of large language models for education. *Learning and Individual Differences*, *103*, 102274.

Kautzmann, T. R., & Jaques, P. A. (2019). Effects of adaptive training on metacognitive knowledge monitoring ability in computer-based learning. *Computers & Education, 129*, 92–105.

Kieran, C. (2001). The mathematical discourse of 13-year-old partnered problem solving and its relation to the mathematics that emerges. *Educational Studies in Mathematics, 46*, 187–228.

Kim, M. Y., & Wilkinson, I. A. (2019). What is dialogic teaching? Constructing, deconstructing, and reconstructing a pedagogy of classroom talk. *Learning, Culture and Social Interaction, 21*, 70–86.

Klašnja-Milićević, A., Ivanović, M., & Nanopoulos, A. (2015). Recommender systems in e-learning environments: A survey of the state-of-the-art and possible extensions. *Artificial Intelligence Review, 44*, 571–604.

Klašnja-Milićević, A., Vesin, B., Ivanović, M., & Budimac, Z. (2011). E-Learning personalization based on hybrid recommendation strategy and learning style identification. *Computers & Education, 56*(3), 885–899.

Knight, S., Shibani, A., Abel, S., Gibson, A., & Ryan, P. (2020). AcaWriter: A learning analytics tool for formative feedback on academic writing. *Journal of Writing Research, 12*(1), 141–186.

Koichu, B., Berman, A., & Moore, M. (2007). Heuristic literacy development and its relation to mathematical achievements of middle school students. *Instructional Science, 35*, 99–139.

Koichu, B., Schwarz, B. B., Heyd-Metzuyanim, E., Tabach, M., & Yarden, A. (2022). Design practices and principles for promoting dialogic argumentation via interdisciplinarity. *Learning, Culture and Social Interaction, 37*, 100657.

Kolahkaj, M., Harounabadi, A., Nikravanshalmani, A., & Chinipardaz, R. (2020). A hybrid context-aware approach for e-tourism package recommendation based on asymmetric similarity measurement and sequential pattern mining. *Electronic Commerce Research and Applications, 42*, 100978.

Konijn, E. A., & Hoorn, J. F. (2020). Robot tutor and pupils' educational ability: Teaching the times tables. *Computers & Education, 157*, 103970.

Kumpulainen, K. I., & Lipponen, L. (2010). Productive interaction as agentic participation in dialogic enquiry. In *Educational dialogues* (pp. 60–75). Routledge.

Kumpulainen, K. I., & Lipponen, L. (2014). Building on the positive in children's lives: A co-participatory study on the social construction of children's sense of agency. *Early Child Development, 184*(2), 211–229.

Kumpulainen, K. I., & Wray, D. (2003). *Classroom interactions and social learning: From theory to practice*. Routledge.

Kutnick, P., & Blatchford, P. (2014). *Effective group work in primary school classrooms*. Springer Science & Business Media.

Laeeq, K., & Memon, Z. A. (2019). Strengthening virtual learning environments by incorporating modern technologies. In *Intelligent computing: Proceedings of the 2019 computing conference* (Vol. 2, pp. 994–1008). Springer International Publishing.

Lamb, R., & Etopio, E. A. (2020). Virtual reality: A tool for preservice science teachers to put theory into practice. *Journal of Science Education and Technology, 29*(4), 573–585.

Le, C., Shrestha, K. J., Jeong, H. D., & Damnjanovic, I. (2021). A sequential pattern mining driven framework for developing construction logic knowledge bases. *Automation in Construction, 121*, 103439.

Leach, J., Ametller, J., Hind, A., Lewis, J., & Scott, P. (2003). *Evidence-informed approaches to teaching science at junior high school level: Outcomes in terms of student learning*. Paper presented at the annual meeting of the National Association of Research in Science Teaching (NARST).

Lee, S., & Jeon, J. (2022). Visualizing a disembodied agent: Young EFL learners' perceptions of voice-controlled conversational agents as language partners. *Computer Assisted Language Learning*, 1–26.

Lee, S. C., & Irving, K. E. (2018). Development of Two-Dimensional Classroom Discourse Analysis Tool (CDAT): Scientific reasoning and dialog patterns in the secondary science classes. *International Journal of STEM Education*, *5*(1), 1–17.

Lee, S. M., & Wu, J. G. (2024). Preparing teachers for the future: Microteaching in the immersive VR environment. *ReCALL*, 1–19.

Lefstein, A., Snell, J., & Israeli, M. (2015). From moves to sequences: Expanding the unit of analysis in the study of classroom discourse. *British Educational Research Journal*, *41*(5), 866–885.

Lehesvuori, S., & Ametller, J. (2021). Exploring coherence and authorship in pedagogical link-making in science. *International Journal of Science Education*, *43*(17), 2791–2813.

Lin, C. F., Yeh, Y. C., Hung, Y. H., & Chang, R. I. (2013). Data mining for providing a personalized learning path in creativity: An application of decision trees. *Computers & Education*, *68*, 199–210.

Lin, M. P. C., & Chang, D. (2020). Enhancing post-secondary writers' writing skills with a chatbot. *Journal of Educational Technology & Society*, *23*(1), 78–92.

Littleton, K., & Mercer, N. (2013). *Interthinking: Putting talk to work*. Routledge.

Liu, P., Qiu, X., & Huang, X. (2016). Recurrent neural network for text classification with multi-task learning. *arxiv preprint*, arxiv:1605.05101.

Luan, H., & Tsai, C. C. (2021). A review of using machine learning approaches for precision education. *Educational Technology & Society*, *24*(1), 250–266.

Lyster, R., & Ranta, L. (1997). Corrective feedback and learner uptake: Negotiation of form in communicative classrooms. *Studies in Second Language Acquisition*, *19*(1), 37–66.

Ma, W., Adesope, O. O., Nesbit, J. C., & Liu, Q. (2014). Intelligent tutoring systems and learning outcomes: A meta-analysis. *Journal of Educational Psychology*, *106*(4), 901.

Macgregor, S. K., & Atkinson, T. R. (2002). Facilitating learner interactions in the two-way video classroom. *Journal of Educational Technology Systems*, *31*(1), 45–62.

Maldonado-Mahauad, J., Pérez-Sanagustín, M., Kizilcec, R. F., Morales, N., & Munoz-Gama, J. (2018). Mining theory-based patterns from Big data: Identifying self-regulated learning strategies in Massive Open Online Courses. *Computers in Human Behavior*, *80*, 179–196.

Martínez, M. A., Cobo, M. J., Herrera, M., & Herrera-Viedma, E. (2015). Analyzing the scientific evolution of social work using science mapping. *Research on Social Work Practice*, *25*(2), 257–277.

Mazloumian, A. (2012). Predicting scholars' scientific impact. *PLOS One*, *7*(11), e49246.

Mazzoni, E., & Benvenuti, M. (2015). A robot-partner for preschool children learning English using socio-cognitive conflict. *Journal of Educational Technology & Society*, *18*(4), 474–485.

McCulloch, A. W., Hollebrands, K., Lee, H., Harrison, T., & Mutlu, A. (2018). Factors that influence secondary mathematics teachers' integration of technology in mathematics lessons. *Computers & Education*, *123*, 26–40.

McNamara, D. S., Levinstein, I. B., & Boonthum, C. (2004). iSTART: Interactive strategy training for active reading and thinking. *Behavior Research Methods, Instruments, & Computers*, *36*(2), 222–233.

McNeill, K. L., González-Howard, M., Katsh-Singer, R., & Loper, S. (2017). Moving beyond pseudo argumentation: Teachers' enactments of an educative science curriculum focused on argumentation. *Science Education*, *101*(3), 426–457.

Mehan, H. (1979). *Learning lessons: Social organization in the classroom*. Harvard University Press.

Mercer, N. (2000). *Words and minds: How we use language to think together*. Routledge.

Mercer, N. (2008). The seeds of time: Why classroom dialogue needs a temporal analysis. *The Journal of the Learning Sciences*, *17*(1), 33–59.

Mercer, N. (2010). The analysis of classroom talk: Methods and methodologies. *British Journal of Educational Psychology*, *80*(1), 1–14.

Mercer, N., & Dawes, L. (2014). The study of talk between teachers and students, from the 1970s until the 2010s. *Oxford Review of Education*, *40*(4), 430–445.

Mercer, N., Dawes, L., Wegerif, R., & Sams, C. (2004). Reasoning as a scientist: Ways of helping children to use language to learn science. *British Educational Research Journal*, *30*(3), 359–377.

Mercer, N., Hennessy, S., & Warwick, P. (2010). Using interactive whiteboards to orchestrate classroom dialogue. *Technology, Pedagogy and Education*, *19*(2), 195–209.

Mercer, N., Hennessy, S., & Warwick, P. (2017). Dialogue, thinking together and digital technology in the classroom: Some educational implications of a continuing line of inquiry. *International Journal of Educational Research*, *97*, 187–199.

Mercer, N., & Littleton, K. (2007). *Dialogue and the development of children's thinking: A sociocultural approach*. Routledge.

Merigó, J. M., Mas-Tur, A., Roig-Tierno, N., & Ribeiro-Soriano, D. (2015). A bibliometric overview of the Journal of Business Research between 1973 and 2014. *Journal of Business Research*, *68*(12), 2645–2653.

Michaels, S., O'Connor, C., & Resnick, L. B. (2008). Deliberative discourse idealized and realized: Accountable talk in the classroom and in civic life. *Studies in Philosophy and Education*, *27*, 283–297.

Min, B., Ross, H., Sulem, E., Veyseh, A. P. B., Nguyen, T. H., Sainz, O., Agirre, E., Heintz, I., & Roth, D. (2023). Recent advances in natural language processing via large pre-trained language models: A survey. *ACM Computing Surveys*, *56*(2), 1–40.

Minaee, S., Mikolov, T., Nikzad, N., Chenaghlu, M., Socher, R., Amatriain, X., & Gao, J. (2024). Large language models: A survey. *arxiv preprint*, arxiv:2402.06196.

Mohammadhasani, N., Fardanesh, H., Hatami, J., Mozayani, N., & Fabio, R. A. (2018). The pedagogical agent enhances mathematics learning in ADHD students. *Education and Information Technologies*, *23*, 2299–2308.

Molinari, L., Mameli, C., & Gnisci, A. (2013). A sequential analysis of classroom discourse in Italian primary schools: The many faces of the IRF pattern. *British Journal of Educational Psychology*, *83*(3), 414–430.

Morgan, C., Craig, T., Schütte, M., & Wagner, D. (2014). Language and communication in mathematics education: An overview of research in the field. *ZDM*, *46*, 843–853.

Mortimer, E., & Scott, P. (2003). *Meaning making in secondary science classrooms*. McGraw-Hill Education (UK).

Moussalli, S., & Cardoso, W. (2020). Intelligent personal assistants: Can they understand and be understood by accented L2 learners? *Computer Assisted Language Learning*, *33*(8), 865–890.

Muhonen, H., Pakarinen, E., Poikkeus, A. M., Lerkkanen, M. K., & Rasku-Puttonen, H. (2018). Quality of educational dialogue and association with students' academic performance. *Learning and Instruction*, *55*, 67–79.

Muhonen, H., Rasku-Puttonen, H., Pakarinen, E., Poikkeus, A. M., & Lerkkanen, M. K. (2016). Scaffolding through dialogic teaching in early school classrooms. *Teaching and Teacher Education*, *55*, 143–154.

Muhonen, H., Rasku-Puttonen, H., Pakarinen, E., Poikkeus, A. M., & Lerkkanen, M. K. (2017). Knowledge-building patterns in educational dialogue. *International Journal of Educational Research*, *81*, 25–37.

Murphy, M. J., Seneviratne, R. D. A., Remers, O. J., & Davis, M. H. (2009). 'Hawks' and 'doves': Effect of feedback on grades awarded by supervisors of student selected components. *Medical Teacher*, *31*(10), e484–e488.

Nassaji, H., & Wells, G. (2000). What's the use of "triadic dialogue"? An investigation of teacher-student interaction. *Applied Linguistics*, *21*(3), 376–406.

National Institute of Child Health and Human Development Early Child Care Research Network. (2002). The relation of global first-grade classroom environment to structural classroom features and teacher and student behaviors. *The Elementary School Journal*, *102*(5), 367–387.

Nichd, E., & Bonnie, K. (2005). A day in third grade: A large-scale study of classroom quality and teacher and student behavior. *The Elementary School Journal*, *105*(3), 305–323.

Norman, K. (1992). *Thinking voices: The work of the National Oracy Project*. Hodder and Stoughton.
Nystrand, M. (1997). Dialogic instruction: When recitation becomes conversation. In *Opening dialogue: Understanding the dynamics of language and learning in the English classroom* (pp. 1–29). Teacher College Press.
Nystrand, M., & Gamoran, A. (1991). Instructional discourse, student engagement, and literature achievement. *Research in the Teaching of English*, *25*(3), 261–290.
Nystrand, M., Wu, L. L., Gamoran, A., Zeiser, S., & Long, D. A. (2003). Questions in time: Investigating the structure and dynamics of unfolding classroom discourse. *Discourse Process*, *35*(2), 135–198.
O'Connor, C., & Michaels, S. (2007). When is dialogue 'dialogic'? *Human Development*, *50*(5), 275–285.
O'Connor, C., Michaels, S., & Chapin, S. (2015). "Scaling down" to explore the role of talk in learning: From district intervention to controlled classroom study. *Socializing Intelligence through Academic Talk and Dialogue*, 111–126.
O'Connor, C., Michaels, S., Chapin, S., & Harbaugh, A. G. (2017). The silent and the vocal: Participation and learning in whole-class discussion. *Learning and Instruction*, *48*, 5–13.
OECD. (2019). *OECD future of education and skills 2030: OECD learning compass 2030*. OECD Publishing.
OECD. (2020). *Education responses to Covid-19: Embracing digital learning and online collaboration*. OECD Publishing.
Olsson, F. (2009). *A literature survey of active machine learning in the context of natural language processing*. Swedish Institute of Computer Science.
Ouyang, F., Wu, M., Zhang, L., Xu, W., Zheng, L., & Cukurova, M. (2023). Making strides towards AI-supported regulation of learning in collaborative knowledge construction. *Computers in Human Behavior*, *142*, 107650.
Oxford University Press. (2002). *Shorter Oxford English dictionary*. Oxford University Press.
Palincsar, A. S., & Brown, A. L. (1989). Classroom dialogues to promote self-regulated comprehension. *Advances in Research on Teaching*, *1*, 35–71.
Paquette, L., Ocumpaugh, J., Li, Z., Andres, A., & Baker, R. (2020). Who's learning? Using demographics in EDM research. *Journal of Educational Data Mining*, *12*(3), 1–30.
Pardo, A., Jovanovic, J., Dawson, S., Gašević, D., & Mirriahi, N. (2019). Using learning analytics to scale the provision of personalised feedback. *British Journal of Educational Technology*, *50*(1), 128–138.
Park, Y., & Doo, M. Y. (2024). Role of AI in blended learning: A systematic literature review. *The International Review of Research in Open and Distributed Learning*, *25*(1), 164–196.
Parker, C., & Bickmore, K. (2020). Classroom peace circles: Teachers' professional learning and implementation of restorative dialogue. *Teaching and Teacher Education*, *95*, 103129.
Paul, C. D., Bukaty, C. A., & Dieker, L. (2020). Teacher professional learning using simulation: A Delphi study. *Teacher Development*, *24*(1), 21–32.
Pehmer, A. K., Gröschner, A., & Seidel, T. (2015). How teacher professional development regarding classroom dialogue affects students' higher-order learning. *Teaching and Teacher Education*, *47*, 108–119.
Pianta, R. C., Hamre, B. K., & Allen, J. P. (2012). Teacher-student relationships and engagement: Conceptualizing, measuring, and improving the capacity of classroom interactions. In *Handbook of research on student engagement* (pp. 365–386). Springer.
Podschuweit, S., Bernholt, S., & Brückmann, M. (2016). Classroom learning and achievement: How the complexity of classroom interaction impacts students' learning. *Research in Science & Technological Education*, *34*(2), 142–163.
Pohl, M., Wallner, G., & Kriglstein, S. (2016). Using lag-sequential analysis for understanding interaction sequences in visualizations. *International Journal of Human-Computer Studies*, *96*, 54–66.

Poon, L. K., Kong, S. C., Wong, M. Y., & Yau, T. S. (2017). Mining sequential patterns of students' access on learning management system. In *Data mining and big data: Second international conference, DMBD 2017, Fukuoka, Japan, July 27–August 1, 2017, proceedings 2* (pp. 191–198). Springer International Publishing.

Pouyanfar, S., Sadiq, S., Yan, Y., Tian, H., Tao, Y., Reyes, M. P., Shyu, M. L., Chen, S. C., & Iyengar, S. S. (2018). A survey on deep learning: Algorithms, techniques, and applications. *ACM Computing Surveys (CSUR)*, *51*(5), 1–36.

Pöysä, S., Vasalampi, K., Muotka, J., Lerkkanen, M. K., Poikkeus, A. M., & Nurmi, J. E. (2018). Teacher – student interaction and lower secondary school students' situational engagement. *British Journal of Educational Psychology*, *89*(2), 374–392.

Radeva, I., Popchev, I., Doukovska, L., & Dimitrova, M. (2024). Web application for retrieval-augmented generation: Implementation and testing. *Electronics*, *13*(7), 1361.

Raiaan, M. A. K., Mukta, M. S. H., Fatema, K., Fahad, N. M., Sakib, S., Mim, M. M. J., Ahmad, J., Ali, M. E., & Azam, S. (2024). A review on large Language Models: Architectures, applications, taxonomies, open issues and challenges. *IEEE Access*, *12*, 26839–26874.

Randall, N. (2019). A survey of robot-assisted language learning (RALL). *ACM Transactions on Human-Robot Interaction (THRI)*, *9*(1), 1–36.

Resnick, L. B., Asterhan, C. S., & Clarke, S. N. (2015). *Socializing intelligence through academic talk and dialogue*. American Educational Research Association.

Resnick, L. B., Michaels, S., & O'Connor, C. (2010). How (well structured) talk builds the mind. In *Innovations in educational psychology: Perspectives on learning, teaching and human development* (pp. 163–194). Springer.

Reznitskaya, A., & Gregory, M. (2013). Student thought and classroom language: Examining the mechanisms of change in dialogic teaching. *Educational Psychologist*, *48*(2), 114–133.

Ricci, F., Rokach, L., & Shapira, B. (2022). Recommender systems: Techniques, applications, and challenges. In *Recommender systems handbook*. Springer.

Richards, M., Waugh, K., Slaymaker, M., Petre, M., Woodthorpe, J., & Gooch, D. (2024). Bob or bot: Exploring ChatGPT's answers to university computer science assessment. *ACM Transactions on Computing Education*, *24*(1), 1–32.

Rocca, K. A. (2010). Student participation in the college classroom: An extended multidisciplinary literature review. *Communication Education*, *59*(2), 185–213.

Rojas-Drummond, S., Littleton, K., Hernández, F., & Zúñiga, M. (2010). Dialogical interactions among peers in collaborative writing contexts. *Educational Dialogues: Understanding and Promoting Productive Interaction*, *1*, 128–148.

Rojas-Drummond, S., Pérez, V., Vélez, M., Gómez, L., & Mendoza, A. (2003). Talking for reasoning among Mexican primary school children. *Learning and Instruction*, *13*(6), 653–670.

Rojas-Drummond, S., Torreblanca, O., Pedraza, H., Vélez, M., & Guzmán, K. (2013). 'Dialogic scaffolding': Enhancing learning and understanding in collaborative contexts. *Learning, Culture and Social Interaction*, *2*(1), 11–21.

Rosita, Y. D., Rosyida, E. E., & Rudiyanto, M. A. (2019). Implementation of dijkstra algorithm and multi-criteria decision-making for optimal route distribution. *Procedia Computer Science*, *161*, 378–385.

Roy, S., & Garg, A. (2017, October). Predicting academic performance of student using classification techniques. In *2017 4th IEEE Uttar Pradesh section international conference on electrical, computer and electronics (UPCON)* (pp. 568–572). IEEE.

Ruiz-Primo, M. A. (2011). Informal formative assessment: The role of instructional dialogues in assessing students' learning. *Studies in Educational Evaluation*, *37*(1), 15–24.

Sani, S., & Aris, T. N. (2014, January). Computational intelligence approaches for student/tutor modelling: A review. In *2014 5th international conference on intelligent systems, modelling and simulation* (pp. 72–76). IEEE.

Sartori, G., & Orrù, G. (2023). Language models and psychological sciences. *Frontiers in Psychology*, *14*, 1279317.
Saville-Troike, M. (2003). Extending "communicative" concepts in the second language curriculum: A sociolinguistic perspective. In *Culture as core: Interdisciplinary perspectives on culture in the second language classroom* (pp. 3–17). Information Age Publishing.
Schwab, G. (2011). From dialogue to multilogue: A different view on participation in the English foreign-language classroom. *Classroom Discourse*, *2*(1), 3–19.
Sharma, K. K., & Seal, A. (2021). Multi-view spectral clustering for uncertain objects. *Information Sciences*, *547*, 723–745.
Shelton, B. E., Duffin, J., Wang, Y., & Ball, J. (2010). Linking open course wares and open education resources: Creating an effective search and recommendation system. *Procedia Computer Science*, *1*(2), 2865–2870.
Shi, W., Zhuang, Y., Zhu, Y., Iwinski, H., Wattenbarger, M., & Wang, M. D. (2023, September). Retrieval-augmented large language models for adolescent idiopathic scoliosis patients in shared decision-making. In *Proceedings of the 14th ACM international conference on bioinformatics, computational biology, and health informatics* (pp. 1–10). Association for Computing Machinery.
Shin, J., Balyan, R., Banawan, M. P., Arner, T., Leite, W. L., & McNamara, D. S. (2023). Pedagogical discourse markers in online algebra learning: Unraveling instructor's communication using natural language processing. *Computers & Education*, *205*, 104897.
Sigaud, O., & Wilson, S. W. (2007). Learning classifier systems: A survey. *Soft Computing*, *11*, 1065–1078.
Sinclair, J., & Coulthard, R. M. (1975). *Towards an analysis of discourse: The English used by pupils and teachers*. Oxford University Press.
Siriwardhana, S., Weerasekera, R., Elliott, W., Kaluarachchi, T., Rana, R., & Nanayakkara, S. (2023). Improving the domain adaptation of retrieval augmented generation (RAG) models for open domain question answering. *Transactions of the Association for Computational Linguistics*, *11*, 1–17.
Smith, M. K., Jones, F. H., Gilbert, S. L., & Wieman, C. E. (2013). The classroom observation protocol for undergraduate STEM (COPUS): A new instrument to characterize university STEM classroom practices. *CBE – Life Sciences Education*, *12*(4), 618–627.
Sokolova, M., & Lapalme, G. (2009). A systematic analysis of performance measures for classification tasks. *Information Processing & Management*, *45*, 427–437.
Song, D., & Kim, D. (2021). Effects of self-regulation scaffolding on online participation and learning outcomes. *Journal of Research on Technology in Education*, *53*(3), 249–263.
Song, Y., Chen, X., Hao, T., Liu, Z., & Lan, Z. (2019). Exploring two decades of research on classroom dialogue by using bibliometric analysis. *Computers & Education*, *137*, 12–31.
Song, Y., Cheng, B., Zhu, J., & Hu, X. Y. (2022). Exploring the collective process of classroom dialogue using sequential pattern mining technique. *International Journal of Educational Research*, *115*, Article 102050.
Song, Y., Hao, T., Liu, Z., & Lan, Z. (2020). A systematic review of frameworks for coding towards classroom dialogue. In *Emerging technologies for education: 4th international symposium, SETE 2019, held in conjunction with ICWL 2019, Magdeburg, Germany, September 23–25, 2019, revised selected papers 4* (pp. 226–236). Springer International Publishing.
Song, Y., Lei, S., Hao, T., Lan, Z., & Ding, Y. (2021). Automatic classification of semantic content of classroom dialogue. *Journal of Educational Computing Research*, *59*(3), 496–521.
Song, Y., Zhang, S., & Liu, B. (2023). Investigating the dialogic patterns of mathematics lessons in different stages of education. *The Journal of Educational Research*, *116*(2), 77–89.

Soter, A. O., Wilkinson, I. A., Murphy, P. K., Rudge, L., Reninger, K., & Edwards, M. (2008). What the discourse tells us: Talk and indicators of high-level comprehension. *International Journal of Educational Research*, *47*(6), 372–391.

Steen-Utheim, A., & Wittek, A. L. (2017). Dialogic feedback and potentialities for student learning. *Learning, Culture and Social Interaction*, *15*, 18–30.

Suresh, A., Jacobs, J., Perkoff, M., Martin, J. H., & Sumner, T. (2022, July). Fine-tuning transformers with additional context to classify discursive moves in mathematics classrooms. In *Proceedings of the 17th workshop on innovative use of NLP for building educational applications (BEA 2022)* (pp. 71–81). Association for Computational Linguistics.

Svensson, G. (2010). SSCI and its impact factors: A "prisoner's dilemma"? *European Journal of Marketing*, *44*(1/2), 23–33.

Sychev, O., Penskoy, N., Anikin, A., Denisov, M., & Prokudin, A. (2021). Improving comprehension: Intelligent tutoring system explaining the domain rules when students break them. *Education Sciences*, *11*(11), 719.

Tan, S., Cho, Y. W., & Xu, W. (2023). Exploring the effects of automated written corrective feedback, computer-mediated peer feedback and their combination mode on EFL learner's writing performance. *Interactive Learning Environments*, *31*(10), 7276–7286.

Tang, K. S., Tan, A. L., & Mortimer, E. F. (2021). The multi-timescale, multi-modal and multi-perspectival aspects of classroom discourse analysis in science education. *Research in Science Education*, *51*(1), 1–11.

Tasche, D. (2018). A plug-in approach to maximising precision at the top and recall at the top. *arXiv preprint*, arXiv:1804.03077.

Tegos, S., & Demetriadis, S. (2017). Conversational agents improve peer learning through building on prior knowledge. *Journal of Educational Technology & Society*, *20*(1), 99–111.

Van den Berghe, R., Verhagen, J., Oudgenoeg-Paz, O., Van der Ven, S., & Leseman, P. (2019). Social robots for language learning: A review. *Review of Educational Research*, *89*(2), 259–295.

van der Veen, C., de Mey, L., van Kruistum, C., & van Oers, B. (2017). The effect of productive classroom talk and metacommunication on young children's oral communicative competence and subject matter knowledge: An intervention study in early childhood education. *Learning and Instruction*, *48*, 14–22.

van der Veen, C., & van Oers, B. (2017). Advances in research on classroom dialogue: Learning outcomes and assessments. *Learning and Instruction*, *48*, 1–4.

VanLehn, K. (2011). The relative effectiveness of human tutoring, intelligent tutoring systems, and other tutoring systems. *Educational Psychologist*, *46*(4), 197–221.

Varadarajan, S., Kasravi, K., & Feldman, R. (2003). Text-mining: Application development challenges. In *Applications and innovations in intelligent systems X: Proceedings of ES2002, the twenty-second SGAI international conference on knowledge based systems and applied artificial intelligence* (pp. 247–260). Springer London.

Vertemati, M., Cassin, S., Rizzetto, F., Vanzulli, A., Elli, M., Sampogna, G., & Gallieni, M. (2019). A virtual reality environment to visualize three-dimensional patient-specific models by a mobile head-mounted display. *Surgical Innovation*, *26*(3), 359–370.

Vista, A., Awwal, N., & Care, E. (2016). Sequential actions as markers of behavioural and cognitive processes: Extracting empirical pathways from data streams of complex tasks. *Computers & Education*, *92*, 15–36.

Vrikki, M., & Evagorou, M. (2023). An analysis of teacher questioning practices in dialogic lessons. *International Journal of Educational Research*, *117*, 102107.

Vygotsky, L. (1978). Interaction between learning and development. In M. Cole (Ed.), *Mind in society: The development of higher psychological processes*. Harvard University Press.

Wang, S., Xu, T., Li, H., Zhang, C., Liang, J., Tang, J., Yu, P. S., & Wen, Q. (2024). Large language models for education: A survey and outlook. *arxiv preprint*, arxiv:2403.18105.

Wang, X., Liu, Q., Pang, H., Tan, S. C., Lei, J., Wallace, M. P., & Li, L. (2023). What matters in AI-supported learning: A study of human-AI interactions in language learning using cluster analysis and epistemic network analysis. *Computers & Education, 194*, 104703.

Wang, Z., Pan, X., Miller, K. F., & Cortina, K. S. (2014). Automatic classification of activities in classroom discourse. *Computers & Education, 78*, 115–123.

Weaver, R. R., & Qi, J. (2005). Classroom organization and participation: College students' perceptions. *The Journal of Higher Education, 76*(5), 570–601.

Webb, N. M., Franke, M. L., Ing, M., Turrou, A. C., Johnson, N. C., & Zimmerman, J. (2019). Teacher practices that promote productive dialogue and learning in mathematics classrooms. *International Journal of Educational Research, 97*, 176–186.

Webb, P., Whitlow, J. W., & Venter, D. (2017). From exploratory talk to abstract reasoning: A case for far transfer? *Educational Psychology Review, 29*, 565–581.

Wegerif, R. (2007). *Dialogic education and technology: Expanding the space of learning* (Vol. 7). Springer Science & Business Media.

Weisleder, A., & Fernald, A. (2013). Talking to children matters: Early language experience strengthens processing and builds vocabulary. *Psychological Science, 24*(11), 2143–2152.

Wells, G., & Arauz, R. M. (2006). Dialogue in the classroom. *The Journal of the Learning Sciences, 15*(3), 379–428.

Wertsch, J. V. (1993). Sociocultural setting, social languages, and mediated action. In *Voices of the mind: A social cultural approach to mediated action* (pp. 119–148). Harvard University Press.

Wiebe Berry, R. A., & Kim, N. (2008). Exploring teacher talk during mathematics instruction in an inclusion classroom. *The Journal of Educational Research, 101*(6), 363–378.

Wilkinson, I. A.G., Reznitskaya, A., & D'Agostino, J. V. (2023). Professional development in classroom discussion to improve argumentation: Teacher and student outcomes. *Learning and Instruction, 85*, Article 101732.

Wilmes, S. E., & Siry, C. (2021). Multimodal interaction analysis: A powerful tool for examining plurilingual students' engagement in science practices: Proposed contribution to RISE special issue: Analyzing science classroom discourse. *Research in Science Education, 51*(1), 71–91.

Wilson, J., & Czik, A. (2016). Automated essay evaluation software in English Language Arts classrooms: Effects on teacher feedback, student motivation, and writing quality. *Computers & Education, 100*, 94–109.

Wilson, J., & Roscoe, R. D. (2020). Automated writing evaluation and feedback: Multiple metrics of efficacy. *Journal of Educational Computing Research, 58*(1), 87–125.

Wong, J., Khalil, M., Baars, M., de Koning, B. B., & Paas, F. (2019). Exploring sequences of learner activities in relation to self-regulated learning in a massive open online course. *Computers & Education, 140*, 103595.

Xie, Z., & Cao, X. (2010, June). Construction three-dimensional observation system of teacher-student interaction behavior in classroom and practice. In *2010 2nd international conference on education technology and computer* (Vol. 4, pp. V4–271). IEEE.

Xu, W., Wu, Y., & Ouyang, F. (2023). Multimodal learning analytics of collaborative patterns during pair programming in higher education. *International Journal of Educational Technology in Higher Education, 20*(1), 8.

Yacobson, E., Toda, A. M., Cristea, A. I., & Alexandron, G. (2024). Recommender systems for teachers: The relation between social ties and the effectiveness of socially-based features. *Computers & Education, 210*, 104960.

Yanfen, L., & Yuqin, Z. (2010). A study of teacher talk in interactions in English classes. *Chinese Journal of Applied Linguistics (Foreign Language Teaching & Research Press), 33*(2), 76–86.

Yang, F. J. (2011). A virtual tutor for relational schema normalization. *ACM Inroads, 2*(3), 38–42.

Yang, X., Guo, X., & Yu, S. (2016). Effects of cooperative translation on Chinese EFL student levels of interest and self-efficacy in specialized English translation. *Computer Assisted Language Learning*, *29*(3), 477–493.
Young, T., Hazarika, D., Poria, S., & Cambria, E. (2018). Recent trends in deep learning based natural language processing. *IEEE Computational Intelligence Magazine*, *13*(3), 55–75.
Zawacki-Richter, O., & Latchem, C. (2018). Exploring four decades of research in Computers & Education. *Computers & Education*, *122*, 136–152.
Zhao, J., Gupta, R., Cao, Y., Yu, D., Wang, M., Lee, H., Rastogi, A., Shafran, I., & Wu, Y. (2022). Description-driven task-oriented dialog modeling. *arxiv preprint*, arxiv:2201.08904.
Zhong, S., Geng, Y., Liu, W., Gao, C., & Chen, W. (2016). A bibliometric review on natural resource accounting during 1995–2014. *Journal of Cleaner Production*, *139*, 122–132.
Zupic, I., & Čater, T. (2015). Bibliometric methods in management and organization. *Organizational Research Methods*, *18*(3), 429–472.

Index

Note: Page numbers in *italic* indicate a figure and page numbers in **bold** indicate a table on the corresponding page.

FSC
www.fsc.org
MIX
Papier | Fördert
gute Waldnutzung
FSC® C083411

Kolibri 360 GmbH
Ferdinand-Jühlke-Straße 7
99095 Erfurt, Deutschland
produktsicherheit@kolibri360.de